Business
Agreements

Also by John J. McGonagle, Jr.

Managing the Consultant: A Corporate Guide

John J. McGonagle, Jr.

Business Agreements

A COMPLETE GUIDE TO ORAL AND WRITTEN CONTRACTS

CHILTON BOOK COMPANY   RADNOR, PENNSYLVANIA

To Priscilla Erin Colleen

Published in Radnor, Pennsylvania 19089, by Chilton Book Company
and simultaneously in Canada by Fleet Publishers,
a Division of International Thomson Limited,
1410 Birchmount Road, Scarborough, Ontario M1P 2E7
Designed by Jean Callan King/Visuality
Manufactured in the United States of America

Portions of Chapter 4 originally appeared in
Managing the Consultant (Chilton Book Company, 1981)
in slightly different form. "Submission to Arbitration"
and "Demand for Arbitration" were supplied by the
American Arbitration Association. The publisher
gratefully acknowledges permission to reprint them here.

Library of Congress Cataloging in Publication Data

McGonagle, John J.
  Business agreements.

  Bibliography: p. 265
  Includes index.
  1. Contracts—United States. I. Title.
KF801.Z9M37 1982   346.73'02   82-71298
ISBN 0-8019-7223-X   347.3062   AACR2

1 2 3 4 5 6 7 8 9 0   1 0 9 8 7 6 5 4 3 2

Contents

Chapter 6 Writing an Agreement   120

Chapter 7 Preprinted and "Standard" Form Agreements   150

Notes   251

Glossary   253

References   265

Index   270

Business Agreements

1
Introduction

This book is both a reference for the lay person (as well as for the lawyer) on one of the core activities of businesses, the making of agreements, and a sourcebook that provides sample language and sample agreements for the more common forms of business contracts. The book proceeds step by step through the process of entering into a business agreement, drafting it, reading and interpreting it, and finally, dealing with any disputes that arise from the agreement itself.

Every day the average businessperson enters into numerous agreements, and often he thinks he has entered into others, which may or may not be legally binding. Exactly what are these agreements, and how do they come about? Aside from such carefully negotiated agreements as mergers, consider the following more ambiguous actions, each of which can result in a business agreement:

A company truck is parked in a public lot and the driver is issued a parking stub.

A purchase of surplus government goods is made at an auction.

A copier is left at your business as a demonstration model for you to consider.

A potential employee completes and signs an employment application.

At a stockholders meeting, a stockholder objects to the way a vote was taken and demands that it be taken again in accordance with the bylaws.

An electrician is called in to fix a short-circuit.

A person unknown to you submits a proposal for an article for the company newspaper. He asks you to check your decision on the article on an enclosed form.

Each of these is an agreement, and the terms of the agreement are established often without any verbal communication.

You are given a contract to administer. Do you know how to read it and interpret it? You are asked to review and suggest modifications for a draft of a contract currently being negotiated. Do you know how to do that? A contract under which you are operating does not cover a particular problem. You and the supplier work out a solution. Should the contract be amended in writing? How do you do that? What if you do not do so?

You are sued for breach of contract by a purchaser, but you are sure he has no case. How can you be sure? Or you win a judgment for a breach-of-contract action. Do you know how to go about collecting it? You are sued for a consumer contract dispute in small claims court. Do you handle that any differently from a regular suit?

This book is designed to help you answer these and other related questions.

How to Use This Book

This book is intended to be used in several ways. First, by reading through it completely, you will begin to see the interrelated aspects of business agreements in context. For example, clear drafting of an agreement requires an understanding of basic contract law, the interpretation of agreements, and the structure of the deal. Throughout, checklists and forms for many common situations are reproduced. Included in the Appendix is a glossary of the terms most frequently used in business agreements and a list of references on legal and contract issues, form books, and guides for handling particular business situations.

Finally, this book can be used as a text either in a formal academic program or in an in-house training context. It is designed to lend itself to the study of particular agreements. For example, an engineering firm may use this book and its own forms to educate new managers and contract specialists.

Throughout the book are examples of actual cases, some of which have been tried in various courts. They are selected to make a difficult point clear, not because they represent important precedents. No citations to the underlying cases are given because this is not a legal text. Citations would lead you to cases often more than a century old. Interpreting cases is difficult and, given the existence of good legal reference books, unnecessary.

The key to using this book is to refer to it frequently. The more it is used, the better a resource it will be. Make notes in it. Refer to your own business forms or to those used in your profession. Add your own references to the Appendix.

The Law and How to Find It

This book will not attempt to teach you everything the average lawyer knows about legal research. Rather, it will refer you to places where you can find information that will help in determining or understanding the law. Two useful aids in legal research are Marcus Cohen's *Researching the Law (In a Nutshell)* and *West's Law Finder.* The first is a handbook written for law students, but it is used by lawyers as well. The second is a brochure prepared by the largest legal publisher in the United States.

Another basic source for the businessperson is primarily for lawyers but can be found in most libraries. Each year, the Martindale-Hubbell Company publishes a multivolume directory of lawyers and law firms. The last volume in this annual set contains general information on a number of topics, including summaries of the laws of each state, prepared and updated by a law firm in that state. The summaries are designed to help the lawyer key into more detailed sources for information, such as statutes, court rules, and recent cases. They also provide information on specific, practical questions, including the courts, the rules for creating partnerships, the proper form of an affidavit, and how a deed is recorded. In some cases they note which states have adopted one of the "uniform" laws. These model statutes are also reproduced in the directory. If you use it, make sure you have the most current edition.

Another source of information is general texts on contract law. Written for lawyers, they summarize the law, point out new trends, argue against developments that the authors find disturbing, and refer the lawyer to cases and other original sources. The ones used most often by lawyers are multivolume treatises, which are of little use to the businessperson. More useful are one-volume references such as those noted in the References. These are often written for law students, but they are used by many lawyers in practice. Although they are brief and try to make points in broad general terms, they can be technical and difficult to use. But they are preferable to the multivolume treatises.

A final source is publications dealing with specific legal areas. Generally these works, some of which are in the References, are prepared by lawyers for lawyers specializing in a particular area. They are printed by companies directing their trade to lawyers. In them, you will find typical agreements and related forms. In addition, some discuss the legal background of the transactions, touching on tax law, tort law, and litigation, as well as on contracts. Because these books have been prepared for lawyers, they tend to focus on the document first, not on the deal. After reading them, you will begin to see why lawyers are so document-oriented. Never fall into the same trap: Use the forms as checklists for structuring your deal. Don't let the form dictate the deal; let the deal determine what goes into the agreement.

If you are searching for a solution to a legal issue and exhaust these sources, go to a law library if you do not have your own attorney. The first place to look for a library is at a local law school. Also, in many states the local bar association may have a library that is open to the public. Call the local bar association or a public librarian to find a good law library.

Being a Good Client

In 1980 and 1981 the American Bar Association and other legal organizations released reports critical of the performance of lawyers. Among the areas that were sharply criticized was the training the lawyers received in interviewing, counseling, and negotiating. One result is that law schools are offering courses in these areas to sharpen the skills of licensed lawyers.

But the solution to this problem cannot be found by improving lawyers' skills alone. A good lawyer and a good client form a partnership. If you are an informed client, your lawyer will be more effective. If you are prepared and understand what the lawyer can and cannot do for you, he or she can do a better job of protecting your interests. Almost as important, if you are a good client, you will seek legal help only when you need it and not spend money for legal assistance when it is not necessary. Sometimes the best thing a client can do is *not* to call on a lawyer. The benefit may not be worth the cost.

One of the aims of this book is to make you a better client and thereby a better businessperson. A good client understands how to prepare the information his lawyer needs to offer effective counsel. A good client understands what the lawyer can and cannot do. A good client knows when to see a lawyer.

In the area of business agreements, a good client is one who knows:

What a business agreement is

How a business agreement is made

How to prepare a business agreement

What a business agreement should cover

How to read a business agreement

How to live under a business agreement

What to do if a dispute arises

To know these things, the client must know his own business and its practices, the law that applies to the business and to contracts in general, and what the law will do in creating, interpreting, applying, and enforcing contracts. These factors make up the environment in which business agreements are made.

To help you understand how to read, write, and understand business agreements, a number of samples of typical agreements and clauses are included. Some have been prepared in "readable" or "plain language" form to show how basic agreements can be framed to be understandable and complete. Others are framed in the more typical legalese. This is because not all agreements that you will encounter will be readable, not even all of the newer ones. Of course, most of the older agreements will not be in readable form; rather, they will be collections of boilerplate riveted together with additions and small modifications by each drafter.

Perfect agreements could have been included in the text, at least insofar as the author is concerned. But it is more difficult to learn from perfect agreements. Therefore, agreements and portions of agreements have been included that are either badly worded, too long, ambiguous, or contradictory.

Whenever possible, the specific defects in language in an agreement are pointed out. In each case the language is taken from agreements that have been prepared by lawyers and signed by businesspeople. They show not the failings of the lawyers alone, but the failings of the clients who did not think out their deal or did not take the time to understand the entire agreement. Too often clients defer to their attorneys on particular contract clauses, either in terms of their necessity or in terms of their meaning under the circumstances. With the help of this book and its lessons, it is hoped that you will be able to avoid these mistakes and become a better businessperson and client.

2

Basic Contract Law

A contract is a contract is a contract, or so a poet might say. The law defines a contract as a legally enforceable agreement between two or more parties involving mutual promises to do or not to do something. Contract law is where the law and day-to-day business most often meet.

There are numerous types of contracts, both written and oral. The most common business contract is the express contract, but almost all of the other types can also be found in business situations. For example, in one case, an employee working on a pier told his supervisor that he had an idea for a device to speed up loading and unloading the ships there. The device would save money and lower the accident rate. The supervisor liked the idea and promised that the company would pay the employee one-third of what the company saved by using the device. The supervisor suggested that the idea be patented, and he offered to be the employee's partner in exploiting it.

A number of these devices were put into operation by the company. From time to time, the employee asked his supervisor about his money, and he was always assured that he would be paid. In the meantime, another company supervisor fired the employee.

The employee sued. The courts concluded that, while the supervisor could not make a contract for the company, and there was no express contract, a doctrine known as unjust enrichment or quasi-contract did apply. Under this doctrine, since the company had profited from the employee's unique invention, it was obligated to pay him fair compensation for it.

Contracts (or agreements) initially can be divided into three types, depending on whether they can be enforced in court, the ultimate test of a contract's validity: (1) valid contracts, (2) voidable contracts, and (3) void contracts.

A valid contract meets all applicable legal requirements. If one party to it does not perform according to its terms, the party injured by the nonperformance can seek enforcement or damages in court.

A voidable contract is apparently valid and enforceable, but because of a defect in its creation, one party can resist its enforcement and assert that it is invalid. The contract continues to be valid until a court determines otherwise. You resist enforcement of such a contract at your own risk because if a court decides the contract is not voidable, you have breached it. That means you owe the other party damages.

A void contract is the term applied to a contract that cannot be enforced by either party. It is not a contract at all, and never was one, since it was never created as a result of a legal defect. For example, if two people agree to do something illegal, the contract between them is void.

A valid contract can be either an executed contract or an executory contract. An executed contract is one in which both parties have carried out and performed all their individual obligations. An executory contract, on the other hand, has yet to be fully performed. The lack of complete performance may lie with one or both parties. If one party to an executory contract fails or refuses to perform within the time established in the contract for that performance, that party has breached the contract. Having breached the contract, he may be liable for damages sustained by the other party as a result of the breach.

The discussion so far is premised on a contract between two parties, although contracts may have substantially more parties to them. Contracts between two parties can be either unilateral or bilateral. A bilateral contract, which is the most common, is created by an exchange of promises between two parties. Commonly, one of the parties makes an offer to enter into a contract, and the other, knowing of that offer, accepts it and agrees to perform. This exchange of promises is the foundation of the contract, establishing the obligations of each party to it. If either party fails to perform its promises, the other may seek relief for any losses based on that breach of contract. The relief may include or be limited to money damages against the offending party.

A unilateral contract, in contrast, is a sort of one-way agreement. It is traditionally defined as the exchange of a promise for an act. The contract does not become effective until the act is performed. Similarly, the promise made need not be performed until the act is completed. When the act is performed, the promise must also be performed. For example, if you offer a reward to anyone aiding in the arrest of a shoplifter, you have created a unilateral contract. The promise is the offer of a reward, and the acceptance is made when a shoplifter is arrested with the help of a third party. In a bilateral contract, each party must go forward or be in breach. In a unilateral contract, the person making the promise can withdraw the promise at any time before the act is performed, without being liable for damages to the other.

A final set of distinctions is among express, implied, and quasi-contracts. An express contract, which can be either oral or written, sets forth the intention and legal commitments of the contracting parties. An implied contract is the result of a legal commitment created by the actions or the conduct of the two parties. This contract comes into being when one party provides goods or renders a service, with a reasonable expectation of a payment, and the other party accepts the goods or services, knowing of the conditions involved. No actual agreement, or "meeting of the minds," has occurred, but the courts imply a contract in fairness to the party that provided the goods or service; that is, the courts assume that the party receiving the goods or services intends to pay for them.

A quasi-contract is one that is implied by operation of law, not as a result of the actions of the parties. The courts impose a contract even if one party never promised to pay. It results from a legal determination that a contractual relationship is necessary to prevent unjust enrichment, or unfair or unconscionable benefits from flowing to one party at the expense of another. When one party receives services or goods, including money, the courts have determined that he should pay for what he received. Usually when the party providing the goods or services cannot recover in a lawsuit because no express or implied contract exists, he may be allowed to sue on the basis of a quasi-contract, implied by operation of law. This is not a true contract: Rather, it is a legal fiction designed to correct overreaching or other inequitable conduct.

Types of Contracts

ORAL AND WRITTEN CONTRACTS

A tremendous amount of business is conducted through oral (or verbal) contracts. Even though they are not put in writing, they are legally binding obligations enforceable by the courts. Some contracts must be written to be enforceable, but not all written contracts are enforceable, either because they are illegal or against public policy, or because the parties are not legally competent to make them.

Why a Written Contract May Be Better

Written contracts are in many cases preferable to oral ones. The prime reason is that it can be difficult to establish the terms of an oral contract. If you sue for breach of an oral contract, as plaintiff, the burden of proof is on you to persuade the court that your version of the facts, including the terms of the oral contract, is correct.

The difficulties of proving the terms of oral contracts led to the enactment of the statute of frauds, discussed later in the chapter. Basically, this statute requires certain contracts to be written if they are to be enforced by the courts.

Whether or not a prospective contract is covered by the statute of frauds, every businessperson should as a matter of course put it in writing.

It seems that lawyers would be the most meticulous in using written agreements instead of relying on oral ones. The reverse is true. One state bar association distributed a booklet to its members giving hints on avoiding malpractice claims. The first of the ten major steps was:

I. Always Put the Terms of the Attorney-Client Relationship in Writing

While it is not necessary to have a written contract between the attorney and client, the details of the representation should at least be confirmed by letter to the client. This written standard is a helpful reminder to the attorney as to the service that must be performed, as well as defining a measure of performance for the benefit of the client. After the relationship has gone on for a period of time, it is possible both parties will find it difficult to remember the exact terms of the representation absent the written statement. If the attorney does not accept the representation, it is equally critical to send a non-engagement letter.[1]

This advice should be respected not only in dealing with attorneys, where a written agreement can serve the client's interest, but in any on-going business relationship with professionals who provide services, such as engineers, doctors, lawyers, consultants, architects, and repairmen.

Typical retainer letters used by lawyers are included in the Appendix. The first deals with a business, nonlitigation matter. The second is a contingent-fee retainer letter. In most states any contingent-fee arrangement must be signed by the client, acknowledging receipt of the letter and agreeing to its terms.

VOIDABLE AND UNENFORCEABLE CONTRACTS

A contract may be written, signed by legally competent parties, and yet be void. A common ground for declaring that a contract is void is that it is "against public policy."

A voidable contract is one that can, but will not necessarily, be set aside by a court. If one party to the contract is incompetent—for example, senile—the contract will not be enforced against that party if the defense of incompetency is raised when the lawsuit is brought or if that party simply refuses to perform as required by the contract. If that defense is not raised, or if the party performs all of its obligations, the contract will stand. In the same way, contracts induced by fraud or mistake can be set aside, or avoided, if the party who contracted because of the other party's fraud wishes to get out of it. That party has the option to live up to the contract if he desires.

In an unenforceable contract, there is no remedy if it is breached. For example, because the statute of frauds requires written contracts to pay someone the debts of another, an oral contract to pay a customer's debts is unenforceable. Also, if a valid written contract is breached by one party, but the injured party waits twelve years to sue, that party will find his suit barred by the statute of limitations. Even if the written contract was valid and binding when made, and even if one party has been injured by the breach of another, no suit can be brought because the injured party waited too long to sue.

UNILATERAL AND BILATERAL CONTRACTS

Contracts can be either unilateral or bilateral. A unilateral contract is made up of a promise by one party and an act by the other, carrying out the terms contained in the promise. Under the definition that a contract is a legally enforceable agreement between two or more persons involving mutual promises to do or not to do something, a one-sided or unilateral contract may seem to be excluded. Nevertheless, there are many such contractual situations. For example, in one case a purchaser received an order from a potential buyer. The order stipulated the immediate delivery of certain equipment, noted the price to be paid, and specified that the price would be paid on or before delivery. The seller, on receiving the order, shipped the equipment within two days. The day after shipment, the buyer wrote the seller, cancelling the order. In a lawsuit by the seller for breach of contract, the Iowa Supreme Court determined that this was a unilateral contract. Since the seller shipped the goods before the order was withdrawn, there was a contract. The performance of the requested actions by the seller completed the deal. The seller was allowed to collect damages for the buyer's refusal to accept and pay for the equipment.

The more familiar bilateral contract consists of the exchange of mutual promises. If the seller in this case had sent the buyer a telegram accepting the order, there would have been a bilateral contract. This is because one promise, a promise to sell and deliver, had been exchanged for another promise, one to pay for the goods when delivered.

EXPRESS AND IMPLIED CONTRACTS

In an express contract, which can be either oral or written, the terms have been agreed on between the parties.

Implied contracts are obligations undertaken without either party mentioning the words *agree* or *contract*. For example, a regular customer may walk into a store, pick up an article, and show it to the clerk. The clerk nods, and the customer leaves. The customer now owns the article and has promised to pay, without a word being said. This is an agreement evidenced by the actions of the parties.

There are two types of implied contracts: those implied in fact, as in the example of the customer and the clerk, and those implied in law. Contracts implied in law are not really contracts because there is no agreement between the parties. But to do justice, in certain situations the law will impose an agreement on the parties, as in the case at the beginning of the chapter. This implied contract was created when the employee performed a service, in the justifiable belief that he was to be paid by the other, and by that performance benefited the other party.

Another example would be when one spouse, the wife, asks a contractor to repair a driveway on property owned in the other spouse's name only. The party benefiting from the work is the husband, since he owns the property. Thus the husband would be required to pay for the repairs, even though he never spoke to the contractor.

Elements of Enforceable Contracts

Enforceable means that the courts will order legal remedies to protect one party if the other party fails to honor the contract. Some contracts appear to be enforceable but are not because they are regarded as moral obligations. For example, a supervisor might save an employee's life by dragging him away from a dangerous machine. In so doing, the supervisor gets hurt. The grateful employee's promise to pay for the supervisor's injury would be regarded as a moral obligation. If the employee failed to pay, the supervisor could not sue and force him to pay.

There are six essential elements of an enforceable contract:

1. There must be mutual assent by the parties to the contract
2. There must be consideration
3. The object of the contract must be lawful
4. The contract must require performance within an agreed period of time
5. The contract must be written when required by law
6. The parties must be legally competent to enter into a contract

MUTUAL ASSENT

Mutual assent is the most basic element of any contract. The parties to the contract must agree on what the contract is about. In legal terms this is called "meeting of the minds." When there is a mutual mistake, there is no "meeting of the minds." An example of a mutual mistake might be where both a buyer and a seller agree on the sale of wine from a particular estate. If that estate produces no wine, the parties have no agreement. The court would rule that there was no meeting of the minds because of a mutual mistake in the terms of the contract.

Because of this, when making an agreement, every item should be accurately included. A binding and enforceable contract reflects the mutual assent of the parties. It covers all the terms that the two parties have agreed on, and only those terms.

Mutuality of assent can be expressed as a requirement that there is a firm offer and a firm acceptance of that offer. Offer and acceptance make up assent. For example, a buyer's purchase order includes a clause requiring all disputes about it to be arbitrated. The seller fails to sign the order, as required on the order. Instead, he sends his own sale memorandum to the buyer. That memo does not mention arbitration. After the goods are shipped, a dispute arises and the buyer demands arbitration. In this case, the New York courts refused to order arbitration, because the facts did not show that the parties had agreed to it. Here there was no agreement because one party had not agreed to arbitrate; one offer was countered with another offer. Since the buyer said nothing, he was bound by the terms of the counteroffer after he accepted the goods.

In situations when there is some doubt as to the existence of mutuality of assent, the courts will try to determine what the parties actually meant: Did they intend to be bound or not to be bound when they exchanged promises? In commercial cases the courts now are not so strict in requiring that an acceptance exactly match the offer to form a contract.

CONSIDERATION

In an enforceable contract, consideration underlies and induces the promise. A mere promise does not constitute a contract and cannot be enforced against the promisor, the party making the promise. To make a promise enforceable, *something* must be given up by the promisee, the party to whom the promise is made. Something given up by the promisee before the promise is made will not support the promise.

Many business agreements, particularly leases and sales agreements, recite that they are made "for $1 and other good and valuable consideration, the receipt of which is hereby acknowledged." This language is included to make the contract enforceable, even when no money is actually exchanged. This written assertion of consideration can be challenged and disproved under limited circumstances, but its existence may support a contract that has no other apparent consideration. This is because the courts are reluctant to go behind the written terms of a contract and question the written recital that the parties gave and received consideration. The bald assertion that there is consideration is also protected by the parol evidence rule, described in Chapters 5 and 9. This rule of evidence makes it difficult to challenge the language of a written contract by oral testimony.

Strong reliance on contract formality is made by charities seeking pledges during their fund-raising campaigns. Some ask donors to sign a pledge "in consideration of" the pledges of other contributors. This language is designed to make the donors believe the pledge is an enforceable contract so that they will make the promised payments. That pledge is merely a voluntary unilateral promise. Some courts may enforce this, particularly if the pledge is a large one and the charity to which it was made acted in reliance on it, perhaps by signing a contract to build a new laboratory. But in general, if the donor changes his mind, he cannot be sued by the charity for breach of contract.

LAWFUL OBJECT

The commitments that the parties agree to in a contract must be lawful. Some contracts, although in writing and signed by the parties, are by themselves illegal because the nature of the contract requires something illegal to be done. Such a contract is void.

Examples of contracts commonly regarded as void because of illegality would be a gambling contract or a contract that has as a part of its terms the clear intent to restrain trade (see Chapter 8). Other contracts can be regarded as void in part because they verge on illegality:

1. A contract that cannot be performed without committing some wrong, or tort, while completing it.
2. Although still heavily litigated, in general a contract that completely excludes a party from all liability to a third party is held to be

void. An example of this is a contract clause providing that "the contractor exempts himself from liability for injuries to person or property caused by or resulting from the negligence of such contractor." This is discussed in more detail in "Limitations on Liability" later in the chapter.

3. A court may refuse to enforce a contract if it feels that the contract was "unconscionable" when it was written and signed. See "Unconscionable Contracts" later in the chapter.

4. A contract that was made knowing that one of the parties would have to commit an illegal act to bring the contract to its conclusion.

TIME OF PERFORMANCE

To be enforceable, a contract must provide a time within which it is to be performed. If it does not, it is viewed by the courts as unenforceable because of the lack of specificity. In the case of most contracts, particularly oral ones, the courts will infer that the parties intended that the contract was to be performed within a reasonable time. A reasonable time depends on the nature of the acts to be performed and the customs and practices of the business and the community.

IN WRITING: THE STATUTE OF FRAUDS

The requirement that certain types of contracts must be in writing to be enforceable was first adopted by the English Parliament in 1677 in a law called the Statute of Frauds. Almost every state has adopted its basic provisions. These laws, called by the same name as their ancestor, provide that no legal action may be taken to enforce the following contracts unless they are in writing and signed by the party against whom enforcement is sought:

1. A contract by an executor or administrator of an estate to pay the debts or liabilities of the deceased from the executor's or administrator's own assets.

2. A contract to pay someone else's debt or debts.

3. A contract that promises something upon someone's marriage, called a contract made in consideration of marriage.

4. A contract for the sale of real estate or the transfer of any interest in land.

5. A contract that cannot be performed within one year of the date it was signed by the two parties.

In addition, every state except Louisiana has adopted provisions akin to the statute of frauds when they adopted the Uniform Commercial Code (discussed in more detail in "Buying and Selling Goods," later in this chapter). The UCC provides that, in the case of the sale of goods worth $500 or more, some written memorandum of the contract of sale must be signed by the party to be charged or by his agent, except when (1) the buyer accepts part of the goods and actually receives them; or (2) he gives something in part payment.

The practical implications of this can be seen in the common case where a business accepts a telephone order for more than $500 in goods. If there is no written contract, the buyer can later back out. One way to prevent this is to follow up on such orders promptly with a written confirmation. If the buyer does not object to the confirmation, the contract can be enforced.

The parol evidence rule, while different, supports the operation of the statute of frauds and of the UCC by preventing the introduction of oral evidence to change or contradict the terms of a written agreement. It would be futile to require that certain agreements be written to be enforceable if they could be amended orally.

THE CAPACITY TO MAKE A CONTRACT

For a contract to be enforceable, all the parties to that contract must be competent to contract at the time the contract is made.

Corporations
A corporation is a legal entity whose existence is authorized by the state. Its powers are limited to those specifically set forth in its articles of

incorporation and to those necessary to carry them out. A corporation has no other powers. If you have a contract with a corporation that requires it to do something it is not empowered to do in its articles of incorporation, the contract is beyond the corporation's powers, or *ultra vires.* Such a contract can be regarded as void because the corporation has the defense of legal incapacity.

Today, it is not likely that this would be a problem because most corporations are created with the widest possible powers. In fact, some state laws permit the articles of incorporation to provide that the corporation be given all of the powers available to corporations under that state's law. The only problem today would be in dealing with a corporation that is established for a limited purpose, and whose articles of incorporation may therefore limit what it can do.

Minors and Others Lacking Capacity

Certain groups of individuals are regarded as lacking the capacity to enter into a contract. The contracts they enter into while in this state, called a legal disability, may be disavowed by them or on their behalf, or affirmed by them or on their behalf, if and when the disability is removed. Such contracts are voidable at the option of the legally disabled party, but not at the option of the other party.

The most common situation involves the legal disability of a minor. A minor is deemed not to be legally competent to enter into a contract. This means that the minor, if sued for breach of contract, can argue that he lacks the legal capacity to make a contract. The courts will generally accept this defense and refuse to enforce the contract. The age of minors varies from state to state; in most states it is eighteen.

Minors who leave home or whose parents have refused to support them are considered emancipated. Their contracts are also voidable, unless the contracts are for the necessities of life: food, shelter, clothing, medical assistance, and education. Thus entering into a contract with a minor always poses the risk that the contract can be disavowed in the future.

The right of a minor to plead lack of legal capacity while still a minor and either ratify or avoid the contract on achieving majority is personal to him or her. If the minor dies, all of his contracts may be avoided by his heirs or representatives. If the minor becomes insane, this can be done by the minor's guardian.

The other party to the contract with a minor is always viewed as able to protect himself. If that party is under no legal disability, he is bound by the contract if the minor chooses to hold him party to it.

Similar protection is provided for insane persons or for persons obviously under the influence of alcohol or narcotics. Their contracts, except for necessities, are voidable.

After a Contract Is Signed

ASSIGNING A CONTRACT

Generally, rights under any contract can be assigned, unless the contract is for personal services. Personal service contracts are those made with a specific individual who presumably possesses unique skills. If the services to be rendered under a contract are personal, the contract may be assigned only with the consent of both of the original parties to the contract.

Other contracts are freely assignable, unless the law or the contract itself forbids the assignment or requires it to be in writing. An example of a typical assignment is a full-fare airline ticket. The ticket is the evidence of the airline's contract to carry the purchaser as a passenger. That ticket is assignable by either the purchaser or the airline. The purchaser can sell or give the airline ticket to someone else simply by delivering the ticket. This act constitutes the assignment. If the airline is acquired by another airline, the successor airline assumes the obligation to carry the purchaser or the individual to whom the ticket has been assigned.

Because of the freedom to assign contracts, a contract may include a clause specifically providing that it may not be assigned, or it may set forth a set of conditions under which it may be assigned. If the contract is valid, such limitation on assignment will be enforced by the courts. A typical nonassignment clause is paragraph 10 of the sample employment agreement in the Appendix.

Discharging a contract occurs when both parties perform according to the terms of the contract. No further obligations remain between the two parties. Because conditions may change or relationships between the parties may be altered, the law recognizes nine methods of discharging a contract when there has not been full performance:

1. Failure of consideration

2. Inability to perform

3. Rescission

4. Cancellation and surrender of the contract

5. Substitution of a new contract

6. Novation

7. Accord and satisfaction

8. Account stated

9. Release

Failure of Consideration

Consideration, the giving up of something to support a promise, is critical to the existence of a contract. If a contract requires the transfer of a particular thing, the destruction of that thing excuses performance. For example, a contract to paint a specific building is discharged if the building is destroyed.

Inability to Perform

Some contracts can be discharged if their performance has become impossible. This can happen where the law changes after the contract is signed, thus preventing performance. For example, if a township passes an ordinance stopping new well drilling, a drilling company is discharged from its contract to drill a new well under a contract signed before the ordinance was passed. If one party cannot perform, the law does not require that party to do what it cannot do.

Rescission

A contract can be rescinded by the parties. For example, a company may hire an architect to design a new plant. Before the architect does anything, the company changes its mind and decides that it does not need the plant. The company and the architect may just agree that their deal is off; there would no longer be a contract. If the architect had done some work before the decision was made, rescinding the contract would require the company to pay for the work already done as the consideration for the architect giving up his rights under the contract.

Cancellation and Surrender of the Contract

Cancellation of a contract and surrender of the contract itself are similar. Marking "cancelled" on a deposit check given as a down payment on a copier and returning that check to the buyer discharges the contract and the buyer's obligations under the contract, if the buyer accepts the check. If the company selling the copier had a note signed by the customer, surrendering that note must be accompanied by a new agreement between the company and the customer releasing the customer's obligation under the contract.

Substitution of a New Contract

Substituting a new contract discharges the old one. A new contract can retain some of the terms of the original contract and include new terms as well as an entire agreement covering the same transaction. In either case the second contract is substituted for the first, and the first is discharged. Neither party can then enforce the old contract.

Novation

Substitution of new parties, called novation, also discharges the contract. For example, one party owes a second party $5,000. A third party and the first two agree that the debtor will be discharged and the new party will become the debtor. The original debtor is now discharged.

Accord and Satisfaction

When one party is not satisfied with the performance of the other, the contract can be discharged through accord and satisfaction. For example, a debtor owes you $2,000. You both agree that the debtor will resurface your parking area to satisfy the debt. The agreement is an accord. When the lot is resurfaced, there has been an accord and a satisfaction. The $2,000 debt has been discharged.

Account Stated

A monthly business checking or NOW account statement is one of the most common examples of an account stated. The statement shows deposits that the company made and what checks the bank has paid out against that account. If the company raises no questions about the statement when it is received or within a reasonable time after receipt, a legal action against the bank—example, one filed two years later a mistake in the account—will be dismissed by the courts unless the company can show the bank acted in bad faith or defrauded the company.

Another example of an account stated is a quarterly bill from an office-equipment supplier that is accompanied by a list of all items purchased and charged to the company's account. Payment of the bill, or a failure to question improper charges on it within a short time, can deprive the company of the right to sue for a breach of contract. The payments are considered a discharge of the contract between the supplier and the company.

Release

If a creditor is willing to release a debtor from a contractual obligation, they are both effecting a release. If the creditor is owed money under a note but the debtor disputes the amount still due, the creditor may be willing to forgive part of the amount it believes it is owed in exchange for avoiding the costs of a lawsuit to collect the disputed amount. In such a situation the creditor should sign a release stating that the debtor is released from completing the contract and that the creditor agrees not to sue the debtor for the balance. Preparation of a release is discussed in Chapter 7.

BREACHING A CONTRACT

A breach of contract is an unjustified failure to perform the terms of the contract when that performance is due. There are two types of breach: partial breach and total or material breach. An example of a total breach would be the unilateral termination of the contract by one party, where the contract does not give that party the power to do so.

If there is any likelihood that the agreement will be terminated, the termination must be clear. A 1981 case in Wyoming illustrates this. An individual signed an agreement to build a mobile-home court for a land-owner. After the agreement was signed, the landowner sent a letter saying he intended to terminate the agreement because the land surrounding the property had been purchased by a coal company. The builder sued, claiming that the landowner had breached their contract by terminating and repudiating it.

The Wyoming Supreme Court concluded that there was no breach of contract. The letter, it said, expressed only an intention to cancel and did not constitute an "unequivocal termination" of the contract. In other words, saying you intend to terminate is not the same as saying you *have* terminated.

Special Issues

BUYING OR SELLING GOODS

A sale or a purchase of goods is a contract, so the law of sales is governed by many of the principles of the law of contracts, as modified by a key statute, the Uniform Commercial Code. The UCC has been adopted by every state except Louisiana. But despite its name, it has not been adopted uniformly.

As with any other contract, certain elements are required if the purchase or sale of goods is to be legal:

1. Mutual assent, resulting from an offer and acceptance of that offer, communicated to the person who made the offer

2. Legally competent parties to the contract

3. Consideration

4. Legal subject matter of the contract

If any element is lacking, the purchase or sale will not be enforceable in the courts.

If you order a book by phone or place a written order and that order is accepted, a contract of sale arises. When you go to an office-supply store and place an order for a particular dictating machine that the dealer does not have in stock but will get for you, you may have to sign a contract to buy the machine.

The UCC in each state provides whether the specific contract to be entered into must be in writing. This depends on the value of the purchase. In almost every state, if the value exceeds $500, the contract must be in writing to be enforced by the courts. A sales slip or receipt will generally meet the requirement for a written agreement. If you are buying something of considerable value, you should require a more formal contract, specifying what you are buying, the price, when payment is to be made, and when and where delivery is to be made.

TITLE AND OWNERSHIP

What is important in a typical sale or purchase is when the goods become the buyer's, or "when title passes." Until the goods are the buyer's, the seller bears the loss if anything happens to them. The parties can agree on when the goods become the buyer's. If there is no clear agreement, either because the intent of the parties is not clear or because the parties never discussed it, the courts have applied a set of rules to determine title and the risk of loss:

1. A buyer agrees to purchase a specific item, such as a copier, from a dealer. The buyer has no place to put it for a month, so the buyer leaves it in the store. Title passes to the buyer at the time the sale agreement is made, so if the store and copier are destroyed in a fire, the loss of the copier is the buyer's.

2. If the copier being sold is secondhand and requires repairs, the

dealer retains title. The dealer bears any loss if the store and copier are destroyed before the repairs are finished.

3. If the dealer gives the buyer the option of returning the copier after a thirty-day trial instead of paying for it, the buyer gets title on delivery. During the time the buyer uses the copier, the loss is his if it is damaged. If he returns it within the thirty days, title returns to the dealer and any future losses are borne by him. If no time was set by the parties for the trial period, the courts will permit it to be kept for a reasonable time. If it is returned within that reasonable time, the risk of loss is returned as well.

4. If the agreement provides that the dealer deliver the copier to the buyer on approval, the title passes to the buyer when he indicates approval, or if and when he retains the copier beyond a reasonable time without giving a rejection notice.

5. If the buyer goes to a building-supply company and places an order for a certain kind of roofing, which the buyer is to pick up at the yard the next day and take to the plant in its own truck, the roofing is deemed to be "unconditionally appropriated" to the contract. Title then and there passes to the buyer. If the company's warehouse burns during the night, the buyer suffers the loss of the value of that roofing.

6. If the lumberyard agrees to deliver some lumber to the buyer's plant or to pay for the cost of transportation to the plant, title does not pass to the buyer until the lumber has actually been delivered to the plant.

7. If a dealer of flowers and shrubs places a firm order for 2,000 rosebushes to be shipped by an airline specified by the buyer, title passes to the buyer when those bushes have been delivered to that airline.

Shipment and Liability for Loss

There are a variety of arrangements governing commercial shipment of goods, and often they are expressed by initials. The most familiar is a COD shipment, standing for "cash" or "collect on delivery." A buyer pays no money when he orders the goods, but the seller's delivery man is ordered not to hand them to the buyer until he receives payment, usually in cash, unless the seller has previously agreed to accept a check. If the delivery truck is in an accident on the way to the buyer and the goods are destroyed, the loss is the buyer's.

If a buyer orders a machine from a factory in the United States or abroad, two methods of payment are used, each of which has a different significance for the risk of loss. A document used in connection with the shipment is the bill of lading. The bill of lading encompasses the instructions given by the shipper to the shipping company or common carrier. It is both a receipt given by the carrier to the shipper and a contract between the shipper and the carrier covering the terms of the transportation to be provided. A copy of the bill of lading is sent to the buyer, since it also indicates ownership. The person who presents the bill of lading at the designated place of delivery is entitled to receive the shipment from the carrier.

A contract with the manufacturer of the machine may be FOB (free on board) or FAS (free alongside ship). Under such a contract, the buyer receives title when the seller delivers the machine to the carrier. If the Sascha Machine Tool Corporation, with a factory in Camden, New Jersey, contracts to sell one of its machines "FOB Camden," title to that machine passes to the buyer when the machine is delivered to the railroad freight yard in Camden. Any damages to the machine during shipment are the buyer's responsibility.

If a buyer in Seattle orders a machine from a Japanese manufacturer, the contract may read "CIF Seattle." CIF means cost, insurance, and freight. The manufacturer must deliver the machine to the carrier and pay the freight to Seattle, the point of destination. He must send the buyer the invoice or contract, an insurance policy covering the entire shipment, the bill of lading, and a receipt showing that the freight has been paid. Title passes to the buyer only when the manufacturer has done all of these things.

If the Seller Does Not Own the Goods Sold

The law provides that a seller cannot usually give a buyer a better title, or greater ownership, to goods than the buyer actually has. In particular, a thief cannot pass along good title to a stolen item. If the rightful owner finds his goods in someone else's possession, he has the right to get the goods back. The courts will order the return of the stolen goods to the rightful owner, even when the person who bought them from the thief acted in good faith—that is, the buyer was an innocent purchaser for value. The buyer's only recourse is to sue the thief for the price he paid for the stolen goods, providing he can find the thief.

QUALITY AND WARRANTIES

There is always concern over the rights and remedies of a buyer when the goods purchased are found to be of poor quality or dangerous, or if they do not meet the expectations of the buyer. In any contract each party has the duty to perform his obligations according to the understandings, either express or implied, between them. The understandings concerning the quality of the goods purchased or sold are called warranties. A furnace purchased for an office building carries with it a warranty that it will heat the air in the building. If it does not do this, the buyer has an action against the seller of the furnace for a breach of warranty. To win in an action for breach of warranty, the buyer cannot just show that he was dissatisfied with the product's performance. The buyer must show that the product did not do what it was supposed to do to the satisfaction of a reasonable person.

Warranties are of two types, express and implied. If you sell a suit labeled "pure wool," you, as merchant, have made an express warranty that, in fact, the suit is wool. A buyer has several options if he finds that it is *not* wool. He may (1) return the suit and sue you for the purchase price; (2) keep the suit and sue you for the difference between what the buyer paid for the suit and what it is actually worth; or (3) refuse to accept the suit on delivery, if the buyer finds out after the purchase but before it is delivered, and sue for breach of warranty.

Implied warranties have been created by the courts to protect consumers. Today, if a consumer purchases a can of spoiled fruit that makes him sick, he can sue the manufacturer because the law implies a warranty of quality. Here the warranty is that the fruit is reasonably fit for the purpose for which it was sold—that is, the fruit is fit to eat—and that it is of saleable or merchantable quality.

There are three common implied warranties in the UCC:

1. The seller has the legal right to sell the goods, and the buyer therefore has exclusive use and possession of them
2. The goods are fit for the purpose that the buyer and the seller had in mind in making the sale
3. If the buyer orders from a sample or a description, the product received must be the same as the sample or as described by the seller

In addition, federal and state laws now specify what warranties consumer goods must carry and how the consumer is to be made aware of them.

Not all promises about the quality of goods are warranties. Salespersons are allowed to build up the product being sold, exaggerating its qualities and good features. This overemphasis is often called "puffing." The courts have ruled that puffing does not constitute a warranty. The reasoning is that extreme statements by the seller are to be treated as mere exaggerations and taken with a grain of salt. The buyer is expected to protect himself against puffing by making reasonable inquiries about the goods or by arranging that any promises of performance be incorporated in the agreement.

BAILMENTS

Bailments usually do not spring to mind when thinking of business agreements because few businesspeople recognize the term. And those who do may not realize that many of the terms covering a bailment are not negotiated by the parties but rather are established by law. Simply stated, a bailment is created when one person is in rightful possession of the personal property belonging to another person. Possession as used in the law of bailments implies control, but the bailee (the one receiving the property) may not use it for his own purposes. If he does, he is responsible for any damages to it.

There are basically three types of bailments created by agreement between parties:

1. Bailment for the sole benefit of the bailor (the owner of the property)

2. Bailment for the sole benefit of the bailee

3. Bailment for the mutual benefit of the bailee and the bailor

More commonly, these are identified as storage, borrowing, and rental of personal property.

The bailment for the sole benefit of the bailor does not have to be accepted by the bailee, since he is not compensated. If he were, it would be a bailment for their mutual benefit. Once the bailee accepts the property, however, a contractual obligation is created. The bailee is liable to the bailor if he is negligent in the maintenance or care of the personal property given to him. However, since he is not being paid, the bailee is held to a low standard of care. He is liable to the owner of the property only for acts of gross negligence. The bailment can be terminated by either party at will. For example, assume that a company truck breaks down at your home. A neighbor comes by and offers to fix it, saying that it seems to be a problem with the fuel pump. You let him fix it and he takes out the pump. Because you could not force the neighbor to do the work, it is a bailment for your sole benefit. But having taken the pump, the neighbor must then return it. If he does not, or if he damages it through gross negligence, he is liable to you for the resulting damages.

In a bailment for the sole benefit of the bailee, there is also no compensation. But since the personal property of the bailor is being loaned to the bailee, and since it is for the exclusive benefit of the bailee, the law requires that the bailee have a higher standard of care than in the previous case. In this case, even slight negligence on the bailee's part would make him liable to the bailor for damages.

In business the most common bailment is that for the mutual benefit of the parties. Here each side gets something from the deal. One is paid and the other receives services of some kind. This relationship requires the bailee to exercise ordinary care in the maintenance and use of the property. He must return the property on demand, and if he fails to do so, he is presumed to be liable for its loss. However, if the bailee can show that the loss was caused by circumstances beyond his control, he is not liable so long as he used ordinary care.

The purpose of this agreement is usually either to repair or to store the bailor's property. For example, if you take your car to a garage to be fixed, you have created a bailment when the mechanic accepts it. If the car is subsequently stolen from the garage, the garage is not liable, providing it took reasonable precautions to safeguard the car. For example, if the garage left the car outside with the keys in it, it would be liable to you for the loss.

If the bailee is to render services to the property, he must perform these services with reasonable care and in conformance with the agreement of the parties. If the personal property is transferred for a specific purpose and the bailee uses the property for some other purpose, he is liable for any damages resulting from that use. For example, your company may rent a power drill and some wood bits, stating that it will be used in redoing an office. If the drill burns out in use, you are not liable. If, however, you used the drill for another purpose, such as drilling into concrete, you will be responsible for the damage to it, since this use was not the purpose of the bailment.

In many cases of bailment for mutual benefit there will be a written rental agreement between the parties governing the use of the personal property and the liability of each party. Unless that agreement provides otherwise, the owner of the property is responsible for major repairs that become necessary during the rental period. If the rental covers a truck, that means the owner, or bailor, would be responsible for the repair of defective brakes, fuel pumps, and engines. The renter, or bailee, would be responsible for fixing a flat tire. To limit the liability of the bailee, the contractual provisions have to be reasonable and have to be known to the bailor, which usually means a written agreement is necessary.

The mere passing of an item of personal property from one person to another can create an agreement even though no document is signed and no discussions of liability and standards of care are held. The law supplies all of these, and it requires only the act and limited communication to create an agreement.

LIMITATIONS ON LIABILITY

In one of Charles Schulz's *Peanuts* cartoons the characters are confronted by Lucy. She holds out a piece of paper and asks each of them to sign it. When asked about it, she says, "No matter what happens any place or any time in the world, this absolves me from all blame." This cartoon makes a serious point: In today's increasingly complex world, parties entering into contracts try to define and ultimately limit their liability and exposure to liability from the other party and even from persons who are not parties to the contract. Done in the context of an arm's-length bargaining, clauses that allocate responsibility between the parties are generally valid. While these parties cannot keep third parties from suing them, they can require that another party to the contract repay them if they are held liable to a third party. This concept is called *indemnification.* Essentially, one of the parties operates like an insurance company. It will make good on certain defined losses and take responsibility for certain lawsuits.

The effort to limit liability has often gone too far. Frequently, the businessperson and consumer will be faced with documents that severely limit or even pretend to eliminate the liability of another for certain losses. These are disclaimers—that is, attempts to limit the liability between the two parties. The general rule is that where a third party is involved—the one who did not sign the contract—these disclaimers are illegal and cannot be enforced. The courts characterize them as "against public policy."

Disclaimers and limitations of liability can also be void and against public policy even if they involve only the two parties to a transaction. For example, an exculpatory contract is one that has no warranty on the goods purchased. State and federal laws now require that there be at least a limited warranty on consumer goods. The courts have held that the sale of a product without any warranty is permitted if the parties were able to bargain on the terms of the sale. Otherwise, this limitation on liability is void.

UNCONSCIONABLE CONTRACTS

The courts and state legislatures have also designated some contracts as "unconscionable." These agreements are regarded as unfair and commercially unreasonable, either at the time a party seeks to enforce the contract or at the time the contract was made. Among unconscionable contracts that generally try to limit or eliminate liability are the small print on bank signature cards, parking lot tickets, sales contracts, credit cards, and credit charge slips. These are not always unconscionable, however. The test is whether or not the agreement between the parties is oppressive and unfair.

Similar to these is the contract of adhesion, which is not illegal but generally is hard to enforce by the one who offered it. The most common contracts of adhesion are form agreements, presented on a take-it-or-leave-it basis. The courts have applied a number of tests, but they usually try to determine whether or not there was an opportunity for the two parties to bargain over the terms of the contract. If not, and if the terms are overly harsh or one-sided, the entire agreement may be reinterpreted in favor of the party who lacked the ability to bargain. Most of the changes in landlord-tenant law in the past two decades have resulted from court determinations that particular leases were contracts of adhesion. Having determined that, the courts refused to enforce restrictive terms, particularly those absolving the landlord from liability to the tenant.

The most common contract of adhesion today is the insurance contract. This contract is typically offered for sale on a take-it-or-leave-it basis. The insurance company drafts the contract, and there is ordinarily only a very narrow range within which a business can negotiate modifications to the insurer's offer. In the case of insurance contracts that must be approved by state insurance departments before they can be used, the insured may not be allowed to negotiate any change. Rather, he has only the choice of "adhering" to the contract or rejecting it.

Because this contract is considered one of adhesion, and because it is drafted by the insurer, it is usually construed in favor of the insured and against the insurer when there is any ambiguity. While standardized insurance policies—those whose language is prescribed in part or entirely by state law—should be treated differently because the clauses were not drafted by the insurer, most courts still treat them as contracts of adhesion and construe them against the insurer.

An attempt to use the language in a contract to escape liability for your acts is limited in virtually every context when there is fraud. The basic rule is that any contract language that protects a person against his own fraud is unenforceable because of "public policy." Thus this type of clause cannot be used by the party it favors to prevent the other party from proving fraud in order to avoid liability under a contract. For example, many contractual disputes involve a contract clause such as "No representations or warranties of any kind shall be binding on the seller unless incorporated in the agreement." The courts have held consistently that this clause will not stop a fraudulent seller from being held responsible for his fraud.

The definition of fraud varies. Among the most common cases of fraud are material misrepresentations of a present or former fact made with the intention that the buyer can rely on it. As a result of the misrepresentation, the buyer did rely on it, acted, and was damaged. The classic situation is in the sale of property. Here fraud can allow the buyer to cancel the transaction. However, the courts have held that the buyer must have been reasonable in relying on the fraud. For instance, if the buyer made an independent investigation of the property being sold, he will be presumed to have relied on the results of that investigation and not on the misrepresentations of the seller.

PARLIAMENTARY PROCEDURE

One of the areas that few people think of as creating contract rights is parliamentary procedure. If a business adopts rules of parliamentary procedure as part of its bylaws, that procedure becomes a contract between the shareholder (or member) and the corporation (or association), just as the constitution, articles of incorporation or association, and bylaws themselves are a contract between the organization and its shareholders. They are also a contract among the shareholders themselves.

When a business corporation, union, trade association, or charity adopts rules of procedure or a parliamentary manual as part of its bylaws, any shareholder or member of that organization has a right, by contract, to insist that the rules be applied and applied properly. This is true even though the bylaws permit a majority of the members to change the rules. Thus a majority can impose a contract on the minority, unlike other contracts, which cannot be imposed on unwilling persons.

Because this is an unusual kind of contract, the remedies available in the case of a breach are limited. If a member alleges that the organization has breached its contract with him, he will still have to adhere to the rules of the organization in seeking relief. His relief will probably be limited to an order forcing the organization to comply with the rules in question. If the organization alleges that the members violated this contract, it cannot sue for damages. Instead, its remedy is to punish the member in the manner and to the extent provided in the rules of the organization. The usual punishment is expulsion or suspension.

3

Making an Agreement

Negotiating an Agreement

Negotiating is an art all to itself. Whenever you are about to negotiate an agreement, prepare yourself beforehand. Never base a new agreement on an old contract and begin negotiations from that. The contract should be tailored to the deal; the deal should never be constructed from the contract. Whether you are negotiating a multimillion-dollar deal to ship goods internationally or simply arranging for the purchase of office supplies, enter the contract negotiations with a clear idea of your goals.

The following outline sets forth some of the key steps involved in negotiating a business agreement:

1. Determine your goals and attitudes.

   How important is the deal to you?

   Why is this particular party important?

2. Determine the other party's goals and attitudes.

   What does he want from this deal?

   How does he see your strengths and weaknesses?

3. Gather a team of experts to advise you on the deal and clarify contract language.

   Who should you negotiate with? (Team members to establish your needs).

   What do you know about the other party? What are his business practices, competitive conditions, customer relations?

   Does he have the authority to make a binding deal?

   What trade-offs are you willing and able to make and for what?

4. Set up the negotiations.

   What documents do you need? (Performance specifications, previous contracts, purchase orders, credit history.)

5. Determine your strategy.

   Do you have a checklist of topics to be covered and an agenda for the negotiations?

   Have you reviewed standard and form agreements on the subject?

   In light of these agreements, should you revise your agenda or checklist?

   What are the other party's counterpositions likely to be?

6. The actual negotiations.

7. Drafting the agreement.

   Memorialize the deal in a written agreement as soon as possible.

   Record your reasons for trade-offs. This is useful for future contracts. Also, in case of litigation, you will have a record of why the parties rejected as well as why they accepted.

   Prepare the agreement according to your checklist/agenda.

Modify your standard form contract, if appropriate, or outline a new agreement.

Get the agreement signed as soon as possible.

THE NEGOTIATING TEAM

In complex negotiations or in negotiations involving a large purchase, consider using a team of experts in the subject matter of the proposed contract. They will help you get what you want and highlight problems in proposed contract language before the deal is closed. When a businessperson gives an executed agreement to technical personnel to administer, the personnel should not have to ask what it means or ask for clarification of any specific and unique terms and concepts. If the contract uses a concept or term in a manner *different* from the way technical personnel use it, it invites misunderstanding, improper performance, disputes, and litigation. Using a team made up of those who must live with the contract helps to eliminate this.

USING A CHECKLIST/AGENDA IN NEGOTIATIONS

Some legal-form books now incorporate checklists that are useful in preparing for specific contract negotiations. They can also assist you in preparing the final agreement.

In addition to the specific terms that are unique to a particular transaction (see Chapter 4), certain basic elements should be included in every checklist. Ask the following questions as you set up the checklist:

Who are the parties involved in the deal?

Does the person signing the contract have the authority to do so?

Can the contract be assigned? How? To whom?

What are the parties to do?

What is the consideration for the deal? What is each side getting from it or giving up?

Is one party's obligation dependent on the other doing something first?

What constitutes performance?

What happens if an outside force, such as a strike, makes performance hard or impossible?

Is any money or property to be put into escrow? Why?

Who bears the risk of loss and when?

Who is responsible for compliance with laws such as OSHA rules or patent laws?

Where is the contract to be performed?

Where are goods to be delivered? What services are to be performed?

What law governs the contract?

When is performance to take place?

What is the duration of the agreement?

Are there automatic renewals?

Is there a right to terminate? For what reasons? By whom?

Is time of the essence? If something cannot be done within a specific length of time, should the contract be cancelled?

When are the parties paid? How?

How is the contract set up?

Is there any right to cancel for breach of contract?

Are any other documents incorporated by reference?

Are all prior communications merged into the agreement?

Can the agreement be changed orally or only in writing? By whom and how?

What constitutes a waiver of a contractual right?

Is any indemnification needed?

Are there any warranties?

Is there to be a deposit? Should the deposit serve as liquidated damages?

How will disputes be handled? Is there to be an arbitration clause?

Preparing an Agreement

The manner in which you agree to pay a supplier of goods or services or the manner in which you agree to be paid has an important bearing on the contents of an agreement. Selecting among several standard methods of compensation means that you must include the following in the contract:[1]

1. Firm fixed-price contract:
   Scope of Work
   Schedule
   Terms and Conditions
   Price

2. Cost plus fixed-fee contract:
   Scope of Work
   Schedule
   Terms and Conditions
   Estimated Cost
   Fixed Fee

3. Incentive Contracts
   A. Fixed-price incentive contract:
      Scope of Work
      Schedule
      Terms and Conditions
      Special Clauses
      Target Cost
      Target Profit
      Ceiling Price
      Sharing Ratio (formula for profit)
   B. Cost plus incentive contract:
      Scope of Work
      Schedule
      Terms and Conditions

Special Clauses
Target Cost
Target Fee
Minimum Fee
Maximum Fee
Sharing Ratio (formula for fee)
C. Cost plus award-fee contract:
Scope of Work
Schedule
Terms and Conditions
Estimated Cost
Base Fee (a fixed amount that does not vary with performance)
Award Fee (determined after subjective evaluation of performance)
Fee Payment Plan

MEMORIALIZING THE AGREEMENT

Even when two parties have reached agreement on all the issues, the process of making an agreement is not complete. The danger of informality in business agreements has been pointed out by the American Institute of Architects to its members:

A clear understanding between the Architect and his client [the Owner] as to their mutual relations and obligations is of utmost importance. . . .

A letter form of agreement with an attached or referenced statement of services to be performed and compensation to be paid is sometimes used. When accepted by the Owner, it constitutes a contract, but unless the services and compensation are fully defined, such an agreement may become burdensome to both parties as the Project progresses. . . . At the outset of a Project, amicable relations may prevail. However, relations between the parties may change or one of the parties may die, and if the agreement is not clear or comprehensive in its provisions, both parties or their successors will suffer because of these inadequacies.

In most cases it is also possible to have a legally binding oral agreement, but such agreements are highly undesirable because of the likelihood of misunderstandings with respect to what was agreed upon and the inherent incompleteness of such agreements. This is true to a lesser extent with agreements contained in an exchange of letters.[2]

DRAFTING THE AGREEMENT

Clear writing and clear thinking go hand in hand. All too often, clouded writing reflects clouded thinking. If you do not fully understand all the elements of the transaction, you may tend to hedge your bets in drafting. You will be vague instead of specific, perhaps adding unnecessary clauses that might affect the deal in an unexpected way.

Approach writing an agreement just as you would any other document. The document is merely the full expression of what you have just agreed on. It is designed to govern the conduct of the parties, both in operations and in disputes. Follow the same basic rules for preparing an agreement as you would for a report:

1. Make sure you fully understand what you have to do.
2. Use your checklist and notes as your outline.
3. Allow enough time to do the job properly.
4. Organize your thoughts before you write. Who is it to be written for? What are the most important elements? How should the document be organized? How will it be used?
5. Write simply and clearly. Use active verbs. The Appendix lists active substitutes for passive verbs.
6. Eliminate unnecessary expressions. Some of the most common words and expressions to avoid are listed in the Appendix.
7. Read what you write aloud. If you lose your place, your reader will too. If it sounds stilted and confusing, it probably is.
8. Do not be afraid to keep the agreement short. Longer is not always better.

Unfortunately, not every agreement is made up of one document. Often you will be faced with the problem of assembling an agreement from a set of documents or of amending an existing agreement. In both cases, the practical problems are the same.

Each part of the agreement, including amendments, should be referred to in one place if possible. For example, the document could state: "This Agreement is made up of the following items, all of which are incorporated into this by reference." Then list each item. If this is not possible, the documents that amend a central document, such as a rider to a master lease, should be labeled as amendments. For example, they can be labeled as "Amendment to a lease dated _____ between _____ and _____ ." The amending document should be signed, or at least initialed by the parties. Again, if you can, indicate on the agreement itself that there are other parts to it, for example by adding "Paragraphs 8–11 are on an attached page" after the text of paragraph 7.

Special Cases

NEGOTIATING BY PHONE

Generally, you should not negotiate a deal and agree to the terms of an agreement over the phone. With a few exceptions, a verbal agreement is as binding as a written one. In the case of a telephone deal, the likelihood that one party does not understand the other is greater than in a face-to-face negotiation. For example, on the phone one speaker may be distracted, but the other does not know it. The second speaker, making a point, interprets the other's silence as assent. Actually, the first missed the point entirely. Also the parties are probably not looking at the same thing, whether it is a sample, a chart, a price list, a form, or a set of conditions. Misinterpretations can go undetected.

If you have to negotiate an agreement over the phone, always remember that you have a contract when you are finished. The following suggestions will help you handle this situation:

1. Make an outline or list of the points to cover before calling.
2. Have everything you need at your desk, such as files, forms, notes, and a calculator.
3. Make sure the other person has the authority to bargain and make a contract.
4. Take notes on the conversation.
5. Repeat what you think you have agreed to.
6. Don't agree to any final elements unless you and the other party clearly understand what you have done.
7. Identify what you have not covered so that there is no misunderstanding.
8. Confirm the full extent of the agreement in writing as soon as possible after the call. Make this the agreement if possible.

REPLY FORMS

Some business agreements are now being made more formal, whereas in the past they relied on a tacit understanding between the parties involved. For example, free-lance writers usually submit an idea for an article in the form of a query to a magazine for its consideration. After reviewing the query, the editor would either decline the article or ask that the author submit the full article for consideration. One free-lance business writer, Mike Major, has proposed using a standard form contract to clarify the terms of submission at the query stage.

Major feels the form will help an author to get a fair deal from editors. He explains:

> The form has three parts. The first refers to the "speedy reply" aspect; the second, the author's terms; the third, the author's guarantee. The form helps you [the author] negotiate a fair deal because it commands respect. It conveys the impression that you are organized, professional and businesslike. The editor can indicate any one of the four responses with only a flick of a pen, and his

Speedy Reply/Agreement Form

(Please check your preference, and, if you wish to make an assignment, sign below. Keep one form for your records and return the second in the enclosed SASE.)

☐ Yes, this looks good, and your terms are acceptable. You have an assignment. See my signature below.

☐ Sorry, this looks good and your terms are acceptable, but we're overstocked now. Try us again with this in _____ months.

☐ Sorry, we can't use this one, but we respect your professionalism and your terms are acceptable, so we encourage you to try us with another query.

☐ This is not for us.

The terms of agreement between the Author, MICHAEL J. MAJOR, and the Publication, _____

for the Author's proposed work, titled, _____

are: a payment of $_____ minimum, plus normal expenses; for the leasing of first North American serial rights only for the written work; and, if photos are included, one-time editorial use in one issue only for the photos; a response to all communications within 30 days; and the printing of the byline, "Mike Major," beneath the title of the published work. Also, it is understood that the Author's proposed work will be done on assignment, which means that the Publication will pay the Author, in full, within 30 days of its receipt of the Author's completed work, according to the terms of this agreement, and that this payment will be nonrefundable. If, within one year of the Publication's leasing the Author's work, the Publication does not publish this work, all rights revert to the Author. The Publication also agrees to send the Author three copies of the issue in which his work appears.

"I have read and agree to the above terms."

signed, _____

The Author, MICHAEL J. MAJOR, guarantees that his proposed work will meet the highest editorial standards, that, if the Editor finds the work in any way unsatisfactory, the Author will make all the necessary corrections for no added charge. Unless other arrangements are made, the proposed work will be delivered within three months of the assignment. If the Editor wants the work sooner, the Author will make every effort to comply. He will certify, in writing, the new, agreed-upon deadline. The Author affirms that he has never missed a deadline.

signed, MICHAEL J. MAJOR, PRESIDENT
MAJOR ENTERPRISES

signature if he makes an assignment [that is, a contract to have the author prepare the article].[3]

The form is an offer to enter into a contract. If you, as editor, sign it, you have agreed to its terms. If you are interested in the proposal but do not want to agree to all the terms, write back and tell the author what terms you wish to change. Do not sign the agreement and then write telling what else you want. If you do, you will have agreed to his terms and offered to amend those terms. If he does not accept the proposed changes, then you are under contract with him on his terms. When you both have agreed on the proper terms, prepare an agreement and sign that new agreement, or type the changes on the form, sign the old form, and initial the changes. Then have him do the same.

PRICE QUOTATIONS

When you make a price quotation to a potential customer, you have extended an offer, which the customer can accept on the terms you state. If you and the customer have not specified all the terms of the agreement, many terms can be included by implication. Because of this, the price quotation by itself may be sufficient to constitute an offer. This means that you should make sure that your price quotations are conditioned. For example, is the price good for only thirty days? If you do not say so, the customer may accept this offer even though you have since changed the price. Even months later, the party can claim that the original contract price still applies. Unless you limit the time the price is good or communicate a new price to the customer, if there is a lawsuit, the courts will hold that your price offer remains open for a "commercially reasonable amount of time." The time depends on the practice of the parties in the past, the pattern of price changes of the seller, and general industry practice. In an era of rapidly changing prices, past patterns of price changes may no longer provide protection and flexibility. Always be sure to specify how long the price quote is open.

EMPLOYMENT APPLICATIONS

It is surprising how many forms business agreements can take and the circumstances under which they are made. Consider these three paragraphs from a typical employment application:

> I hereby certify that the facts contained in the employment application are true and complete to the best of my knowledge. I understand that, if I am employed, a falsified statement on this application shall be grounds for dismissal.
>
> I hereby authorize the investigation of all statements I made in this employment application. I authorize the references I have given in this employment application to give you any and all information containing my previous employment and any pertinent information they may have, personal or otherwise. I hereby release all parties from all liability for any damages that may result from furnishing the same to you.
>
> I understand and agree that, if I am hired, my employment is for no definite period and may, regardless of the date of payment of my wages or salary, be terminated at any time without any prior notice by you.

These three paragraphs constitute the terms of an employment agreement. By signing, you as employee, have agreed that your employer can fire you for false statements on the application. You also agree that your employment can be terminated by the employer at any time "without prior notice." This means that you have given up your right to a notice period, which is based on how frequently you are paid.

You also have agreed not to sue anyone who gives information to your employer arising out of the investigation of your application. Your signature gives the employer your signed consent to have your references give him information about you without having to contact you. Finally, notice that this consent is not limited in terms of time. Conceivably, the employer could investigate your application years later and dismiss you for a misstatement on it.

EMPLOYEES

Every time you as an employer hire a new employee, you have entered into a contract. Very little may have been discussed between you, and virtually nothing may be in writing. Yet it is a contract just the same. As with all other contracts, some of the terms are implied if there is no contrary agreement between the parties. Other terms cannot be varied by the parties at all. You should be aware of all of these terms so that in hiring you can make clear where your employer-employee relationship varies. They will also help you understand when and how to prepare a more formal employment agreement.

Basically, the agreement covers the following broad topics:

1. It binds you as employer and the specific employee.

2. The employee is to work at a specified wage for a given number of hours. If the wage is not specified, there is an implied understanding that the worker will get the payment usual for that area for someone with his degree of skill.

3. The employer can terminate the employee for good cause and not be liable for further wages. If the employee quits, the employer must pay salary up to the time the employee leaves. The employer can deduct from the wages any losses suffered as a result of the employee's departure, if the departure was without good cause. Previously, the employer could also fire the employee without good cause or even as retaliation. Today, however, more and more employees are protected against abusive discharge.[4]

4. The employer must provide a safe workplace.

5. If the employee is authorized to do certain acts for the business, such as purchase supplies, the employer is bound by the employee's actions and is responsible for any purchases or commitments he makes in doing his job.

6. If the employee injures someone while working for you, you as employer are liable to the injured person for any resulting damages.

7. A new worker can expect the same treatment as those currently

working for you and similar businesses. For example, if nothing is said about vacations and your present employees customarily get two weeks during the first year at work, the new employee has a right to expect two weeks. If most other local businesses close during severe snowstorms but pay their employees, your employees have that right because they are hired under the conditions common to the area, unless there is a clear understanding to the contrary.

8. The employee must obey instructions given by the employer. He must be diligent, prudent, and careful so that his actions do not cause a loss or harm to any other person.

9. A material omission of a fact or condition related to the job on the job application may be grounds for the employer to discharge the employee, if the employer learns about it in the future.

10. A departing employee may not disclose trade secrets or customer lists to competitors. That employee is free to use the technical knowledge he gains on the job to the benefit of your competitors.

11. The employer can make reasonable rules about the job, and the employee must adhere to them. These can even bar taking a second job that interferes with work for the employer, either because of the time and attention required or because it is for an actual or potential competitor.

12. Unless state law requires it, an employer does not have to give a former employee a reference.

SKILLED WORKERS

Skilled workers at one time were referred to as artisans, a term denoting their historical origins in the craft guilds of Europe. Today, the term *artisan* covers a worker or craftsperson skilled in an art or trade, including plumbers, electricians, carpenters, repairmen, mechanics, and other skilled workers. When you have a contract with an artisan, most of the terms are implied. You may have a written agreement or merely an agreement on a few critical terms, but usually there is no formal agreement.

Without a written agreement, a contract with an artisan includes the following:

1. By accepting the assignment, the artisan has agreed to perform it satisfactorily.
2. If goods are left with the artisan, the artisan has an obligation to take good care of them. *Good care* means the same care he would take of his own property.
3. If there is no agreed-upon date for completion of the work, the artisan is expected to complete it in a reasonable time.
4. If the artisan and customer agree on a price or on specific amounts of work, the customer is not obligated to pay for any additional work.
5. If the artisan does not complete the work, the customer owes the artisan nothing. If the customer has to hire someone else to complete the job, the customer may bring a lawsuit for any added costs that result from this hiring.
6. When the work is completed in a satisfactory manner, the customer has an obligation to pay promptly. If the customer does not, the artisan may be able to get a mechanic's lien against the property in his care. This means the property does not have to be returned until the bill is paid. If the customer does not pay the bill, the artisan can take legal steps that will permit him to sell the property and pay himself for the work from the proceeds of the sale. Any balance after payment goes back to the customer.
7. If the work is not completed because the customer tells the artisan to stop, the artisan has a right to be paid for the work already done.

TRADE CUSTOM AND USAGE

The content of an agreement often depends on the context of the deal. Most businesspeople assume that the parties should both demonstrate some agreement and state the terms of the agreement in order for it to be binding. But custom in the business community can determine both when a deal is made and what its terms are. Of course, when you sign a document setting forth the terms and conditions, you have an agreement. But, think of an auction, where the auctioneer calls off prices. You respond by an agreed-upon gesture. That gesture means the following:

1. You are bidding on the item displayed.
2. The item will be purchased as is, generally without any warranties as to its condition, because you will have had a chance to examine it before bidding started.
3. If the auctioneer accepts your bid, you are bound and cannot then withdraw it.
4. Your bid can be preempted by a higher bid.
5. If your bid is accepted, you will pay for the item that day, in cash, and take it with you.
6. There are no returns, exchanges, or refunds.

Your single gesture has these meanings because they have been agreed to in the profession of auctioneering.

What makes up a contract can vary from industry to industry. One of the most interesting industry practices in this regard is found in the wholesale diamond business in New York City. Here virtually all transactions are unwritten. At most, there may be a written note prepared by someone who weighed a diamond, setting forth its weight. By tradition and custom, a deal is closed by a handshake and one party uttering "mazel und brucha." Once these words have been spoken, the deal as discussed is made. This means that diamond dealers are very careful in their speech, for the fast pace of that market can mean that a passing offer to sell a diamond can be accepted quickly by the words and offer of a handshake. Once done, the deal is made. Murray Schumach, a reporter for the *New York Times*, related the following story, illustrating the pervasiveness of trade practice and custom in the diamond industry.

Today, the mazel und brucha code is so much a part of Forty-Seventh Street [the center of the diamond trade] that it has become an ornament in the Street's self-mocking humor. . . .

The tale is that once there was a diamond dealer on Forty-Seventh Street, who no matter how much money he made, never stopped complaining. His gripe was always the same—his wife. She was a nag. She was a spendthrift. She had no understanding of how hard he worked. She could always find a woman friend whose husband was making more money then he was.

One day, as he was whining in the Diamond Club about his wife to another dealer, the listener, who had heard these complaints many times, finally interrupted and said, "I don't know. It seems to me that you have a very good wife. She's intelligent. She's attractive. She dresses with taste. I don't know why you're always moaning about her."

The husband was astounded at this defense. "Would you take her?" he demanded.

The other man remained silent.

The husband pressed him. "If you think she's so wonderful," he said, "how much would you give for her?"

The friend pondered for a while. Then he said, "Nothing."

The husband grasped his friend's hand, shook it, and shouted, "Mazel und brucha! It's a deal."[5]

SUBCONTRACTING

In general, the terms and conditions of a subcontract will be determined by the contents of the prime contract. Therefore, to create an outline or checklist for negotiating a subcontract, you will have to re-familiarize yourself with the prime contract and all related documents.

When preparing a subcontract, keep in mind the following:

1. What does the prime contract require you to subcontract? (In government contracts a portion may have to be subcontracted to a defined economic or ethnic group.)

2. What does the prime contract forbid you to subcontract?

3. What does the prime contract require from subcontractors: that is, a bond, financial statement, prior approval by the one who gave out the prime contract?

4. Will you have to meet regularly with the subcontractor? Where? Will the subcontractor have to assign someone to the subcontract and/or the contract site on a part-time or full-time basis?

5. Who will deal with the subcontractor? Is this how they usually work? That is, will the subcontractor have to make any changes in his management or accounting operations to function efficiently under the subcontract?

6. Do you need any information from the subcontractor for your own use or protection? For example, will you need proof that he has workers' compensation insurance? Should you require a bond to assure his work?

SIGNATURES

Every agreement in writing has to be signed by the party to be charged—that is, the party against whom enforcement is sought. So goes the legal jargon. But exactly what is a signature? As between merchants, a signature is a symbol used by someone with the intent to authenticate a document. If the signature is not the traditional penned name, the law requires that the signatory to the agreement be able to be identified by oral evidence. That means that the signature does not have to be a name, if it can be identified as the mark of a particular person or business. In addition, the symbol that passes for a signature must be consistent with the accepted practice in that field.

For example, all of the following have been accepted as signatures on legally binding contracts:

1. Initials

2. A trade name, if used instead of a signature

3. A facsimile produced on a copier or transmitted over the telephone lines

4. Imprints on large-volume forms

5. Codes or other symbols agreed on by a buyer and a seller that are designed to be read by a computer

THE CORPORATE SEAL

Some documents that are executed in the name of a corporation must have the corporate seal affixed to them. This is most often true for documents dealing with the transfer of real property. The reason for this is that authority to sign agreements with the name of the corporation can be limited by the Board of Directors—that is, given only to certain individuals and for certain kinds or sizes of agreements only.

An individual entering into a major agreement with a corporation needs to know that the person signing for the corporation, even if it is the president of the corporation, has the authority to sign the agreement. The presence of the corporate seal on an instrument that purports to be executed by the authority of the corporation in some states creates what is called a rebuttable presumption that the instrument was so executed. If the corporation disputes that it is bound by the agreement, it has the burden of showing that for some reason the agreement does not bind it. This is essentially a rule of evidence, not of contract law. Some states have passed laws abolishing the old legal requirements that certain classes of legal documents have to have a seal to be valid.

4

Specific Business Agreements

Analyzing different business agreements will enable you to apply the lessons learned in Chapters 2 and 3 to specific cases. The following cases illustrate how to look at the applicable law, analyze the commercial questions, and solve the drafting problems in several typical business situations: the hiring of personnel and consultants, the purchase of computer software, partnerships, stock purchases and sales, and the purchasing or sale of a business. In general, tax questions are not discussed in detail because they vary so much according to the deal and the situation of each party.

Even if you do not anticipate dealing with a particular transaction discussed in this chapter, read the chapter for practice in thinking through a business-legal problem and resolving it by an agreement. Using a checklist to think through a transaction is critical. A variety of checklists is included in the Appendix.

Employment Agreements

In the past an employment agreement with a key employee or executive protected a corporation against the disclosure of trade secrets, against the employee working for a competitor for a number of years after leaving, or against the loss of a substantial investment if the employee accepted a position elsewhere. From the employee's perspective, the agreement provided security and predictability. As a result of these needs, employment agreements took on a basic form and thus gave rise to similar questions of interpretation. A sample employment agreement is included in the Appendix.

Employment agreements are now being used for other situations as well. In some companies retired employees bid for short-term employment or consulting contracts to serve the company on task forces dealing with identified problems for a fixed amount of time. When the contract expires, the employee can bid for another, look elsewhere, or do nothing. For the company, this provides a means to use the talents of its retired workforce. For the retired worker, it is an opportunity to continue a relationship with his previous employer, but to have more control over the nature and extent of his work.

The slow but steady rise of flexible work schedules may also give impetus to more and different employment contracts. Both the employer and the employee may wish to assure that certain work schedules will be met, particularly as more work schedules become nontraditional. The traditional employment agreement is not easily adapted to these new developments; and the employment agreement in the Appendix should not be used blindly for these new situations. As with any other agreement form, start with the transaction, not with the form.

The sample form (page 235) shows the problems involved in combining various forms. It is clear from Paragraph 3.1 that the agreement is primarily aimed at employing a particular individual as a company president, with special responsibilities for a particular subsidiary. But the definitions state (Paragraph 1.1) that "Company" means the corporation signing the agreement as well as its subsidiaries, affiliates, and other related companies. Is the executive being employed to be president of only the signing company? Will the document be satisfied if the executive is the president of one or more subsidiaries, including the named subsidiary? Within the literal terms of the agreement, the answer is yes. But the intent of the parties is that the executive be president of one particular entity. This form could easily be clarified if Paragraph 3.1 stated: "The Executive shall serve as President of [the company]."

EMPLOYMENT AGREEMENTS BY IMPLICATION

The conduct of management alone can result in an employment agreement. Most companies believe that management must enter into a signed agreement to have its inherent managerial discretion limited. This is not true. As in other areas, conduct and speech can result in a binding agreement.

For example, in one case an assistant sales manager filled in as the sales manager for several months while his superior was ill. The company president and several board members complimented him and on several occasions promised extra pay. That extra pay was not forthcoming, so the employee sued to recover the money. The courts held that, even though it was not mentioned in the employee's current written agreement, the repeated promises of extra pay constituted a binding agreement. The same could hold true even if there had been no employment agreement. The actions of the officers and directors of the company, who could commit the company, constituted an agreement to provide extra pay. Even if the amount was not specified, a court would enforce that agreement, setting a "reasonable" amount of additional pay, reflecting the work done, the pay of the person being replaced, and the company's past practices in similar situations.

CONDUCT OF THE EMPLOYER

If you as employer have an existing employment agreement with an employee, you will have to exercise extreme care in your dealings with that employee. In the past some employers extricated themselves from unsatisfactory employment agreements by making the conditions and location of employment as unpleasant as possible, within the limits of the agreement. Recent cases now bring this practice into question. Courts, labor arbitration panels, and the National Labor Relations Board regard resignations made under such circumstances as *constructive discharges.* Applying the same logic to the employment agreement case would mean that if the company deliberately made the employee's working conditions so intolerable that he was forced to quit, the company is as liable as if it had formally fired the employee. A hasty acceptance of the resignation of an employee, which the employee tendered in anger when none was intended, can now be considered a constructive discharge. Even engaging in a pattern of late payments that causes the employee to quit can be considered the same as termination by the employer.

This principle extends into other nonpunitive areas as well. For example, refusing a transfer can be grounds for termination. However, if an employee's contract commits the employer to keep him at a particular work location, management cannot terminate him for failing to accept the transfer.

INVENTIONS

Many companies in high technology and research and development have employment agreements that purport to cover their rights to inventions developed by the employee. Generally, they provide that the company will own the invention if it was created by the employee in the scope of his employment. This can create a circular problem: If the employee invents something, isn't it his job to do so? The solution is to specify in the employment agreement that one responsibility of the employee is to produce inventions. In that case the company owns the invention if it was produced using company facilities or time. Without an agreement, the employee and the company have these rights (known as "shop rights"):

1. If the invention is made by the employee on his own time, using his own equipment and facilities, the employee owns the invention.

2. If the employee uses the company's facilities or time, but the invention is *outside* the scope of his job, the employee owns the invention. However, the company can use the invention regardless of what the employee does with the patent.

3. If the employee uses company facilities or time, and the invention is *within* the scope of his job, then the company owns the invention.

Of course, once the employee under an employment agreement has been improperly terminated, all bets are off so far as the employer is concerned. For example, if a clause in the employment agreement obligates the employee not to compete with the company for a period of years after his departure from the company, the company may have difficulty enforcing it if the company improperly terminated the employee. The reason: The company would be prevented from using the terms of the contract that it breached against the employee.

Consultants' Contracts

Given the disparate approaches to consulting and the fact that the consultant is a creature of the modern business world, the legal nature of a consulting relationship must be understood. The status of consultant is one conferred only by the agreement between two parties.

The consulting agreement falls between the employment relationship and the independent contractor relationship. It is substantially closer to the latter, but it has elements of each. For example, when a corporation receives the services of an expert, it does not surrender all supervisory powers. Rather, the consultant has the status of an independent contractor, but the parameters of the consultant's task may be subject to continuing definition or even modification by the corporation as the task proceeds. In the case of the employment contract, the employer retains the right to select the employee, is responsible for payment of his or her wages, provides direction and has the right to control the employee's method of doing work, has control over the workplace, and has the right to supervise and dismiss the employee. With these managerial prerogatives also come legal obligations arising from a whole complex of legal notions generally encompassed under the phrase *employment relationship.* These legal doctrines include the following:

Agency: When an employer hires and supervises an employee, the employee acts only in the employer's interests. While subordinate to the employer, the agent can legally bind the employer.

Vicarious liability: The damages an agent or employee inflicts on others are the responsibility of the employer. The employer, not the employee, must compensate the victim of the employee's mistake.

Regulation of the workplace: Employers are required to provide safe workplaces for employees and to provide worker's compensation insurance to injured workers for business-related accidents or illnesses.

Under the classic independent contractor relationship, an employer hires an expert to do a certain job but retains no supervision over the means by which the expert accomplishes the task. This means that the employer has no direct control over the expert's own employees. Thus the employer is insulated from certain legal and managerial liabilities in exchange for relinquishing certain managerial prerogatives. The reasons for entering into this relationship are similar to those generally given for hiring consultants:

1. A need for limited or one-time use of specialized skills

2. A need for unique areas of expertise

3. Limitations on corporate wage scales

4. The unavailability of specific skills in a current labor market

5. Rapid access to the latest technology and to experience in its application

6. Multiple exposure to alternative solutions to new problems

7. Credibility as an outsider

8. Limitations on executive time

From a management point of view, there are many reasons to hire consultants. There may be a shortage of expertise among existing staff and the work to be done does not warrant hiring additional personnel, even on a temporary basis. Or there may be a shortage of staff and resources, usually because of personnel and budget restrictions, or of time. Consultants are also hired to provide an objective perspective or fresh ideas and insight. In light of the special nature of the consulting relationship, several key elements should be included in a consulting agreement:

1. The nature and scope of the work to be performed

2. The status as an independent contractor, including handling of the work product

3. The payment of compensation and costs

4. The duration of the relationship

5. The termination of the relationship

6. Modification of the relationship and the work to be performed

7. Restrictive covenants to protect the corporation

8. Settlement of disputes and interpretation of the duties and compensation

9. Remedies on default or failure to perform

10. The manner of giving notice or changes in assignments

A simple agreement retaining a consultant is included in the Appendix.

Two other issues, which may require including additional clauses in the contract, should also be considered when hiring a consultant: access to information and awareness of company policies. In general, the consultant needs relatively unfettered access to people and information. As the project develops, limitations on the availability of data or access to people may hinder the consultant as he continues his work. However, the more access to information that he is given, the greater the concern on the part of the business in protecting the confidentiality of this information, both during the assignment and after its completion.

To function effectively, the consultant should be made aware of all formal and informal corporate policies and procedures that could have an impact on his performance. He must be made aware of other policies so that he can be sensitive to personnel interaction, which can be vital if he is to obtain the complete cooperation of those assigned to work on the project with him. The consultant should transgress these policies and practices only when it is necessary to the effective performance of his job. At all other times they should be respected.

Because of the complexity of the consulting relationship, the agreement should never be oral because it may be virtually impossible to enforce. The main problem is created by the statute of frauds, which in most states provides that a verbal contract is void if, by its terms, it is unable to be performed within one year of the time the contract is made. A 1970 decision by an appellate court in New York State is instructive in this regard. In this case an individual alleged that he was to be employed by the Corning Glass Works for the period May 1, 1966, through April 30, 1967, as a management consultant for a fee of $25,000. The agreement was an oral contract and was entered into based upon discussions that were alleged to have taken place in February and March of 1966. The court ruled that this agreement was void, since by its terms it was not to be performed within one year of its making, even though the alleged term of the contract was only one year.

The application of this doctrine to the consulting relationship is particularly critical. Many consultants are hired on an intermittent basis, or they are hired for one project and then rehired to continue with another aspect of the same project. Alternatively, some consultants are put on a retainer by a corporation to assure their availability. If these agreements are partially or wholly oral, they may be declared void and unenforceable.

In preparing any agreement between a consultant and a corporation, the hiring person should never be styled as an employer. This designation could undermine the contention that the consultant is an independent contractor. This is particularly critical, since the wrongs of an independent contractor cannot be attributed to the person who hired him. However, merely stipulating in an agreement that the contractor is an independent contractor does not automatically create that relationship.

By establishing the independent contractor relationship, the corporation is giving up the right to control the consultant and the consultant's employees, both on the task to be accomplished and the result to be obtained. However, the corporation must respect this allocation of control. For example, if the courts are faced with a question whether the wrongs, or torts, of the consultant are the responsibility of the corporation, they will not stop at the document. If they determine, based on the facts, that the corporation has actually been exercising control over the consultant or the consultant's employees, they may well find that, despite the language of the agreement, the relationship is that of an employer to an employee. For example, a corporation hires an overseas marketing consultant to secure a certain contract. Under their agreement the consultant is an independent contractor. He is given a large advance for expenses and not required to account for it. The corporation and the consultant are in continuous communication. When it is disclosed that the contract had been awarded to the corporation because of bribes, the corporation denies liability, stating that the consultant acted as an independent contractor rather than on behalf of the corporation. In spite of this, the corporation could be held liable because it was actually directing the consultant's actions by stressing the need to secure the contract and by providing a large expense account for which it did not require an accounting.

Noncompetition Agreements

The agreement not to compete is used frequently in a variety of circumstances:

1. The sale of a going business with its goodwill
2. Agreements that limit the ability of an employee to compete after termination of employment
3. Agreements not to solicit customers
4. Agreements not to disclose confidential information
5. Agreements assigning future inventions

From the employer's standpoint, the purpose of these agreements is to obtain protection from dishonest competitors and disloyal employees who may make use of trade information or customer relationships at its expense. From the employee's standpoint, these agreements limit his economic mobility and weaken his bargaining power with both his present and prospective employers.

In analyzing these restraints, the courts have shown that they are influenced by the concept of freedom of contract, business ethics, industry developments, specialization, and flexibility of employment. These factors have led the courts to analyze the application of these restraints and to accept them within limitations of space, time, activity, and considerations of public policy. Examples of clauses that are regarded as noncompetition agreements are found in the Appendix in the Employment Agreement (Paragraph 9) and the Consulting Agreement (Paragraph 7).

SALE OF A BUSINESS WITH GOODWILL

A sale of a business incorporating the "goodwill" built up by the owner may necessitate an agreement by the owner not to compete in the particular business area after the sale. Such an agreement is viewed as necessary to protect the value of the interest being purchased. In fact, it may be viewed as a logical result of the obligation that the seller of the business will deliver the business "as is." Because the parties to this kind of sale are usually of equal standing, and because the seller has bargained for and received money or other consideration from the sale of the business, such agreements in business sales are liberally construed and generally enforced by the courts.

POSTEMPLOYMENT RESTRICTIONS

In contrast with the sale of a business is the restriction placed on an employee preventing him or her from engaging in an identical or even a similar occupation. A postemployment restraint is not itself essential to the value of the employment, since there is no inherent obligation placed on the employee not to compete after the termination of employment. The two parties, employer and employee, are usually of unequal bargaining power, and the employee, in accepting such a restriction, surrenders his skill, economic mobility, and bargaining position for future alternate employment. Thus, as a general rule, postemployment restraints are more difficult to enforce than restraints on competition, which are part of the sale of an on-going business. If they are part of an employment agreement, when there has clearly been bargaining on a more equal basis, they are generally enforced by the courts.

AGREEMENT NOT TO SOLICIT CUSTOMERS

The courts tend to view the employer's position more sympathetically in this limited version of general postemployment restrictions, since the company's clients are an asset acquired by the company's efforts and expenditures over time.

AGREEMENT NOT TO DISCLOSE CONFIDENTIAL INFORMATION

This postemployment restriction is usually easy to enforce. When particular information is not known to be confidential, and the employee has not been notified that it is confidential, the employee may not be bound to keep it secret. Many employment, consulting, and independent contractor agreements provide that the signatories agree not to reveal or use any of the employer's trade secrets. What constitutes a trade secret is an important issue in the application of such clauses.

Recently, courts have ruled that a company cannot sue former employees and bar them from using trade secrets if they are not treated as such by the company seeking to enforce one of these clauses. In one case a court was faced with a lawsuit by a company against a number of its former employees over the use of a company production process in a competing business they had set up. The court did not let the company stop them from using the process because (1) the company had never warned its employees about the importance of secrecy, and (2) the specifications for the equipment and the processes involved had been posted on the walls of the plant, so even competitors who had toured the plant could have seen them. The court decided that the process had not been treated as a trade secret, so it could not be called one in a lawsuit.

One lesson from this case is that in preparing such a restriction you should not make it too broad: for example, preventing the "use of any and all information gained during employment." Such a broad restriction will be regarded by the courts as unreasonable, and thus they will not enforce it because it could forbid disclosure of material that would be common knowledge.

RESTRICTIONS ON INVENTIONS

Closely related to the problem of trade secrets is the question of what can be done with an invention or an improvement developed by an employee in the course of authorized work and research for a former employer. Specifically, can the employee utilize it in a competing business? Without a contract covering this, the usual rule is that the invention is the property of the employer if the employee was expressly hired to make or develop that item. When the employment is more general, and the employee comes up with the invention in the course of his employment, the employee is entitled to the invention, but the employer has so-called shop rights in it.

An agreement requiring the assignment of inventions or patents to the employer will be interpreted strictly against the employer. Therefore, such a clause in an employment agreement should provide that, in consideration of all compensation to be paid to the employee, all inventions and discoveries made by the employee during the time of his employment are the property of the employer. It should also provide that the employee must properly disclose all such inventions and improvements to the employer.

Whether or not an injunction is available to enforce drafting restrictions is the baseline test for their validity. If a clause cannot be enforced through an injunction, it is no good. Enforcement depends on the reasonableness of the agreement, measured in terms of the limitations imposed over activity, area, and time, as well as against considerations of public policy. In other words, the clause should reflect the needs of the business and not be put into an agreement simply because the employer has superior bargaining power.

Limits on Activity

The prohibition on future activities is subject to a determination of whether or not the restriction is necessary for the protection of the employer or simply damaging to the future interests of the employee. With the increases in specialization, it would be held unreasonable if an employee highly trained for a narrow task was prohibited under the terms of an agreement from working in that field after leaving his present employer. A similar result would be reached when an employee's duties are general, such as a senior executive. Because his activities are ill-defined, an attempt to restrain him from similar activities in the future could be regarded as too broad and thus not enforceable.

These problems can be avoided by specifying in the agreement the exact nature of the tasks to be performed and the reasons for their performance. Inserting language on these points can enhance the enforceability of agreements not to compete, not to solicit, and to assign future inventions.

Limits on Area

In agreements not to disclose confidential information or to assign future inventions, area or geographical restrictions are upheld, within reason. Agreements not to compete or to solicit within a given region formerly served by the employee for the employer will be upheld unless obviously unreasonable. If the employee worked at the employer's main business location, a geographical limitation surrounding that location is reasonable. In fact, the failure to specify the area involved may make the restriction unenforceable because it could be read to apply everywhere.

Limits on Time

Agreements not to disclose trade secrets or to assign future inventions are usually enforceable without limitations as to their duration. In other types of restrictive agreements, the key determination is the amount of time that has to pass for the risk to the employer to be reasonably moderated. The courts treat this as a factual question, so it is hard to set forth guidelines. One standard used by the courts in dealing with agreements not to compete or to solicit customers may be whether the time specified is that necessary for customers to become accustomed to dealing with a new employee.

Emerging Public Policy Considerations

While there is no clear pattern yet, a series of cases in Pennsylvania and elsewhere has sought to add a new test, "public policy." As applied in Pennsylvania, courts also look at noncompetition agreements to determine the impact on the public. To date, these cases have dealt with doctors who have agreed not to compete with their former partners. In addition to other tests, the courts also look at the availability of local medical services. If they are limited in the area covered by the noncompetition agreement, Pennsylvania courts have refused to enforce these clauses. They reason that public policy forbids them to give effect to noncompetition agreements that adversely affect the public at large.

How far this reasoning could be extended is unclear, but it may mark a new attempt to limit the use of these clauses, at least with respect to those who provide essential services.

Computer Software Agreements

Computer software (or programs) is an increasingly active market because of the wide-ranging use of the minicomputer and microcomputer by businesses and individuals. To meet the increasing demands of these users, numerous companies and individuals develop and sell custom-made or off-the-shelf software. Usually, a software package is copied and sold to a number of people. As a result, title to the package is not sold. Instead, the purchaser obtains a license to use the package. This means the following questions must be asked before preparing an agreement:

1. Does the seller own the program? Is he authorized to grant licenses for it? In addition, the buyer may want a hold harmless clause from the seller to protect himself if it turns out that some part of the software he bought belongs to someone else. (A hold harmless clause provides that the seller will not hold the buyer liable for claims made by third persons against the buyer, based on the seller's product. For example, if the buyer were sued because a third party claimed to own the program, any damages that the buyer might sustain would be paid by the seller.)

2. Does the software have to be modified for your own use? If so, retain all rights to your modifications. Most seller's agreements will automatically provide that the seller owns all modifications. The change can protect you in two ways. First, your work, to the extent it is valuable to others, will not be given away. Second, if the seller gets the modifications and resells them legitimately, you could be sued by a later user of the software if your modification did not work.

If the software is to be custom tailored for your needs, consider the following:

1. Will the seller give you a warranty that the software developed for you does not infringe on any other ownership rights? Have a hold harmless clause written into the contract for the reasons given above.

2. Get back all work papers—the human-readable version of the software (the source code) and the machine-readable version (the object code). Make sure that the seller marks all of these as your property as he receives and uses them.

3. Are you willing to allow the seller to sell the program to others? If

not, negotiate a clause to prevent him from reselling parts of the program. If you feel that the program is marketable, you may wish to authorize the seller to license or reuse parts of the software he developed for you. If you do this, make sure that you arrange for royalty payments.

A checklist for preparing computer service and equipment contracts is included in the Appendix.

Partnerships

Most state partnership laws define a partnership as an association of two or more persons to carry on as co-owners of a business for profit. A partnership comes into existence when the parties sign a partnership agreement. But a written document is not necessary to establish a partnership. In fact, a partnership may arise by means of an oral agreement, a handshake, a nod, or even by two parties acting as though they are partners.

If there is no formal agreement, the law sets up a basic pattern for the operation of the partnership, its management, ownership, and division of profits and losses. The partners need only identify themselves and the subject of their partnership. For this reason, many businesspeople find that they have slipped into partnerships without even realizing it.

In the past, partnerships were considered entities created between two or more individuals. But corporations also can become partners. So the modern businessperson must be aware that, by a casual word on the telephone, his corporation may become a member of a partnership. This is most likely when the businessperson is the president of a small corporation. His oral consent to a marketing deal (for example) with another corporation can make them partners.

The key elements of a partnership are fairly well known. Unlike a corporation, a partnership subjects each partner to personal liability for the debts of the business. This means that all of the assets of each partner can be called on to pay the debts of the partnership if necessary. In a corporate partnership, the corporation's assets, but not those of its shareholders, are exposed.

Unless special arrangements are made, the partnership ends on the death or retirement of any partner. Since there are no shares of stock in a partnership, you cannot transfer your interest in a partnership the way you can your interest in a corporation. In the absence of any agreement on the point, a simple management structure is created for the partnership. All partners have an equal voice in the management of the business. Each partner is also a general agent for the partnership. That means each has the broadest authority to engage in the business of the partnership.

Because a partnership is created by an agreement, its duration should be carefully thought out. Specific terms agreed on should go into the agreement. If no term or duration is specified in the agreement, the partnership will last indefinitely. Only expulsion, resignation, or the death of a partner will dissolve it automatically. Because of this automatic termination possibility, partners often set up some sort of purchase provision, so the interests of a departing partner can be purchased by one or more of the remaining partners and the partnership continued.

The creation of a partnership requires no minimum capital. When partners contribute to the partnership's capital, their contributions can be in the form of services, goods, or money. Because of the variety of capital contributions, the agreement should cover how these contributions are valued and how they can be returned in case of dissolution. Unless there is an agreement on this point, no partner is entitled to a salary for managing the regular business of the partnership. And unless there is an agreement to the contrary, the partners share all profits equally. Losses are divided in the same manner as the profits, unless there is a different provision in the partnership agreement.

Managing a partnership can present special problems, since all partners have equal rights in the control and management, unless the agreement provides for some other arrangement. Any disputes concerning the partnership's operation must be decided in accord with the decision of a majority of the partners, regardless of whether or not this is a majority of the owners of the capital of the partnership. Here again, the agreement can change what the law provides.

A detailed checklist of issues involved in creating a partnership is included in the Appendix. It covers the following broad topics:

1. The parties
2. The proposed name of the partnership
3. The nature of the business
4. Whether it is a new or existing business
5. The location of the business
6. The term of the partnership
7. Capital contributions
8. Distributions of profits and paying salaries
9. Time devoted to the business
10. Management and control
11. Accounting and banking
12. Voting and disputes
13. New partners
14. Termination on a partner's death, resignation, disability, or expulsion
15. Dissolution of the partnership

This list can be modified for any business situation where two or more parties will be cooperating on a project, such as in a joint venture or in forming a new corporation.

Stock Purchase and Sale Agreements

In a closely held corporation (one with few shareholders), it is desirable to ensure a market for a shareholder's stock on his retirement, death, or termination of employment with the corporation. Unless a market is provided, a retiring minority shareholder or the heirs of a deceased shareholder will be left to the mercy of the remaining shareholders, both with regard to the price to be paid for the shares and the amount and frequency of dividends. Conflicts can arise with the surviving shareholders, if they are also employees, because they may wish to distribute the corporation's earnings as salaries, not as dividends.

A buy-sell agreement, the solution to the problem, is also important to the continuing shareholders in a closely held corporation. Without some provision for acquiring shares on retirement or death, the remaining shareholders may be faced with a hostile new shareholder. With a buy-sell agreement, these shareholders can keep control of the corporation, despite retirement, death, or termination of employment of any other shareholder.

The buy-sell agreement also ensures against an inadvertent termination of the Subchapter S election, a special tax status available to businesses with a small number of shareholders. The agreement provides protection because election of Subchapter S and its continuation are contingent on the consent of all shareholders. Without an agreement or a by-law that restricts the transferability of shares, prompt consent must be secured from the new owners of the stock, or the special tax status will automatically be lost.

DRAFTING MAJOR PROVISIONS

To illustrate the issues involved in a typical buy-sell agreement, sample clauses from a basic agreement are included in the discussion. The entire agreement, entitled "Share Transfers," is reproduced in the Appendix.

Price

One of the most important decisions that must be resolved by the shareholders in a closely held corporation is how to determine the price of shares, since there is no public market for the stock. The usual methods of establishing a price are (1) specified price, (2) book value formula, (3) capitalization of earnings formula, and (4) appraisal at the time of sale.

Specified Price. Stating in advance the price that will apply to any future purchase and sale of stock permits the corporation and shareholders to plan for that time. A firm price set too high, however, may be a burden to the remaining shareholders who have to pay it. By using a set price, the remaining stockholders know what they will have to pay and can limit the price of the stock in the future. If the shareholders prefer a fixed price, they can state in the agreement that it be reviewed regularly to reflect changes in the corporation's value. If you take this approach, write it into the agreement; do not rely only on the good intentions of the parties that this will be done. Choosing a fixed price is not always the right decision, however, since inflation can reduce the actual value of the stock if the price was set too far in the past.

Book Value Formula. Using a formula avoids some of the rigidities of the fixed price method, but a formula also can become obsolete. In addition, relying strictly on the book value as the basis for the price, an alternative to a fixed price, is limiting. In most businesses, the book value of stock does not represent the actual value of the business, in part because of the difficulty in establishing a price for "goodwill," which is a key element here.

If you use a formula based on the book value, spell out clearly certain items. You should indicate the date of the evaluation—for example, the month ending just before the date the shareholder died, retired, or was terminated. This clause should state both how the book value is to be calculated and by whom. This determination may be made by your certified public accountant, in accord with the manner in which he prepares the corporation's annual statements.

Capitalization of Earnings Formula. If the average earnings of the business over two or three years are multiplied by the appropriate capitalization rate of earnings, the total should produce a figure approximating the total value of the business. The formula would then be applied to value each shareholder's interest in the corporation. The main problem with this formula is that other factors also have a bearing on the value of a business, including sources of new capital, business trends in general, and the trends in the particular markets served by the business.

Because of the need for a sophisticated analysis, over which there can be sharp differences, this type of formula is not often used.

Appraisal at the Sale. By providing for an independent appraisal at the time of the sale, both the retiring and the continuing shareholders are assured that the price will be reasonably related to the existing value of the business. This will mean a fair price for the stock involved. However, this places retiring employees at the mercy of the economy at some future time. When the appraisal method is used, the buy-sell agreement must cover who is to make the appraisal, as of what date it is to be made, and what factors are to be considered in making it.

In the Share Transfers agreement in the Appendix, the pricing is a modification of a fixed price, with annual redeterminations. Given that a unanimous redetermination may be unlikely, the agreement adds a protective clause, providing a formula to update the last agreed-on value:

(7) The value of each share of this corporation is for all purposes fixed at fifty dollars ($50) per share. Such value includes an amount representing the goodwill of the Corporation as a going concern. Within thirty (30) days following the end of each fiscal year of the Corporation, the shareholders shall by unanimous mutual agreement redetermine the value of each of said shares, for the next fiscal year, and endorse said value in the Schedule to this agreement, which is made a part thereof.

In the event that, for any reason whatsoever, no such advance redetermination is made for any fiscal year, the value of each of said shares shall be the value as last fixed under this agreement, increased or decreased as the case may be, by the proportionate amount, allocable to the shares whose value is being determined, of the algebraic sum of the net earnings and net losses, before all federal corporate income, state franchise, income, business personal property, and municipal (including, but without limitation thereto, real property taxes) taxes, of the Corporation from the date of such last value until the date of the death of the shareholder, offer, or request, as the case may be.

The determination of the net earnings and losses shall be made by the Corporation's regular accountant, in accordance with generally accepted accounting principles, on a basis consistent with that normally used in determining the Corporation's net earnings and losses.

This valuation process also applies to any other proceeding where the value of the stock has to be set. For example, in certain situations involving the sale of the business, a shareholder would have the right to insist that the corporation buy his stock back at a fair price. In such circumstances, Clause 4 of the agreement sets the price:

(4) In the event that any shareholder becomes entitled to payment of the fair value of his shares under Chapter 11 of the New Jersey Business Corporation Act, or any amendment thereto, or related or similar statute, the fair value of his shares for all purposes thereunder shall be conclusively presumed to be the price hereinafter fixed, and the shareholder shall be bound to accept any offer of the Corporation to pay said amount in exchange for his shares.

The Purchaser

Either the corporation or the remaining shareholders can buy the stock. The most significant reason for providing that the corporation will buy the stock is that it can use corporate funds. Another advantage is that it avoids the complexity of revising agreements each time one of the shareholders dies, and unlike continuing shareholders who purchase stock, the corporation will not have adverse tax consequences if it uses appreciated property to buy the stock. There are limits to this, however. For example, if the purchase is not paid in installments, a corporation's contract to repurchase its own stock at the owner's option is unenforceable if the corporation would be made insolvent by the purchase. Because of this problem, it may be wise to give the corporation a right of first refusal and give the stockholders a right to purchase if the corporation does not exercise this right.

Section 1 of the sample agreement in the Appendix provides that the corporation has a right of first refusal on any attempted sale by a shareholder. This right also applies to any shares that the shareholder acquires by other means, by virtue of Section 2. Under the terms of Section 3, if the shareholder dies, the corporation must buy the stock. When the corporation has the option to buy the stock under a right of first refusal and it does not buy, the remaining shareholders can buy the stock and split it among themselves. If one of them does not buy his share, then those who do buy can split his share among themselves.

(1) No shareholder shall during his lifetime sell, mortgage, hypothecate, transfer, pledge, create a security interest in or lien on, encumber, give, place in trust (voting or other), or otherwise dispose of all or any portion of his shares in the Corporation now owned or hereafter acquired, except that if a shareholder should desire to so dispose of any of his shares in the Corporation during his lifetime, he shall first offer to sell all of his shares to the Corporation at the price hereafter provided. Any shares not purchased by the Corporation within thirty (30) days after receipt of such offer in writing shall be offered at the same price to the other shareholders, each of whom shall have the right to purchase such portion of the remaining shares offered for sale as the number of shares owned by him at such date shall bear to the total number of shares owned by all the other shareholders, excluding the selling shareholder, provided, however, that if any shareholder does not purchase his full proportionate share of the shares, the balance thereof may be purchased by the other shareholders equally. If his shares are not purchased by the remaining shareholders within sixty (60) days of the receipt of the offer to them, the shareholder desiring to sell his shares may sell them to any other person but shall not sell them without giving the Corporation and the remaining shareholders the right to purchase such remaining shares at the price and on the terms offered to such other person.

(2) Any person who becomes the holder or possessor of any shares, or share certificates, of this Corporation by virtue of any judicial process, attachment, bankruptcy, receivership, execution, or judicial sale shall immediately offer all of said shares to the Corporation, whenever requested by the Corporation so to do, at the

price herein fixed, and none of said shares shall be entitled to any vote, nor shall any dividend be paid or allowed upon any of such shares, after failure to comply with such request.

(3) Upon the death of any shareholder party to this agreement, the Corporation shall purchase, and the estate of the decedent shall sell, all the decedent's shares in the Corporation, and the parties hereto and the Corporation shall take such action as may be necessary to permit it to make such purchase. Title to all said shares shall be deemed to vest in the Corporation immediately upon the death of any such shareholder. The purchase price of such shares shall be computed as hereinafter provided.

Financing the Purchase

The most common means of financing stock purchases is life insurance. On the death of a shareholder, the proceeds from the policy can provide enough funds to buy his stock from his estate. If the purchase is made during his lifetime, the insurance can help only to the extent that it has a cash surrender value, which the corporation can obtain.

Either the corporation or the other shareholders can buy insurance on a shareholder's life. But this becomes complicated when the prospective buyers of the stock are the surviving shareholders. For example, consider the case when there are more than two shareholders in the corporation. If one dies and his policy is large enough to fund the purchase of stock on the death of another shareholder, the amount of insurance owned by each remaining shareholder will not be enough to cover the purchase price for the shares that would have to be bought on the death of the second shareholder.

To illustrate, take a corporation with three equal shareholders, Mr. Kali, Miss Hashi, and Ms. Prissi. The value of the corporation is $90,000. Each shareholder therefore has a $15,000 policy on each of the others. That is, Mr. Kali has a $15,000 policy on Miss Hashi and one on Ms. Prissi. Say Miss Hashi dies. Mr. Kali would collect $15,000 and Ms. Prissi would collect $15,000. Each could then buy half of her stock, for a total of $30,000. Now Mr. Kali has $45,000 in stock. But the only other surviving shareholder, Ms. Prissi, still has only $15,000 insurance on Mr. Kali, one-third of what is now needed. A solution is for the corporation to take out insurance in the full value of the holdings of each shareholder, with an option to increase the face value of each policy. While the corporation has an insurable interest in the life of an active official of the corporation, the insurance premium will not be deductible for federal income-tax purposes. An alternative is to consider a solution without insurance.

For those circumstances, and also if a shareholder is not insurable, arrangements can be made for a buy-out of stock through the use of a sinking fund. The question of whether the sinking funds will be available for payment can be settled by an escrow arrangement. The burden of a purchase made by the individual shareholders can be substantial. If the price is realistic, the surviving shareholders can liquidate the corporation and acquire the necessary funds. To avoid the substantial and possibly adverse tax consequences of this action, an installment purchase can be arranged. This is an accommodation to the buyers, since the seller faces the risk of nonpayment in accordance with the plan as well as various tax problems. The first can be minimized by requiring a pledge of stock and some other security to guarantee payment and also by the use of an escrow. The second can be minimized by provisions of the federal tax laws that let the seller of the stock avoid paying a tax on the entire gain on the sale of the stock in the year of the sale. The seller can pay it as installment payments are received.

In Section 8 of the sample agreement, financing for the purchase of stock from the estate of a deceased shareholder is provided for by the purchase of insurance by the corporation. Section 11 provides that the party buying the stock may choose to pay in installments. The opening language of Section 11 shows why you must be careful about transferring language from one agreement to another without fully understanding it. This clause contemplates that the stock may be bought from someone who is not a party to the agreement or from his estate. But the stock is owned by the signing shareholders only. This clause was inserted because the agreement is part of a larger one to create a new corporation, in which the shareholders agree to buy stock. When the shareholders buy the original stock, they will pay cash. When the buy-sell agreement is activated, the buyer can choose to pay in installments.

(8) The Corporation shall purchase insurance on the life of each of the parties hereto, payable to the Corporation as beneficiary, and shall pay the premiums thereon, in the respective amounts hereafter shown:

    _____ Face Amount of Policy $_____

    _____ Face Amount of Policy $_____

    _____ Face Amount of Policy $_____

(11) Payment for all shares purchased under this agreement shall, except where the seller is a party to this agreement or the estate, executor, administrator, committee, guardian, heir, next of kin, legatee, or other legal representative of a party to this agreement, be in cash upon delivery of the share certificate or certificates properly endorsed.

Where the purchase is made from a party to this agreement, or the estate, executor, administrator, committee, guardian, heir, next of kin, legatee, or other legal representative of a party to this agreement, in lieu of payment solely in cash, payment may be made, at the election of the purchaser or purchasers as the case may be, in the following manner:

(a) a down payment of ten (10) percent of the purchase price in cash, together with

(b) a note or notes providing for payment of the balance in equal monthly installments without interest over a period of twenty-four (24) months, with acceleration of the entire obligation in the event of nonpayment of any installment when due. The seller shall be bound to deliver the certificate or certificates properly endorsed for all shares to be purchased, upon tender by the purchaser or purchasers as the case may be of the down payment and note or notes as above provided.

Nothing herein shall be construed to validate a sale or other disposition of shares otherwise prohibited by this agreement.

Other Provisions

The balance of the sample agreement contains protective language supporting the obligation of the shareholders to sell their stock to the corporation or other shareholders. Section 5 prevents any transfer outside of the agreement from being made, and it requires the corporation to refrain from transferring any stock in violation of this agreement. This clause needs the corporation's agreement to be effective. Note that Section 9 also limits the ability of the shareholders to avoid the agreement, by having all stock certificates marked with a special notice. This notice serves to warn possible buyers of the existence of this agreement and of its impact.

Section 6 provides that if the corporation itself adopts bylaws that are stricter than the agreement, in terms of limiting transfers of stock, the agreement will not be read as overriding those stricter provisions. Finally, Section 10 provides that if the corporation of shareholders do not buy stock on one occasion—say from an estate, because the stock will eventually be owned by a surviving spouse who wishes to come into the business—this failure to live by the strict terms of the agreement will not prevent the parties from insisting that the agreement be adhered to in the future. Of course, too many waivers can keep the agreement from ever being enforced, no matter what it says.

(5) No purported sale, assignment, mortgage, hypothecation, transfer, pledge, creation of a security interest in or lien on, encumbrance of, gift of, trust (voting or other) of, or other disposition of any of the shares of this Corporation by any shareholder in violation of the provisions of this agreement, the certificate of incorporation or the bylaws shall be valid, and the Corporation shall not transfer any of said shares on the books of the Corporation, nor shall any of said shares be entitled to vote, nor shall any dividends be paid thereon, during the period of any such violation. Such disqualifications shall be in addition to and not in lieu of any other remedies legal or equitable to enforce said provisions.

Further, the parties hereto expressly waive any voting, dividend, or appraisal rights to which they would otherwise be entitled, except as herein provided.

(6) Nothing herein contained shall be construed to limit or render ineffective any other provisions of this agreement, or of the certifi-

cate of incorporation or bylaws of this Corporation consented to by all the parties hereto, further restricting or conditioning the transfer of shares of this Corporation, or providing penalties or disqualifications for violations of said restrictions or conditions.

(9) All certificates for shares of this Corporation shall, in addition to any notice thereon required by the certificate of incorporation or bylaws of this Corporation, bear the following notice conspicuously on the face or back thereof:

> Sale, assignment, mortgage, hypothecation, transfer, pledge, creation of a security interest in or lien on, encumbrance of, gift of, trust (voting or other) of, or other disposition of these shares is restricted by the terms of a shareholder agreement dated _____, 1982, which may be examined at the office of the Corporation, . . .

No shares of the Corporation shall be deemed properly issued, and no shares shall be transferred upon the books of the Corporation, nor shall any dividends be paid thereon, nor shall the holder thereof be entitled to any voting or other rights of a shareholder, unless the certificate evidencing such shares contains said legend.

(10) Failure of the Corporation or of the shareholders to exercise any option to purchase given under this agreement, and any waiver of any rights hereunder as to any transfer, shall not, as to any future transfer of said shares (either voluntary or by operation of law) discharge such shares from any of the restrictions herein contained.

The Purchase and Sale of a Going Business

Although the purchase or sale of a business is not one of the most common transactions, it is instructive in drawing up a basic outline for negotiating the terms of the agreement and for the agreement itself.

These principles apply whether the agreement governs the sale of part of a small business or the acquisition of a giant corporation.

If the seller is a sole proprietorship, the deal will take the form of the sale of the seller's separate assets. If the seller is a partnership, the transaction can either be the sale of a partnership asset or the sale of an interest in the partnership itself. If the business is owned by a corporation, either the assets of the corporation may be sold or the shareholders' stock may be sold.

Using the example of a corporation, an acquisition of a going business can be made in one of three basic ways:

1. The buyer can purchase some or all of the seller's assets
2. The buyer can purchase the shares from the seller's shareholders
3. The buyer and the seller may merge or consolidate their respective corporations

The general objectives of the two parties to the sale of a going business are as follows:

1. The seller wants to get his purchase price without having any liabilities attached to it.
2. The buyer wants to be sure that he is getting the assets he sees and that he will not face a problem of hidden liabilities in the future.

The key issues in the purchase or sale of a business include the following ten broad topics. This list is not all-inclusive, because the specific topics depend on the individual circumstances of the parties and the nature of the business and assets being transferred:

Business Purchase Agreement Checklist
1. Property being sold
2. Transfer of intangible items
3. Price
4. Warranties of the seller

5. Conduct of the business until the sale is closed

6. Conditions of the closing of the sale

7. Survival of warranties

8. The ownership of the seller's name

9. Noncompetition considerations

10. Other provisions

    a. Place of closing

    b. Date of closing

    c. Date to take possession of business

    d. Escrows

    e. Warranties by the buyer

    f. Termination of the agreement

PROPERTY TO BE SOLD

In the sale of assets, you must have a detailed list of the assets purchased and the price allocated to each asset. This is especially important if the seller is not selling all of his assets. Price allocation is important because the tax consequences differ between buyer and seller. The seller will attempt to allocate as much as possible to items like goodwill, while the buyer will seek significant allocations to inventory or depreciable items. Unless the agreement resolves these allocations, the Internal Revenue Service may seek to make its own allocation, which probably will not be satisfactory to either party.

If the agreement covers the purchase of stock, it should describe the stock and state the purchase price per share.

TRANSFER OF INTANGIBLE ITEMS

One problem in an asset sale is securing valuable intangible rights for the buyer, such as patents, leases, contract rights, and mortgages. If anyone other than the seller has an interest in any of these rights, you may need their written consent to any transfer. Therefore, the buyer may make obtaining these consents a condition of the closing or of the purchase itself. A permit such as a liquor license can pose special problems, since it involves an intangible item and is also subject to detailed regulations. Transfers of such licenses are usually controlled by a state agency. Usually the agency requires that the two parties to the proposed sale file a detailed application to obtain the agency's permission to transfer the license. This can take time and rarely is it automatic. Thus you should make sure that both parties will cooperate in getting permission to transfer a license. The agreement should state what the parties have decided about the necessity for obtaining approval of the transfer of any particular license:

1. Must it be obtained in order for the sale to go through?
2. Must the application have been made in order to close the sale?
3. Will the application be made only after the closing?
4. What happens if a transfer is refused or restricted?

PRICE

Determining the price of the sale or purchase is a major consideration. For example, is it to be a fixed price agreed to by the two sides, or will it be based on some formula? Next, the purchase price must be allocated among the assets being sold and the conditions spelled out in the purchase agreement. For example, is the price to be paid over time, or is it conditioned somehow in future earnings of the business?

WARRANTIES OF THE SELLER

A warranty is a statement made as a part of the agreement that certain facts are or will be true. If the warranty is not true, it constitutes a breach of contract.

The buyer should consider the following so that he can negotiate with the seller for warranties:

1. Can the business be carried on as presently conducted?

2. Does the seller have title to the assets being sold?

3. Have the shareholders authorized the sale of the corporation's assets?

4. Are the financial statements and statements of contingent liabilities and actual liabilities accurate?

5. Are there any long-term contracts or other significant obligations outstanding?

6. Can the seller assign its contracts, licenses, patents, leases?

7. What kind of lawsuits are there against the seller, and are there any significant lawsuits that have been threatened but not yet initiated?

8. Is the corporation in existence in good standing and qualified to do business in the states where it operates?

9. In the case of a sale of stock, how many shares are outstanding and owned by each shareholder? Is the title to the stock free of all liens and claims?

CONDUCT OF BUSINESS UNTIL CLOSING

The buyer will usually insist that the business of the seller be conducted as usual and that the seller not dissipate its assets by any last-minute dividends, unusual purchases, or loans. To be assured of this, the buyer may want to have full access and the right to investigate the operations of the business prior to the closing. The buyer and seller should think about probable business events that could occur up to the closing. For example, who gets the benefit of new transactions prior to the date of the closing?

CONDITIONS OF THE CLOSING

The buyer should think about what he wants from the seller at the closing. At a minimum, he will want the seller to:

1. Agree that all the warranties made are true as of the closing.

2. State that there have been no material adverse changes in the business.

3. Provide opinions of counsel if necessary. This is usually required for tax and securities law purposes.

4. Obtain and provide all the necessary consents of shareholders, lenders, landlords, and other parties to contracts.

SURVIVAL OF THE WARRANTIES

The parties should discuss and decide whether or not they want the seller's warranties to survive the closing. If they do, the seller could be liable to the buyer if the warranties turn out to be inaccurate and the buyer finds this out only after the closing. If the warranties are to survive the closing, the seller will want a date set for their expiration. The buyer may want to protect himself against losses arising because of a breach of the warranties by holding back a part of the purchase price or setting up an escrow account.

THE SELLER'S NAME

Does the buyer want to continue using the seller's name? This can be provided for in the agreement. If the buyer wants to use that name, should the seller be prohibited from using a similar name? If so, for how long?

NONCOMPETITION

If the buyer is concerned that the seller or some key personnel of the seller will open a competing business or join a competitor after the sale, the agreement can provide for a promise by the seller not to compete. Some of the other provisions that can be stated in the agreement include:

1. Place of closing

2. Date of closing

3. Date for taking possession of the business

4. Escrows. Are they needed to provide for back taxes or liens?

5. Warranties by the buyer. Is the seller concerned that the buyer may not be able to go through with the sale? This may be a problem if the buyer is a regulated business and needs approval from the regulator to make the purchase.

6. Termination. Under what conditions, if any, can either party call off the sale? Are there any penalties for doing this?

As an example of how these simple principles can be applied, study the Table of Contents from a 1979 agreement under which the Penn Central Corporation bought Marathon Corporation by buying its stock. Marathon was then a company with almost $500 million a year in sales.

AGREEMENT FOR REORGANIZATION

Table of Contents

List of Schedules

List of Exhibits

Source: Joint proxy statement for the Special Meeting of Shareholders of the Penn Central Corporation and Marathon Manufacturing Company (November 23, 1979).

5

Reading and Interpreting an Agreement

To read and understand any agreement, you must know the applicable law and how to draft an agreement. And to draft an agreement, you must also know how to interpret one. The two processes overlap. The key difference is that in drafting you can avoid mistakes made by other parties. In reading and understanding you must find these mistakes and resolve the ambiguities. Unless you are renegotiating an agreement, you have no opportunity to undo what has already been done.

The first step in reading an agreement is to determine what it is made up of. Just because a document is entitled "Agreement" and states that it constitutes the complete agreement of the parties on a particular subject does not mean that you have all of its terms in front of you. For example, have any amendments been made since it was signed? Has there been a change in the way both parties behave under the agreement? Has the underlying law changed since the agreement was prepared?

The second step is to make sure that you have all the documents. Was there an exchange of correspondence or forms at the time the agreement was made? Does the agreement have any attachments? Does the agreement incorporate anything by reference? Is it the same item, particularly in terms of date, that the parties intended to have incorporated? Are there any documents referred to in the recitals? Once you have everything, you can begin to interpret.

Under the rules of interpretation it is important to know how written changes in a printed form are to prevail if they differ from the language of the form, and how specific terms of an agreement are to prevail over the general terms, if there seems to be a conflict. In analyzing any agreement, you must use the tools of interpretation and the techniques of draftsmanship, and you must understand the context of the deal. The tools of interpretation assist you in analyzing fine details in the agreement itself. The techniques of draftsmanship enable you mentally to break down unwieldy sentences into usable segments and to spot ambiguities, either intentional or accidental. Understanding the context, the parties, the deal, and the commercial practice between the parties and of the business puts the transaction in perspective. It would be splendid to be able to say that the rules of interpretation are applied in a particular order, as one breaks down an unknown chemical substance into its component parts. Realistically, the rules are applied to achieve certain ends. As a lawyer would put it, *the rules enable you to tell what the courts will say that your agreement means, and that is what it means.* Never lose sight of this concept.

The courts apply these rules to achieve several goals, which are not always consistent:

1. To carry out the intent of the parties

2. To avoid injustice and overreaching by one or the other party

3. To supply the terms that the parties failed to supply.

Is There an Agreement?

Before determining what an agreement means, you must first determine whether or not there is an agreement and what makes up the agreement. The rules here are elaborations of those introduced in Chapter 2.

INVITATIONS AND ESTIMATES

There is a difference between preliminary negotiations and an actual agreement. If one party suggested the terms of a possible agreement by advertising, a circular, or a letter but does not make a definite proposal, all that exists is an invitation to the other party to make an offer. For example, stating that "The Sascha Company can quote you" is a statement of terms, not an offer. But a quotation can be made specific enough to be an offer. If the quotation includes a statement that it is for "immediate acceptance," it is an offer. For an example of this, see the Proposal form in the Appendix.

Similarly, an estimate by itself is not a binding proposal that, if accepted, results in an agreement. Do not confuse this with a document entitled "Estimate," which contains specific terms as to acceptance and performance. Including language such as "Contractor proposes to furnish the following services," together with "Your signature is an authorization to furnish the services described in the above estimate," makes this an offer. If its terms are accepted, you have an enforceable agreement.

Conversely, if the seller's order form states, "Not valid unless signed as accepted by an officer of the company or the sales manager," the potential buyer does not have a contract merely by accepting it. This type of language gives the seller a chance to negotiate with the buyer or to withdraw from the transaction by not signing the order *after* the buyer accepts it.

PROMISE TO AGREE

A discussion between two parties making an agreement does not necessarily result in a legally binding one. The most common situation is where one party accepts an offer but implies that the terms are still to be agreed upon. For example, one party offers to sell computer time to the other. The second party agrees to buy the time but will have his data processing manager call later to arrange the amount of time and other terms of the sale. There is no agreement here because the "acceptance" implies that the terms, including exactly what is to be purchased and at what price, are yet to be arranged.

Even when a deal is apparently settled, there may be only an "agreement to agree," not a contract. In one case, two individuals exchanged letters and came to an agreement on a contract to sell some land. The buyer, in his last letter, directed the seller to draw up duplicate contracts, sign them, and send him the copies. He closed the letter by saying, "I see no reason why we can't close it right up." The seller did as requested, but the buyer refused to sign. The seller sued for breach of contract. The courts ruled that there was no contract, because the buyer's last letter showed that he did not intend to be bound until he had signed it.

ILLUSORY OFFERS

A proposal clearly made in jest, or a remark made that a reasonable individual would not be justified in treating as an offer to enter into an agreement, cannot be made into a contract simply by accepting it.

A marginal case would be a proposal made under great emotional stress. Some courts have held that the person accepting the proposal cannot take advantage of it if he knows, or should have known, that the one making the offer is incapable of rationally intending to make the agreement. Without that intention, there can be no contract.

MISTAKES IN THE OFFER

A mistake in the terms of an agreement resulting from a slip of the tongue can invalidate it if the person accepting the offer knows, or has reason to know, that the one making the offer did not intend what the words expressed. For example, a wholesale dealer received a telegram from a buyer asking the price of oranges. The dealer wired "offer [variety] oranges one fifty; [another variety] two sixty." When delivered to the buyer, the wire omitted the word "two." The buyer ordered the second variety of oranges, but after they arrived he refused to pay more than $1.60. A court determined that the buyer must have known that the local price was $2.60, so the dealer was not required to sell them at $1.60. In this case, the person seeking to make the purchase could not treat the wire as an offer. This is because a reasonable person would know, or should know, in light of the facts and circumstances, that the seller did not intend to make a sale at the price of $1.60.

Usually, if the mistake was made in transmitting the offer, such as by telegram, and the erroneous offer is accepted, there is an agreement. Unless it is clear that the terms sent are so far out of line that they must be wrong, the party accepting the offer can hold the one making the offer to those terms. The party making the offer assumes the risk of a mistake, even in the transmission of the offer.

If the person making the offer misdirects an offer and it goes to the wrong person, that person cannot accept if he knows or should know that he was not the intended offeree.

AMBIGUITY

When one party to an agreement makes a mistake, that party bears the risk of any loss. If both parties to a transaction make a mistake as to what the agreement covers, neither party should be bound, unless they both intend the same mistaken meaning. This principle is applicable in three different situations:

1. If neither party knew nor should have known of an ambiguity in the offer, there is a binding agreement only if the party accepting the offer gave the same meaning to the words that the party making the offer did.

For example, a farmer agrees to sell a tractor for $3,000 to another farmer. Unknown to either of them, the farm manager for the first farmer purchased a new tractor just the day before. Neither party intends that the agreement cover the new tractor because neither knew about its purchase.

2. If both parties know, or should have known, of an ambiguity in the offer, there is no binding agreement unless both parties gave the same meaning to the ambiguous word or term.

For example, one farmer agrees to sell his "tractor" to another farmer for $3,000. The seller had three tractors, so the agreement is ambiguous when read in this context. The agreement is binding only if each farmer meant that the same tractor was being sold.

3. If the party making the offer knew, or should have known, of the ambiguity in its offer, and the one accepting the offer did not know and should not have known about the ambiguity, there is an agreement. The agreement is on the terms viewed from the accepting party's perspective.

In the previous example, if the buyer did not know the seller owned three tractors, the agreement will be enforced to transfer the one tractor he knew about.

EXPIRATION OF AN OFFER

Even though an offer has been made, its acceptance does not always result in an agreement. No offer remains open indefinitely. Offers expire, if not accepted, under a number of different circumstances:

1. The offer expires after the passage of the time stated in the offer itself. Any communication after that moment is regarded as a counter-offer.
2. If no time is given in the offer, the offer expires after the passage of a "reasonable" amount of time.

3. The offer is terminated by the death of the person or the destruction of a thing essential for the performance of the agreement.

4. The death (or insanity) of the person making the offer terminates the offer.

5. After an offer is made but before it is accepted, the proposed contract becomes illegal. At that moment, the offer is terminated.

6. If the person to whom the offer is made clearly rejects it, the offer terminates. It cannot be revived by a later attempt to accept.

7. A counter-offer is an implied rejection of an offer. It does not include mere inquiries on possible modifications when that party expressly reserves consideration of the offer.

An offer can be made irrevocable by an option agreement. If one party pays to keep an offer open for a fixed period, the offer is irrevocable for that period of time. Indeed, it is not even terminated by the death or insanity of the party making the offer during the option period.

ACCEPTANCE REQUESTING A CHANGE

An acceptance that asks for a change in or addition to the terms of the offer but does not insist on them constitutes an acceptance on the terms as offered. As to the requested changes or addition, you merely have an offer to modify the newly-created agreement. These proposed modifications may be accepted or rejected by the one making the original offer. Insistence, which is necessary to avoid this, may be shown by either a demand that the changes or addition be made or a statement conditioning an acceptance on them.

A WRITTEN AGREEMENT REFERRED TO IN AN OFFER

When one party makes an offer and the other party accepts but insists on a written agreement, there is no agreement at that time. Because the acceptance is not complete and without reservation, it is considered a counter-offer. Since the original offer did not provide for a written contract, the courts must determine if the written agreement was intended merely to make a record of the agreement—that is, to "memorialize" it. The alternative is to conclude that the written agreement is to be the end product of the negotiations. In the former case, there is a binding agreement if the offer has been accepted, even if there is no written contract. In the latter, the offer and acceptance are regarded merely as part of the negotiations, which are not concluded until the written agreement has been prepared and signed.

A determination of whether or not there is an agreement depends on the facts of the particular case. In making that determination, several factors are considered:

1. Does the wording of the offer sound like negotiations or a final offer? For example, if it says "We have available," it is not an offer.

2. Is the agreement required to be in writing, or is it one that usually is in writing? If so, there is no binding agreement until it is.

3. What is the nature or subject matter of the agreement? For example, does it require a formal document because of its complexity, detail, or size?

ACCEPTING BY SILENCE

Normally, if you do not respond to an offer, you cannot be held to have accepted it. Making a contract is a voluntary act; you cannot have a contract forced on you. In three basic cases, however, silence actually can constitute the acceptance of an offer and create an enforceable agreement:

1. When a seller says that he is so sure the buyer will accept that the buyer does not have to say anything. If the buyer does not answer, and if he intends to accept by that silence, there is a contract. Of course, since this kind of agreement depends on whether or not the buyer *intends* to accept, it would be almost impossible to prove in court that it exists.

2. When, because of previous business dealings, one party leads an-

other to understand that silence means acceptance. This is a specific application of the principles of custom and usage discussed later in this chapter.

3. When one party accepts services after having had the opportunity to reject them. This occurs when the services accepted were offered with the expectation that they would be paid for. This constitutes an *implied* contract, discussed in Chapter 2.

What Makes up the Agreement?

Generally, an agreement is thought of in terms of a single document or perhaps a document accompanied by a signed amendment. All too often this is not the case. The agreement may be made up of several pieces of paper, some unsigned. For example, in 1980 an engineering company sued a city in Ohio for breach of contract after the city denied that it had entered into a contract with the company for certain engineering services. The city charter required all contracts with the city to be written. While there was no single, integrated document, the court ruled that enough documents, including letters and work specifications, had been exchanged by the parties to make up a written agreement.

The following sections illustrate common situations and the rules that establish exactly what makes up the entire agreement between two parties.

THE PAROL EVIDENCE RULE

Before signing a written agreement, both parties negotiate the terms and conditions of their deal. The written agreement would be expected to include everything the parties agreed on during negotiations. Thus it would seem reasonable to require that the parties adhere to what they signed, and neither party should be allowed to claim that he agreed to something other than what is in the written agreement.

To protect each party, the law has created a rule of evidence, the parol evidence rule. This rule states that testimony is not admissible in court to vary the terms of a written agreement when that testimony pertains to oral or written statements made before or at the same time the agreement is signed. While it is a rule of evidence, it has the effect of requiring that terms agreed on by the parties must be included in the final written agreement or they may be unenforceable. This means that no agreement should be signed unless it contains all of the terms and conditions that the parties agreed on. As pointed out in Chapter 4, you may want an agreement to include performance standards for a product, if that is the basis for the sale. If the standards are not included, and if the product does not perform as advertised, you cannot sue successfully.

The parol evidence rule applies to all agreements, including such common forms as purchase orders, delivery receipts, acknowledgments, and contractor's binding quotations. There can be several agreements, written and oral, between the same parties, dealing with parts of the same transaction, so long as each one is valid on its own. The rule is limited as follows:

1. It applies only to a written agreement. If the agreement is oral, prior oral statements can modify the final agreement.

2. It applies only when the two parties intended to include or integrate all of the terms of their agreement into the written document.

3. It does not prevent the introduction of evidence on agreements subsequent to the written agreement, even if they amend or explain the written agreement.

Several exceptions to the parol evidence rule are discussed in Chapter 9.

THE MERGER CLAUSE

The practices encouraged by the parol evidence rule have given rise to the extensive use of a standard contract clause commonly known as a merger or an integration clause: "This instrument is intended to be the full and complete agreement of the Parties and there are no understandings, agreements, or undertakings between the Parties on this subject other than those contained herein."

The merger clause means that all prior communications and negotiations between the parties have been merged into the final written agreement. In negotiated agreements it is considered conclusive evidence of integration, which means the parol evidence rule applies. The result is that the text of the agreement must be accepted as a complete expression of the intent of the parties in the absence of fraud or mistake. As one expert in computer sales contracts writes:

> The sign of any successful written agreement is that the contract be a clear reflection of the intent of the parties, a true meeting of the minds. Therefore, when a computer vendor offers the purchaser a preprinted standard contract, it is unlikely that all of the oral representations made during the sales effort will be included, but an integration provision may affect the purchaser's subsequent inducement claims [by preventing him from testifying as to the oral sales representations that induced him to buy].[1]

The manner in which standard form agreements are printed, such as in fine type on the back of another document, may prevent the parties from easily modifying them to reflect special terms. Because of this, the parties may find that these terms are not binding on them. The merger clause usually is not applied to a standard form agreement, particularly an adhesion contract. Because these contracts are so one-sided, special rules have been established.

TERMS ESTABLISHED BY OUTSIDE STANDARDS

The parties to an agreement may refer to some external standard or event to establish some of the terms. For example, commercial loan forms often base the interest rate on the prime lending rate on the day when the money is actually borrowed. This rate varies because it reflects increases or decreases in the prime rate. The lack of a specific price in the agreement itself does not make the agreement invalid. Contracts that refer to such external standards are accepted so long as the method for establishing the price is definite and specific enough for a court to decide what it is.

In a contract that deals with the sale of goods between two merchants, the lack of a clear price will not invalidate it. If the contract's method for setting a price does not produce a definite answer, the courts can substitute a "reasonable" price.

Interpreting the Agreement

If both parties agree on an interpretation and no dispute arises under the agreement, their interpretation never becomes an issue. Only when there is an actual or potential difference are rules of interpretation applied by the courts. (Lawyers apply them too, because if the parties cannot agree and the matter goes to court, the court's rules will be applied.)

THE INTENTIONS OF THE PARTIES

The courts consistently say that the purpose of interpreting an agreement is first to determine and then to give effect to the mutual intention of the parties. In doing this, the courts examine the words and actions of the parties, or what they refer to as *expressed intent.* They give no weight to any secret or undisclosed intentions.

In determining the intent of the parties, the courts may choose among several alternative interpretations, but their choice is made according to which interpretation will best effectuate the agreement. This means they will prefer an interpretation of the words and actions that give a reasonable, lawful, and effective meaning.

THE OVERALL INTERPRETATION

An agreement is read and interpreted as a whole to give effect to every part of it. The courts determine the intentions of the parties from the entire agreement, not merely from isolated words or phrases.

If several writings between the parties pertain to the same transaction, the courts will generally treat them as if they are one complete document. However, this procedure does not apply in several important cases:

1. Major provisions in very small type may not be enforceable.
2. Terms on a preprinted form, such as a bill or invoice or printed on the back of a contract form, may not be considered part of the agreement unless a reasonable person would regard them as such.
3. Provisions or conditions brought to the attention of one party by the other *after* signing may not be valid. For example, if the seller seeks to use additional printed terms on the back of his invoice, the buyer is not bound by them if he did not see them before signing the purchase agreement.

ORDER OF PRECEDENCE

In interpreting a business agreement, you may have to decide which part applies to the issue that concerns you if a conflict arises over terms. This is particularly important when the agreement is memorialized in a number of documents, containing, for example, printed conditions, a typed text, attachments, and handwritten corrections. As among the varying kinds of texts, the courts have determined that the following order should apply in case of a conflict:

1. Handwritten changes and inserts
2. Typed changes
3. Typed agreement
4. Preprinted terms

The theory is that this order best illustrates the actual intent of the parties. It starts with those portions of the agreement that clearly were brought up between the parties in negotiations and resolved. Be certain, however, that your agreement does not already contain its own order of precedence. This is common in many situations, most frequently in contracts with the United States Government, when an agreement by a federal agency to purchase goods or services from a private company may be made up of some or all of the following:

1. A written proposal by the company
2. A schedule of work prepared by a government contracting officer
3. Terms and conditions of the solicitation for bids for this particular product or service
4. A set of general provisions applicable to all contracts of this agency
5. A set of general provisions applicable to all government contracts

For example, in one case, the U.S. Office of Personnel Management solicited proposals to put on a management seminar. The forty-page solicitation contained the following clause:

> *Order of Precedence*
> In the event of an inconsistency between provisions of this solicitation, the inconsistency shall be resolved by giving precedence in the following order:
> (a) The Schedule (excluding the Specifications)
> (b) Terms and Conditions of the solicitation, if any
> (c) General Provisions
> (d) Other Provisions of the contract, when attached or incorporated by reference
> (e) The Specifications

When dealing with any complex agreement, be on the watch for this type of clause, and in preparing your own agreements, try to avoid using such a clause.

The clause implies that the preparer of the documents believes there may be some ambiguities, conflicts, or inconsistencies in the agreement, created by the marriage of several documents. Rather than eliminating these problems, the burden is shifted to the other party to locate them and to resolve the inconsistencies at his own peril. It is a lazy drafter's trick and a dangerous trap for the unwary.

GRAMMAR AND WORDS

Rules of grammatical construction can and should be used to determine the intent of the parties. The courts, evidently recognizing the sorry state of commercial writing, have held that these rules are *not* to be applied when they conflict with the "real" intent of the parties.

In analyzing the meaning of words in an agreement, the courts will accept any definitions that the parties provide in the agreement. Otherwise, words and technical terms are given their ordinary meanings. Local, cultural, or trade usage of terms is applicable, as are the circumstances surrounding the making of the agreement.

USAGE, CUSTOM, AND COURSE OF CONDUCT

Trade usage, custom, and the course of conduct between the parties may be used in two ways: (1) to explain the meaning of words or phrases in an agreement and (2) to imply terms in the agreement when no contrary intent appears from the language of the agreement.

Trade usage is regarded as an established practice or method that has been adopted in an area, trade, or profession. Thus the parties are justified in expecting that it will be observed with respect to the agreement. For example, in hiring a person to sell cars, a company gives the new salesperson the authority to take trade-ins, even if the parties have not discussed this, because the trade usage of taking used cars as trade-ins is so widespread.

Trade usage can also establish who bears the risk of certain losses. In one case, a purchaser bought some lamps that turned out to be defective. He sued the seller. The seller was found not to be liable for the buyer's loss because the buyer was a professional in the lamp business and had personally inspected the lamps before buying them. The court determined that the buyer should have found the defects before he closed the deal. After such a deal is concluded, the defect becomes a business risk that the buyer assumes because it is usual in his business to do so.

Custom is a broader concept, but it is also related to trade usage because it is widely observed. Before custom can be used to interpret an agreement, one of several things must occur:

1. The parties must assent to it
2. One party must know, or have reason to know, that the other intends custom to govern the agreement
3. The custom must be so well known that a reasonable person would be aware of it

For example, in the sale of real estate, custom may set the details of the closing, such as the time of delivery of the deed and the place of the closing itself.

Conduct between the parties is also used to interpret the agreement. The course of conduct may be (1) that of similar transactions prior to the agreement in question, also called "course of dealing," and (2) that involving the actual performance of the agreement, also called "subsequent conduct."

The course of dealing could arise from an ongoing relationship between two companies. For example, a supplier bills one of his buyers regularly. The checks from the buyer are applied to the buyer's account as they arrive. Under one agreement, the buyer receives a defective shipment. In spite of this, he wants to continue to do business with the supplier on a regular basis, merely disputing only this bill. But this may not be enough. Because these two parties have established a regular billing and payment policy, there is a presumption that payment waives any claim of defects. To overcome this presumption, the buyer should send earmarked checks until the dispute is settled. The earmarking can be a note on the back of the check that it is to pay a particular undisputed invoice, identified by date or number. If the check is not marked, the supplier may properly credit the check against the bill that is in dispute and close the matter. The courts look to the course of conduct between the parties as a guide to interpreting an agreement because they presume the parties are correct in their mutual intent in making the agreement.

How a course of conduct can modify a written agreement is shown by a case involving the attempted repossession of a truck. The seller's contract allowed him to take back the truck without notice if the buyer missed any payments. The buyer did miss several payments but then made some late payments, which the seller accepted. Later on, the buyer again missed some payments, and this time the seller tried to repossess the truck. In a lawsuit initiated by the buyer, the court ruled that, in spite of the language in the agreement, the seller could not repossess the truck without first warning the buyer and giving him a chance to make his account current. The court reasoned that, by accepting late payments once before, the seller had led the buyer to believe that late payments would be accepted in the future.

Sometimes not saying or doing enough can result in liability in the same way that saying or doing too much can. For example, in a case decided in 1981, a salad dressing bottler ordered a distinctive lid from a supplier. The supplier's salesperson said it could not recommend using the liner of this lid for a product containing vinegar and salt. But the buyer insisted and the lids were supplied. Later the bottled dressing spoiled and the bottler sued the supplier. The courts held that the supplier was liable for the loss. Even though the supplier had recommended against using the lid, he never told the bottler why. This decision shows that the courts will intervene in commercial disputes to imply obligations or terms that were never even contemplated by the parties.

The application of these rules could result in conflicting interpretations of the agreement. When this occurs, the most widely accepted hierarchy of interpretation is:

1. Express terms of the agreement
2. Course of conduct
3. Course of dealing
4. Trade usage
5. Custom

A logical extension of these rules is to allow evidence about prior agreements between the parties to be used in interpreting a later agreement in dispute. Until recently, this was not permitted, but now more are doing this to resolve ambiguities in routine commercial agreements.

AMBIGUITY

Ambiguity or uncertainty usually means that something is reasonably open to more than one interpretation. In business agreements this means that after using all available tools and rules for interpretation a court cannot, with reasonable certainty, determine the meaning of the word or phrase in question. When this occurs, the courts may look behind the written word of the agreement to oral testimony to explain the ambiguity. (This is discussed further under the parol evidence rule here and in Chapter 9.)

If oral testimony does not eliminate the ambiguity, the courts will interpret the ambiguity against the party that prepared the agreement. This could be called the "If you wrote it, you're stuck with it" rule, and it is applied most frequently in the following cases:

1. When the dispute involves a printed form prepared by one party
2. When the language in question was prepared by an expert who now wants to use that language against the nonexpert to defeat or avoid the agreement
3. When the agreement is generally regarded as an adhesion contract, such as an insurance contract or real estate lease (this is discussed further in Chapters 2 and 4)

PAROL EVIDENCE

As stated before, the parol evidence rule provides that testimony is not admissible in court to vary the terms of a written agreement when that testimony pertains to oral or written statements made before or at the same time the agreement is signed. However, in some situations the rule can be avoided and the court will admit parol evidence. This happens most frequently in the following cases:

1. When there is an ambiguity in a word or clause of a written agreement

2. When a mistake, such as a typographical error in figures, is made while putting the agreement in writing

3. To prove fraud, duress, undue influence, illegality, or lack of capacity to make a contract

4. When important terms are missing in the agreement.

5. When the parties had orally agreed that the written agreement would not be enforceable unless a specific event occurred. This is known as a *condition precedent*.

6. When one party is trying to show that oral changes or additions were made after the agreement was signed. However, the statute of frauds, which requires certain agreements to be written, may prevent such changes from having any legal effect. For example, you cannot use parol evidence to show changes or additions to a deed for real estate, since all transfers involving real estate must be written, and any changes in the written documents also must be written.

Reading a Contract

CASE STUDY I: BUSINESS INSURANCE

To illustrate how to study and understand an agreement, let's briefly analyze a standard insurance agreement, the business interruption policy.

This policy comprises the declaration and the policy form itself, as signed by the insurance company. The declarations, which become part of the policy, are the facts that the insured business states about itself. Generally, in the case of a property and liability policy, these take the form of a description. In the case of life and health insurance policies, they are the application form itself.

Following the declarations, or descriptions, is the body of the agreement. The example starts with two uncaptioned paragraphs that elucidate the insurer's general obligations. But these obligations are

BUSINESS INTERRUPTION FORM NO. 3

Gross Earnings Form for Mercantile or Non-Manufacturing Risks

Insurance attaches to this item(s) only when "Business Interruption," a specific amount and a contribution percentage are specified therefor in this policy, and, unless otherwise provided, all provisions and stipulations of this form and policy shall apply separately to each such item.

1. This policy covers against loss resulting directly from necessary interruption of business caused by damage to or destruction of real or personal property by the peril(s) insured against, during the term of this policy, on premises occupied by the Insured and situated as herein described.

2. In the event of such damage or destruction this Company shall be liable for the ACTUAL LOSS SUSTAINED by the Insured resulting directly from such interruption of business, but not exceeding the reduction in Gross Earnings less charges and expenses which do not necessarily continue during the interruption of business, for only such length of time as would be required with the exercise of due diligence and dispatch to rebuild, repair or replace such part of the property herein described as has been damaged or destroyed, commencing with the date of such damage or destruction and not limited by the date of expiration of this policy. Due consideration shall be given to the continuation of normal charges and expenses, including payroll expense, to the extent necessary to resume operations of the Insured with the same quality of service which existed immediately preceding the loss.

3. **Resumption of Operations:** It is a condition of this insurance that if the Insured could reduce the loss resulting from the interruption of business,

(a) by complete or partial resumption of operation of the property herein described, whether damaged or not, or

(b) by making use of merchandise or other property, at the location(s) described herein or elsewhere,

such reduction shall be taken into account in arriving at the amount of loss hereunder.

4. **Expenses Related to Reducing Loss:** This policy also covers such expenses as are necessarily incurred for the purpose of reducing loss under this policy (except expense incurred to extinguish a fire), but in no event shall the aggregate of such expenses exceed the amount by which the loss otherwise payable under this policy is thereby reduced. Such expenses shall not be subject to the application of the Contribution Clause.

5. **Gross Earnings:** For the purposes of this insurance "Gross Earnings" are defined as the sum of:

(a) Total net sales, and

(b) Other earnings derived from operations of the business,

less the cost of:

(c) Merchandise sold, including packaging material therefor,

(d) Materials and supplies consumed directly in supplying the service(s) sold by the Insured, and

(e) Service(s) purchased from outsiders (not employees of the Insured) for resale which do not continue under contract.

No other costs shall be deducted in determining Gross Earnings.

In determining Gross Earnings due consideration shall be given to the experience of the business before the date of damage or destruction and the probable experience thereafter had no loss occurred.

6. **Contribution Clause:** In consideration of the rate and form under which this policy is written, this Company shall be liable, in the event of loss, for no greater proportion thereof than the amount hereby covered bears to the Contribution (Co-insurance) percentage specified on the first page of this policy (or endorsed hereon) of the Gross Earnings that would have been earned (had no loss occurred) during the 12 months immediately following the date of damage to or destruction of the described property.

7. **Interruption by Civil Authority:** This policy is extended to include the actual loss sustained by the Insured, resulting directly from an interruption of business as covered hereunder, during the length of time, not exceeding 2 consecutive weeks, when, as a direct result of damage to or destruction of property adjacent to the premises herein described by the peril(s) insured against, access to such described premises is specifically prohibited by order of civil authority.

8. **Limitation — Media For Electronic Data Processing:** With respect to loss resulting from damage to or destruction of media for, or programming records pertaining to, electronic data processing or electronically controlled equipment, including data thereon, by the peril(s) insured against, the length of time for which this Company shall be liable hereunder shall not exceed —

    (a) 30 consecutive calendar days; or

    (b) the length of time that would be required to rebuild, repair or replace such other property herein described as has been damaged or destroyed;

whichever is the greater length of time.

9. **Special Exclusions:** This Company shall not be liable for any increase of loss resulting from:

    (a) enforcement of any local or state ordinance or law regulating the construction, repair or demolition of buildings or structures; or

    (b) interference at the described premises, by strikers or other persons, with rebuilding, repairing or replacing the property or with the resumption or continuation of business; or

    (c) the suspension, lapse or cancellation of any lease, license, contract or order unless such suspension, lapse or cancellation results directly from the interruption of business, and then this Company shall be liable for only such loss as affects the Insured's earnings during, and limited to, the period of indemnity covered under this policy;

nor shall this Company be liable for any other consequential or remote loss.

THE PROVISIONS PRINTED ON THE BACK OF THIS FORM ARE HEREBY REFERRED TO AND MADE A PART HEREOF.

NOTE TO AGENTS: Other clauses, such as Automatic Sprinkler Clause or Watchman and Clock Clause, to be added as provided in the rules.

10. **Pro Rata Clause:** The liability under this policy shall not exceed that proportion of any loss which the amount of insurance hereunder bears to all insurance, whether collectible or not, covering in any manner the loss insured against by this policy.

11. **Definition of "Normal":** The condition that would have existed had no loss occurred.

12. **Loss Clause:** Any loss hereunder shall not reduce the amount of this policy.

13. **Work and Materials Clause:** Permission granted for such use of the premises as is usual or incidental to the occupancy as described herein.

14. **Electrical Apparatus Clause (This Clause Void as to Windstorm Insurance):** This Company shall not be liable for Business Interruption loss resulting from electrical injury or disturbance to electrical appliances or devices (including wiring) caused by electrical currents artificially generated unless fire ensues, and if fire does ensue this Company shall be liable only for its proportion of Business Interruption loss caused by such ensuing fire.

15. **Alterations and New Buildings Clause:** Permission granted to make alterations in, or to construct additions to, any building described herein and to construct new buildings on the described premises. This policy is extended to cover, subject to all its provisions and stipulations, loss resulting from damage to or destruction of such alterations, additions or new buildings while in course of construction and when completed or occupied, provided that, in the event of damage to or destruction of such property (including building materials, supplies, machinery or equipment incident to such construction or occupancy while on the described premises or within one hundred (100) feet thereof) so as to delay commencement of business operations of the Insured, the length of time for which this Company shall be liable shall be determined as otherwise provided herein but such determined length of time shall be applied and the loss hereunder calculated from the date that business operations would have begun had no loss occurred.

If any building herein described is protected by automatic sprinklers, this permit shall not be held to include the reconstruction or the enlargement of any building so protected, without the consent of this Company in writing. This permit does not waive or modify any of the terms or conditions of the Automatic Sprinkler Clause (if any) attached to this policy.

16. Liberalization Clause: If during the period that insurance is in force under this policy, there be adopted in this state by the fire insurance rating organization on behalf of this Company, any forms, endorsements or rules by which this insurance could be extended or broadened, without additional premium charge, by endorsement or substitution of such form or endorsement, then such extended or broadened insurance shall inure to the benefit of the Insured hereunder as though such endorsement or substitution of form had been made.

17. Requirements in Case Loss Occurs: The Insured shall give immediate written notice to this Company of any Business Interruption loss and protect the property from further damage that might result in extension of the period of interruption; **and within 60 days following the date of damage to or destruction of the real or personal property described, unless such time is extended in writing by this Company, the Insured shall render to this Company a proof of loss,** signed and sworn to by the Insured, stating the knowledge and belief of the Insured as to the following:

    (a) the time and origin of the property damage or destruction causing the interruption of business,

    (b) the interest of the Insured and of all others in the business,

    (c) all other contracts of insurance, whether valid or not, covering in any manner the loss insured against by this policy,

    (d) any changes in the title, nature, location, encumbrance or possession of said business since the issuing of this policy, and

    (e) by whom and for what purpose any building herein described and the several parts thereof were occupied at the time of damage or destruction,

and shall furnish a copy of all the descriptions and schedules in all policies, and the actual amount of business interruption value and loss claimed, accompanied by detailed exhibits of all values, costs and estimates upon which such amounts are based.

The Insured, as often as may be reasonably required, shall exhibit to any person designated by this Company all that remains of any property herein described, and submit to examinations under oath by any person named by this Company, and subscribe the same; and, as often as may be reasonably required, shall produce for examination all books of account, bills, invoices and other vouchers, or certified copies thereof if originals be lost, at such reasonable time and place as may be designated by this Company or its representative, and shall permit extracts and copies thereof to be made.

18. Subrogation Clause: It is hereby stipulated that this insurance shall not be invalidated should the Insured waive in writing prior to a loss any or all right of recovery against any party for loss occurring to the property described herein.

19. Nuclear Clause: The word "fire" in this policy or endorsements attached hereto is not intended to and does not embrace nuclear reaction or nuclear radiation or radioactive contamination, all whether controlled or uncontrolled, and loss by nuclear reaction or nuclear radiation or radioactive contamination is not intended to be and is not insured against by this policy or said endorsements, whether such loss be direct or indirect, proximate or remote, or be in whole or in part caused by, contributed to, or aggravated by "fire" or any other perils insured against by this policy or said endorsements; however, subject to the foregoing and all provisions of this policy, loss by "fire" resulting from nuclear reaction or nuclear radiation or radioactive contamination is insured against by this policy.

Form No 19G (4-68)

Source: Insurance Services Office, 160 Water Street, New York, N.Y. 10038.

strictly limited by the terms of the entire agreement; they cannot be fully understood without referring to the agreement as a whole.

The intent of the policy is to cover the insured during a period of a total or partial shutdown—in other words, during a business interruption. It is logical to expect that continuing operating expenses as well as profit, if any, are the subjects of the coverage. In this form, coverage applies to the reduction in "gross earnings" less charges that do not necessarily continue (Paragraphs 1, 2, and 4).

Since the subject of the coverage is the business' earnings, one would expect the contract to be interpreted to require that there be earnings to be lost during the interruption. Otherwise, there would be no "loss resulting directly from necessary interruption of business" (Paragraph 1). This very point was the subject of a lawsuit in the Wisconsin Supreme Court. In this case, a business was operating without a net profit. Thus, under normal operations it would not have earned enough to pay continuing expenses. Because of this, the court held that the business had not suffered a loss that was covered by its policy.

Here we can see the impact of the courts. This is a standard form of agreement used by many insurance companies. If this clause is not changed in future versions of the form, the interpretation given it by the Wisconsin Supreme Court in effect becomes a part of the contract.

The impact of courts on contracts can become preponderant. The standard fire insurance policy, 165 lines long, has been interpreted so often by the courts that it has acquired its own private body of law. In fact, the American Bar Association now publishes a book of annotations, or court cases, interpreting this one short document.

Even when clauses seem to govern a situation, you must read them with care. Note Paragraph 7, captioned "Interruption by Civil Authority." The paragraph provides for coverage "when [access is prohibited] as a direct result of damage to or destruction of property adjacent to the premises herein described by the perils insured against." This coverage can run for as long as two weeks. The case it was intended to cover is one such as a fire ("the peril") on the same block ("adjacent to") as the insured's business ("the premises"). If police or firemen cordon off the area, customers are prevented from entering, and the business can come to a complete halt, with virtually the same impact as if the fire had been in the building itself.

The way this policy can be interpreted and applied to new circumstances is illustrated by a case in the District of Columbia following the rioting in April 1968. During the rioting municipal officials imposed a week-long 5:30 P.M. curfew and banned the sale of alcoholic beverages. The owner of a restaurant made a claim with his insurance company for $9,000 in lost revenues under a business interruption policy. There had been no damage to the restaurant, and the riots occurred miles from his property. The claim relied on the "Interruption by Civil Authority" clause.

First, the court noted that the policy specifies coverage for loss from "interruption of business caused by damage to or destruction of real or personal property" (Paragraph 1), which was not the case here. Second, the coverage is for "actual loss sustained [during the time required to] rebuild, repair, or replace such part of the property . . . as has been damaged or destroyed" (Paragraph 2). The court ruled that this also was not the case. The clause specifically covers losses that occur "as a direct result of damage to or destruction of property adjacent to the premises" (Paragraph 7). The court noted that the riots were miles away, so coverage did not apply. The court's conclusion: "Though the loss alleged resulted from the curfew and municipal regulations, these did not prohibit access to the premises because of damage to or destruction of adjacent property." In this case, while the policy covered losses from business interruptions, the various clauses relating to coverage had to be read together. The interpretation that this policy did not cover losses from the closing of an area because of the threat of damage is one that can be derived from a careful review of the language of the policy itself, and one that would be upheld by the courts as a reasonable interpretation of the insurance contract.

It can be said that an insurance policy is an agreement, only more so. One respected authority on insurance summarizes the issues surrounding any insurance agreement:

In a very real sense, the policy incorporates the law of the jurisdiction along with its rules of interpretation and construction of specific terms. The policy language itself is sometimes merely the top of the "iceberg." . . . Many policies are forbidding because they are lengthy. . . . A good share of this increasing length can be traced to provisions that grant greater rights to the insured.

Length may also be liberally combined with complexity. Some policies are so complicated that occasionally the insurer himself does not fully appreciate their meaning until a court decision or claimant "discovers" an interpretation that even the insurer did not foresee. Not infrequently, of course, a court may stretch the meaning of a policy far beyond the reasonable import of its words. . . .

How to be sure that the generalized need expressed by the consumer is fairly and faithfully translated into coverage by his contract is one of the great problems of policy construction, insurance regulation, and insurance marketing. The problem is solved or at least ameliorated by several techniques: (1) . . . ambiguous policy provisions are usually construed in favor of the insured and against the insurer; . . . (2) the court may give judicial recognition to the fact that the policyholder does not read his policy; (3) the policy itself may be regulated or standardized to ensure fairness.[2]

CASE STUDY II: WHEN IS A HOSPITAL NOT A HOSPITAL?

Interpreting one clause in a typical medical insurance policy and attempting to answer the question "When is a hospital not a hospital?" offers further proof on the importance of reading contracts with extreme care. Often buried in definitions are major coverage issues. Here it is important to determine what is *not* said, and you should use some of the same skills in interpreting the agreement that you would use in drafting it.

In one case, an insured patient underwent routine surgery in a hospital that was part of a large urban medical complex. One building in the complex contained all surgical suites and recovery rooms. The insured was moved into this building for the surgery and recovery. Then she was returned to her room in the same building, where she stayed for two weeks. After she was released from the hospital, she filed a claim with her health insurance company under her $50-a-day hospital cash policy.

The insurance company denied her claim for $700 (for a two-week stay) on the basis that she had not been confined to a hospital.

The insured's problem involved the way "hospital" was defined in her policy. Not all health insurance policies have the same definition. While they may look the same, the definitions vary widely and the differences can be critical to the insured. Her policy defined a hospital as an institution that has facilities on the premises for diagnosis and surgery. The hospital she checked into technically did not have its own surgical suite. As increasing numbers of facilities do, it had a contract with the adjoining medical center to use its surgical facilities. The health insurance company asserted that the policy's requirement that there be surgical facilities on the premises was not met by the contract with the adjoining medical center. If this dispute had gone to court, the insurance company would have won. The restrictive definition is regarded as clear and not in violation of public policy.

This illustrates a key point in reading and comparing any insurance policy or other standard contracts. You must know what the policy covers and what it does *not* cover. For example, just because two policies say that they pay $50 per day while you are in the hospital doesn't mean they will pay for confinements in the same hospitals. Hospital cash policies may exclude any or all of the following, even if the word *hospital* appears in the name of the facility:

1. Veteran's or public health service hospital
2. Clinic
3. Continued or extended care facility
4. Convalescent home
5. Rest home
6. Nursing home
7. Home for the aged
8. Treatment center for alcoholism or drug addiction
9. Institutions without surgical or diagnostic facilities on the premises
10. Rehabilitation center

The insurance company is not bound by the name *hospital* if it excludes it from its definition. Some definitions even exclude coverage if the patient is confined in a part of a hospital that primarily serves as a rehabilitation, convalescent, or alcohol or addiction treatment wing. Thus if the patient is transferred to a rehabilitation wing, under such a policy the daily cash coverage stops. This illustrates the importance of a close study of even routine items like definitions.

CASE STUDY III: SUBJECTIVE DETERMINATIONS

The completion of many agreements depends on "satisfying" one party to the agreement. For example, the contract used by the publisher of this book and signed by the author provides that the manuscript, when delivered, "shall be in complete and final form, in content and form satisfactory to Publisher." This raises several questions: (1) When must the publisher decide this? (2) What happens if the publisher rejects the manuscript? and (3) What happens to any advance against royalties? Although these topics are usually covered elsewhere in the agreement, the most critical question is the application of the clause "satisfactory to" the publisher. Under this provision, the publisher's subjective judgment that the manuscript is not satisfactory usually will not be set aside by the courts, even if the work is professional and publishable. The only exception is if the author can prove that the publisher exercised its rights under this clause in "bad faith."

Such a clause gives substantial rights to the party to be satisfied. To minimize this, various options exist. For example, the Authors' Guild suggests that contracts require delivery of a manuscript that "in style and content, is professionally competent and fit for publication." Another alternative is to require that the manuscript be of "publishable quality," still a relatively subjective standard. A final option is to state that the publisher's acceptance of the manuscript "shall not be unreasonably withheld." All of these merely refine a subjective determination standard by giving the appearance of objectivity. If there is an objective standard, use it. But if a subjective standard is what the parties intend to use, the agreement should specify not only how it is to be applied, but by whom and under what conditions.

6
Writing
an Agreement

A contract can be simply worded and still be enforceable. Just make sure that all the elements are contained in the agreement. This contract, taken from A. W. Waite's *The Book of Black Magic and of Facts* (London, 1898), is short and simple, but it is still a binding agreement:

> I promise to grand Lucifuge to reward him in twenty years' time for all the treasures that he may give me. In witness thereof I have signed myself _____ .

This contract had to be written on virgin parchment with a new quill, using an ink made up of ten ounces of gall nuts, three ounces of green copperas, three ounces of rock alum or gum arabic, and enough river water to make a liquid. The pact of course must be signed in blood. While the ink, quill, and parchment are no longer required, this document remains valid.

Plain Language and Readable Agreements

Until a few years ago, the only motivation for drafting a plain and simple agreement was personal style. Since many clients felt that something could not be legal unless it "sounded legal," there was little incentive for lawyers to put agreements in simple language. In addition, many agreements were prepared from form books or from previous agreements. All too often, a sample agreement was merely doctored to meet the needs of the client, usually by adding a few extra clauses, paragraphs, or provisos and deleting those that clearly were not applicable. The result was that lawyers prepared complex documents to create any important legal relationship.

This practice would have continued had it not been for a growing movement toward readability or plain language. The most active area has been personal insurance, where an increasing number of states now require that insurance policies and related documents be in simplified language. To date, more than one-third of the states have initiated some sort of readability law, and more are expected to do so in the future.

New York, Maine, Connecticut, and Hawaii have passed comprehensive plain-language bills, which require all consumer contracts to be in understandable English. At the federal level the Internal Revenue Service and the Census Bureau are experimenting with plain-language forms and instructions. The Office of the Federal Register, which oversees the printing and codification of all proposed federal rules and regulations, has undertaken an effort to encourage federal agencies to draft readable regulations. While it is not at all certain that the readability trend will spread throughout the United States, it is already having an impact on business agreements, and some agreements between businesses are already affected by the plain-language laws. In addition to insurance companies, banks and financial institutions have revised documents ranging from account applications to loan agreements. Unfortunately, many businesspeople assume that because a document is simple and readable it has no legal impact. But it is likely that as more agreements become readable, lawyers and businesspeople will adopt them.

The techniques in this chapter are geared to producing a plain-language, readable agreement. Virtually any agreement can be written in plain or readable language. If you understand how to draft a readable document, you will then also know how to draft and analyze a complex document. The techniques of readability require clarity of thought as well as clarity in expression. If a clause cannot be made readable, more than likely the person drafting the agreement does not understand it. Compare the differences in style between the Sample Share Transfer Agreement and the Consulting Agreement in the Appendix.

Today, a variety of tests are applied to legal documents to see if they are readable. Several of the common ones are discussed in the sources noted in the References. But, ultimately, what is readable is subjective. One expert in legal writing, discussing a particularly complex federal government real-estate-financing clause, states:

> If any instrument written for nonlawyers requires rereading of clauses, sentences, and paragraphs, it should be revised. Documents should be designed for reader comprehension on the first reading.[1]

The Plain-Language Controversy

The controversy about the use of plain language in legal documents has aroused many lawyers to argue against the abandonment of tried and true language for new, untested language, a process that they feel will lead to more, not less, litigation. An American Bar Association Committee on Legal Drafting provides one of the strongest rebuttals to these arguments:

The greatest need for clear drafting is by lawyers in private practice for their clients. Lawyers tend to rely upon language which has withstood the test of litigation. However, it should be realized that, most likely, such language was the subject of litigation initially because it was unclear. . . . [I]n some cases the parties to a contract want it deliberately drafted ambiguously for any number of sound reasons. However, in the absence of such reasons, the client is entitled to a document drafted in language which can be understood by those to whom it is addressed. . . . Some critics have spoken of the romance of the traditional language of the law, stating that clients expect documents prepared by their lawyer to contain such language. The Committee rejects this assertion, and is of the opinion that the use of legalese serves no valid public purpose.[2]

Practicing lawyers are beginning to adopt this position. As a member of this same committee more recently writes:

[An article critical of a particular federal government contract's boilerplate language] is presented . . . as an example of the way the seed of excessive litigation can be planted by "lawyers' language" that has been hallowed by uncritical repetition. That kind of drafting ignores the responsibility of professionals to write so that those to whom documents are addressed can understand them. Lawyers experienced in real estate financing, with some guidance from trained linguists like the author [of the article] . . . could readily translate traditional mortgage clauses into clear English. Then the parties to the transaction, as well as their lawyers, could understand their rights and duties. Such a translation . . . will stand up in court and does not require "rereading of clauses, sentences, and paragraphs." It demonstrates that the lawyer is skilled in communication. . . . Thus the legal profession has a responsibility to present no documents, regulations or statutes that require rereading to be understood. The crushing burden of litigation will then be reduced, and the true intent of the parties will be realized.[3]

Drafting an Agreement

Clarity in writing follows clarity in thinking. In preparing an agreement, this is an all important point. Before you write any legal document, stop and think. This can eliminate many of the problems that arise when you modify an existing document to fit a particular deal. The deal or the transaction comes first. Do the contract from the deal, not the deal from the contract.

Before you draft any agreement, prepare an outline of the transaction to organize the subject matter. The amount of effort that goes into this initial phase will determine the usefulness and accuracy of the agreement. In addition, if the agreement is to be negotiated, an outline is invaluable in making sure that all important points are covered and that the parties in fact do agree on all critical matters. In the drafting stage of the agreement, an outline will help to minimize misunderstandings between you and the other party.

A number of general organizational steps should be taken as you prepare the outline so that the agreement will be clear, complete, and usable. First, establish a single principle of division for separating the subject matter into major topics. Do this by considering who the agreement is written for and what it is to accomplish. For example, if the agreement covers the supply of goods, organize it so that those implementing the agreement, say warehouse personnel, can understand it and operate under it. Thus don't bury the shipment schedule and description of the materials deep in the agreement.

In many cases, the major topics will be apparent, and their identification may cause you to modify your principle of division. If the agreement covers the supply of several kinds of goods, a logical division would be to separate each item. However, if the terms of payment of each item are essentially alike, and payment will be made for you by the same person, you may want to group all the payment terms together. Once you do this, you may want to go back and group other terms, such as all delivery and inspection terms or all supply schedule clauses.

Because the outline is a hierarchy of ideas, use this rule of division at each level of the outline. Unless the agreement is complex, the number of levels should be small.

Second, after establishing the divisions, arrange the items within each topic in a logical sequence. Again, arrange them to be helpful to your audience. A number of rules can be applied here:

1. Place general provisions before specific provisions
2. Place the more important provisions before the less important ones
3. Place the more frequently used provisions before those less frequently used
4. Place permanent provisions before temporary ones
5. Place administrative provisions, such as the effective date of the agreement, addresses for notices, penalties, and arbitration, at the end.

Use a heading for each separate part of the agreement. The heading, which can be a short catch word or phrase that describes the subject, will help the ultimate user to locate applicable provisions more efficiently.

Do not use headings excessively; use them only down to the section level in an agreement, unless a user would miss significant information contained in a section.

Headings should be used with care, because as part of the agreement they can be used to determine its meaning if a dispute ever arises. Be aware, though, that some lawyers frown on the use of headings:

[T]he conscientious draftsman worries about the headings. . . . [T]he heading may imply more (or less) than the provision itself conveys. Gone in the bold language at the beginning of the section or the paragraph are the nuances, cross-references, provisos, and exceptions carefully shaped in the text that follows. Such a concern is invariably met by a provision like this one:

"The table of contents and the headings to the various sections of the Agreement are inserted only for convenience of reference and are not intended, nor shall they be construed to modify, define, limit or expand the intent of the parties as expressed in this Agreement."

* * *

Headings that lead the reader immediately to the point of his search may relieve him from that higher duty to interrelate all the pieces of the entire agreement, to see how the whole thing hangs together. Deprived of headings, the reader will have to develop a greater familiarity with the document before he can be satisfied that he has found what he was looking for.[4]

Despite the language suggested by this lawyer, the courts will use headings to interpret an agreement.

If a short heading cannot be devised for a particular section, you have two options: (1) Do not use a heading, or (2) revise the section into several parts, each with its own heading. If neither works, review the section to determine why it is there and what it does. If you do not understand it, redo it.

When you use headings, indicate the relationship of materials in a series of sections:

Section 1. Statement of Work: Introduction

Section 2. Statement of Work: Scope of Work

Section 3. Statement of Work: Objectives

Section 4. Statement of Work: Specific Tasks and Deadlines

You can also use headings to indicate that a group of related subjects is treated together in a single section. For example:

Section 15. Place of Performance, Place of Payment and Delivery of Notices.

Once you have written the headings, consider using a table of contents if the agreement is lengthy. This enables you quickly to review the agreement and determine if any subjects have been omitted. If you find gaps, they can be filled before signing. The table of contents should look like the outline: Both should indicate everything that the parties have agreed on.

Using a table of contents will help you organize the agreement more logically. Keep in mind that it should be understandable even to those parties who will use it but have not been part of the preparation process. Examine the table of contents in Chapter 4, which is from an agreement covering a major corporate acquisition. Note that it covers all the major elements of any acquisition and groups them in a logical sequence. If you use headings below the section level—that is, at the paragraph level or below—you may want to omit them from the table of contents to avoid making it too long.

PLAIN WRITING IS GOOD WRITING

Most of the examples of contract language here are taken from clauses in certain types of U.S. government contracts. Government contracts were selected not because they are good or bad, but because they are typical. Some provisions are drafted clearly and concisely, others are excessively long and complicated, and some are virtually unintelligible. When studying them, keep in mind that a good drafter, above all, follows the rules of grammar. In fact, it may not be a bad idea to brush up on basic grammar. Many ambiguities in agreements can be avoided by applying basic grammatical rules. Given a choice, keep it simple. For example:

1. Replace long phrases with shorter, simpler ones.
2. Replace long, complex words with shorter, simple words.
3. Do not use any technical term that you do not understand. Know what it means before you use it. If necessary, define it in the agreement.

The Appendix contains a checklist of preferred expressions that are designed to simplify contracts.

When writing (or reading) any agreement, do not become confused by the use of technical legal words and phrases. If you do not understand what a word or phrase means, do not guess at its meaning. Instead, use a good legal dictionary or thesaurus. Several basic ones are listed in the References.

PARAGRAPHS AND SENTENCES

Short sentences and paragraphs are more easily understood than long ones. When both a short and long word can be used to communicate the same thought, use the short one, because it is more likely to be easily understood. By limiting yourself to one or two thoughts in a sentence and to a single relationship of thoughts in a paragraph, you can avoid the difficult problems of resolving ambiguities discussed in Chapter 5. Some authorities of readable documents advise keeping sentences at twenty-five words or less and paragraphs at seventy-five words or less. They also suggest avoiding words with three or more syllables.

A standard clause in a government contract pertaining to rights in computer software states:

Those portions of this technical data indicated as limited rights shall not, without the written permission of the above Contractor, be either (a) used, released or disclosed in whole or in part outside the Government, (b) used in whole or in part by the Government for the manufacture or, in the case of computer software documentation, for preparing the same or similar computer software, or (c) used by a party other than the Government except for: (i) emergency repair or overhaul work only, by or for the Government, where the item or process concerned is not otherwise reasonably available to enable timely performance of the work, *provided* that the release or disclosure hereof outside the Government shall be made subject to a prohibition against further use, release or disclosure; or (ii) release to a foreign government, as the interest of the United States may require, only for information or evaluation within such government or for emergency repair or overhaul work by or for such government under the conditions of (i) above.

The clause contains at least three independent thoughts. Proper drafting would be to break it up into several sentences, perhaps using lists, to help the user see which clause modifies which thought. In addition, the clause contains an excessively detailed exception. The drafter should have considered stating it positively, not negatively.

The user of an agreement always wants to know whether or not a rule or condition of the agreement applies to him before bothering to study the rule or condition. Therefore, if only one or two simple conditions must be met before a rule or condition applies, state the conditions first, then the rule. Examine this clause:

> In preparing reports, the Contractor shall refrain from using elaborate artwork, multicolor printing, and expensive paper and binding, unless it is specifically authorized in the Schedule. Whenever possible, pages should be printed on both sides using single-spaced type.

For clarity, the clause could be revised to read:

> The Contractor should print pages on both sides using single-spaced type whenever possible. Unless it is specifically authorized in the Schedule, the Contractor should not use any of the following in preparing reports:
>
> (a) elaborate artwork
> (b) multicolor printing
> (c) expensive paper and binding

If two complex conditions or more than two simple conditions must be met before a rule applies, state the rule first, then list the conditions. This avoids the confusion that comes from lumping a large mass of conditions together before a rule. Listing provides space between the various conditions, making it visually easier to read. Listing also helps to avoid problems of ambiguity caused by the words *and* and *or*. When you prepare a list, follow these rules:

1. Each item must be in the same classification.

2. Each item must correspond, both in substance and form, to the introductory language of the list.

3. If the introductory language of the list is a complete sentence—

   a. End the introduction with a colon; and

   b. Make each item a separate sentence.

4. If the introductory language of the list is an incomplete sentence—

   a. End the introduction with a dash;

   b. End each item, except the last item, with a semicolon;

   c. After the semicolon in the next to the last item, write *and* or *or* as appropriate; and

   d. End the last item in the list with a period.

The use of lists can also eliminate other problems. For example, the following section is found in many government contracts.

> This clause is applicable if the amount of this contract exceeds $10,000 and was entered into by means of negotiation, including small business restricted advertising, but it is not applicable if this contract was entered into by means of formal advertising.

Its problem is in the statement of preconditions. It can be alleviated by the use of a list.

> This clause is not applicable if this contract was entered into by means of formal advertising. This clause is applicable if—
>
> (a) The amount of this contract exceeds $10,000; and
>
> (b) This contract was entered into by means of negotiation, including small business restricted advertising.

TENSE AND VOICE

While discussing questions of tense and voice may sound like a return to high school grammar, it is upon such questions that many contract lawsuits eventually turn. After reading the numerous illustrations of defective drafting in Chapter 5, it is easy to see how they might result in lawsuits.

A contract speaks as of the time that you apply it, not as of the time that it is drafted. For this reason, agreements generally should be drafted in the present tense. Also, by drafting in the present tense, you can avoid complicated and awkward verb forms. For example, don't write: "Any later payments shall bear interest at the rate of 18 percent per year." Instead, write: "The interest rate on late payments is 18 percent per year."

If you express time relationships in an agreement, observe two rules:

1. Explain events that happen at the same time as the operation of the agreement as if they were present facts

2. Express events that happened before the operation of the agreement as if they were past facts

For example, a contract with one federal department provides:

> State and local government agencies holding Federal contracts of $10,000 or more shall also list their suitable openings with the appropriate office of the State employment service, but are not required to provide those reports set forth in paragraphs (d) and (e).

It can be rewritten, depending on whether the author intended the clause to apply in the case of past or current federal contracts:

> State and local government agencies that hold Federal contracts of $10,000 or more must also list their suitable openings with the appropriate State employment service office. These agencies are not required to provide the reports described in paragraphs (d) and (e).

or:

> State and local government agencies that held Federal contracts of $10,000 or more must also list their suitable openings with the ap-

propriate State employment service office. These agencies are not required to provide the reports described in paragraphs (d) and (e).

If you must include past as well as future events in an agreement, use the present tense, but insert before the appropriate verb the phrase "before (or after) this (section, paragraph, event) takes effect."

Always use the active voice, not the passive. This is particularly important when you intend to impose a duty or confer a power on someone in the agreement. The active voice eliminates potential confusion by forcing the parties specifically to identify an "actor" in the agreement. This makes clear to everyone exactly *who* is to perform the duty or *who* is vested with the power. If possible, name the actor first and then describe the duty or power. For example, don't write: "Each book delivered under this agreement will be covered with a red, white, and blue cover." Instead, write: "The printer will cover each book with a red, white, and blue cover."

CONSISTENCY

Do not use different words to describe the same thing. Variation for its own sake has no place in the drafting of a legal agreement. Using a synonym rather than repeating the term can confuse users. In addition, if the agreement should ever be taken to court, the use of differing words may be interpreted to mean that the parties to the agreement actually *intended* them to be used differently. For example, in a gas contract between an oil company and a pipeline company, a dispute arose as to whether or not the oil company, Gulf, could cancel because the pipeline company had not gotten a Certificate of Public Convenience and Necessity to move the gas. A court reviewing the document noted that in one section Gulf was required to file an "application for a Certificate of Convenience and Necessity," while another section required the pipeline company to file "an application for such authority as may be necessary to enable it to expand the certified capacity of its [gas] line." The court concluded that the difference in language must be purposeful, given the extended negotiations on the contract. The ruling: The pipeline company did not have to file for a Certificate of Convenience and Necessity, but it had met the contract requirement by filing for something else.

Do not use the same word to denote different things. While this sort of ambiguity can be corrected by reference to the context in which the word is used, using one word to express two or more meanings merely increases the possibility of misinterpretation and ultimately a dispute. For example, a standard government contract clause states:

> Except as otherwise provided in this contract, the term "subcontracts" includes purchase orders under this contract.

This clause is just waiting to cause problems. The use of "Except as otherwise provided" is an easy way out in drafting. What it says is that the drafter either added this clause without revising the balance of the agreement to make sure that it was fully integrated, or the drafter does not understand the agreement and is essentially leaving the clarification to the courts. As written, it also defines one concept, "subcontract," to include another, "purchase order." Within this agreement this may make some sense, but it increases the opportunity for good-faith misunderstandings between the parties as to the true meaning of the agreement. A better way to handle this might be to use the following definition:

> The term "Ancillary Agreements" means
>
> (a) Subcontracts between the Seller and third parties to provide goods or services under this contract; and
>
> (b) Purchase orders issued by the Buyer to the Seller under this contract.

If two paragraphs or sections are similar in substance, structure them in a similar manner. This rule will help you improve your accuracy and very often will lead you to discover hidden problems in the language of the agreement you are preparing. For example, don't write:

> When the cargo is delivered—
>
> (a) A receipt must be given;

(b) A count must be made of the number of cartons; and

(c) The cargo clerk shall sign the bill of lading.

Instead, write:

When the cargo is delivered, the cargo clerk must—

(a) Give a receipt to the driver;

(b) Count the number of cartons; and

(c) Sign the bill of lading.

REDUNDANCIES

Legal documents traditionally have been filled with redundancies. One explanation for this is that originally lawyers in England were also scriveners, who were paid by the word for each document they prepared. So the longer the document, the more they collected. Another reason for redundancies is to give emphasis, as if to say "This is what we want, and we really mean it." A third is given by a former editor of the *New York Times:*

> A lawyer friend tells us that sometimes redundancy in legal phrases is a vestigial remnant of the Norman Conquest. Of course, to the lowly worker in the fields, a particular animal was *sheep* in his Anglo-Saxon tongue, whereas to the conquering lord presiding at the table the flesh of that animal was *mutton* in his Norman-French tongue. To insure understanding on all sides, some legal phrases included both languages. An example is *will and testament,* in which the Anglo-Saxon and the Norman-French words are coupled to describe the same document.[5]

None of these is an acceptable reason today. A more current reason is that lawyers tend to adapt existing forms to new situations. They do this by adding language, by merging two or more different documents, and by filling in gaps that the courts have found in agreements in the past. Each of these tactics results in additional words and fewer deletions. The better practice is to decide what you want to say and then say it.

A similar problem, and one with the same roots, is the use of pairs of words, one of which includes the other. Use one term or the other, either the broader or the narrower, to state your intention accurately. A few examples:

1. Authorize and direct
2. Desire and require
3. Means and includes
4. Necessary or desirable

Additional examples of common redundancies are included in the Appendix checklist "Pairs of Words That Have the Same Effect."

DIRECTNESS

If you can accurately express an idea either positively or negatively, express it positively. This clarifies your intent and minimizes the chances of later misinterpretations.

The Department of the Treasury has adopted the following clause on interpreting its contracts, now a fairly standard clause:

> No interpretation of any provision of this contract, including applicable specifications, shall be binding on the Government unless furnished or agreed to in writing by the Contracting Officer or his designated representative.

Put positively, the clause would read:

> The Government is bound only by written interpretations of this contract, including its specifications, which are furnished by or agreed to in writing by the Contracting Officer or his designated representative.

Avoid the use of exceptions. If possible, state a condition or a category directly instead of describing it by stating its exceptions.

Don't write: "All persons except those working 40 hours or more shall . . ."

Instead, write: "Each person working fewer than 40 hours must . . ."

You may use an exception if it avoids a long, cumbersome list or an elaborate description. When you use such exception, state the condition or category first, then state its exception.

Don't write: "The Dealer is permitted to sell in the states of Alabama, Alaska [a list of 47 states] and Wyoming."

Instead, write: "The Dealer is permitted to sell in every state except Arizona, Texas, New Mexico, and the District of Columbia."

Here the category "every state" is established first; then the exceptions are noted.

Avoid the use of *and/or*. Usually one or the other word is sufficient. In some cases, the choice of *and* or *or* may not be adequate. For example, an agreement may provide that

> On default, the lender may proceed against the creditor and/or the guarantor.

Here the lender wants a clause that provides

> On default, the lender may proceed against the creditor, or the guarantor, or both.

ACTION VERBS

Use action verbs in drafting the agreement rather than participles, infinitives, gerunds, or other noun or adjective verb forms. Action verbs are shorter and more direct, and their use more immediately and clearly identifies the "actor" in any clause. A list of common substitutions of action verbs for other forms is found in the Appendix checklists.

Ambiguity is the bane of contract law. In the vast majority of cases, some ambiguity, real or alleged, is involved in the agreement. Ambiguity has at least two common sources in agreements—word order and word meaning. The ambiguity may be completely within the contract, where a sentence or sentences can be interpreted in two or more ways, or it may be the result of its application to a set of facts.

The relative position of words in a sentence is the main way to show their relationship. Group together words that are related in thought, and separate words that are not related. While the root cause of ambiguity often includes a failure to think through a concept, ambiguities resulting from word order and word meanings arise in several ways:

1. Misplaced modifiers

2. Indefinite pronouns used as modifiers

3. Two or more prepositional phrases grouped together

4. Use of a plural noun instead of a singular noun

5. Improper expressions of time

6. Improper expressions of age

7. Excessive use of provisos

Misplaced Modifiers

The careless placement or omission of a modifier may give the same sentence several meanings. For example, the sentence "The security staff shall conduct emergency fire drills which include actual evacuation of employees at least semi-annually" is ambiguous. It can mean either "The security staff shall conduct, at least semi-annually, emergency fire drills which include actual evacuation of employees" or "The security staff shall conduct emergency fire drills which, at least semi-annually, shall include actual evacuation of employees."

Omitted modifiers are just as troublesome. Selling "one-half interest in all minerals" under a certain piece of land may be very different from selling "one-half *of my* interest in all minerals" under that land, when the seller owns less than total interest himself.

Indefinite Pronouns

Avoid the use of indefinite pronouns as references. If a pronoun could refer to more than one person or object in a sentence, repeat the name of the person or object.

Don't write: "After the Contractor appoints a Supervisor, he or she shall supervise . . ."

Instead, write: "After the Contractor appoints a Supervisor, the Supervisor shall supervise . . ."

Prepositional Phrases

Avoid grouping together two or more prepositional phrases in one sentence.

Don't write: "Each subscriber *to* a magazine *in* Washington, D.C. . . ."

Instead, write: "Each magazine subscriber in Washington, D.C. . . ."

Unless you actually mean: "Each subscriber to a magazine published in Washington, D.C. . . ."

AMBIGUITY RESULTING FROM WORD MEANINGS

Singular Nouns

Try to use singular nouns rather than plural nouns. By doing this you avoid the problem of whether the term applies to each member of a class separately or to the class as a whole.

Don't write: "The guard shall issue security badges to the employees who work in Building No. 3 and Building No. 4."

Instead, write: "The guard shall issue a security badge to each employee who works in Building No. 3 and to each employee who works in Building No. 4."

The alternate meaning of the first phrase might also be: "The guard shall issue a security badge to each employee who works in both Building No. 3 and Building No. 4."

If that is what you did intend, say it that way.

Expressions of Time

By drafting expressions of time as accurately as possible, you eliminate potential uncertainty as to when a time period begins or ends.

Don't write: "From July 1, 1982, until June 30, 1983."

Instead, write: "After June 30, 1982, and before July 1, 1983."

If the time period is measured in whole days, use the word *day* instead of *time*. A future user of the agreement might interpret the word *time* to mean an exact time during the day or night when an event occurs.

Don't write: "Thirty days after the time when . . ."

Instead, write: "Thirty days after the day on which . . ."

In general avoid the use of time-relational words such as *now, presently,* and *currently.* Using these words to relate one provision in the agreement to the time the agreement takes effect can create ambiguity. It might be unclear whether or not the provision should change if the "current" facts change after the agreement takes effect. If you intend a provision to remain unchanged after the agreement takes effect, determine what the provision would be on the day the agreement takes effect and write in that specific provision. However, if you intend the provision to change as time passes, always make that fact clear.

Expressions of Age

Expressions of age should be drafted as accurately as possible. The expression "more than four years old" has two possible meanings: A product may be "more than four" on its fourth birthday or on its fifth birthday. Depending on which meaning you intend:

Don't write: "An asset that is more than four years old . . ."

Instead, write: "An asset that is four years old or older . . ."

Unless you mean: "An asset that is five years old or older . . ."

Don't write: "Between the ages of four and seven . . ."

Instead, write: "Four years old or older and under seven . . ."

Provisos

A proviso is a clause that begins *provided that* or *provided however.* The use of provisos is characteristic of highly technical legal drafting, but it is not necessarily good legal drafting. Rather than clarifying a clause, provisos usually result in long and often unintelligible sentences. Too often a proviso merely reflects a last-minute modification in the terms of the deal, or an attorney's attempt to adapt an existing clause to a different set of facts. Today, their use is archaic.

A standard provision in many government contracts states that

> Any claim by the Contractor for adjustment under this clause must be asserted within 30 days from the date of receipt by the Contractor of the notification of change, provided, however, that the Contracting Officer, if he decides that the facts justify such action, may receive and act upon any such claim asserted at any time prior to final payment under this contract.

Use the following conventions to avoid expressions such as *provided however* and *provided always:*

1. To introduce a qualification or limitation to the rule just stated, use *but*
2. To introduce an exception to the rule, use *except that*
3. To introduce a condition to the rule, use *if*
4. If the clause is a separate, complete thought, start a new sentence or a new section

Using these rules, the government contract clause can be rewritten to read:

> Any claim by the Contractor for adjustment under this clause must

be asserted within 30 days from the date the Contractor receives the notification of change. If the Contracting Officer decides that the facts justify it, the Contracting Officer may receive and act upon any claim for adjustment under this clause, which is asserted at any time before final payment under this contract.

SHALL AND MAY

Using *shall* as an auxiliary verb is the most forceful way of showing an obligation to do something. Although other auxiliary verbs are used in conversation and writing to command an act, you must supply additional emphasis for them to indicate clearly an obligation to act. Because the word *shall* carries great force, use it only if you are imposing an obligation to act. An example of this can be found in the General Conditions in service contracts issued by the Department of the Treasury:

> The Contractor shall provide adequate protection for the building, its contents and occupants whenever the contract work is being performed.

Be careful to avoid a false imperative. When your agreement imposes an obligation to act, the subject of that sentence must be appropriate for the imposition of the obligation. When you use *shall,* the subject of the sentence *must* be a person or some other entity that has the power to make the decision or take the action recommended. For this reason, do not use it to declare a legal result or to state a condition. When you write or read a sentence that contains the word *shall,* reread the sentence and substitute the phrase *has the duty to.* If it makes sense this way, *shall* is correct.

Don't write: "The final report shall include a discussion of . . ." Ask yourself whether or not you will fire the report if it fails to include this discussion.

Instead, write: "The contractor shall include a discussion of . . . in the final report."

Don't write: "'Place of business' as used in this agreement shall
   mean . . ."

Instead, write: "'Place of business' as used in this agreement
   means . . ."

NEGATIVE COMMANDS

You can state an obligation *not* to act by using either *may not* or
shall not. But use either phrase consistently throughout the agreement
to state negative commands. Whenever possible, however, state a rule
positively.

CONDITIONS

There are two types of conditions: (1) those that may or may not
occur, and (2) those that relate to time. To avoid ambiguity and confusion, introduce a simple condition, and any condition that may or may
not occur, with the word *if.* Introduce a condition that relates to time
with the word *when.*

"If the Corporation is in default under this Agreement, the
Lender . . ."

"When the goods have been in storage for three weeks . . ."

RECITALS

Recitals are agreements listed in a series of paragraphs beginning
with *whereas* on the first page. Some lawyers dismiss recitals as unim-
portant because the courts usually do not consider them to be part of the
agreement itself. This attitude often leads to sloppy drafting. When
properly used, recitals establish the factual background of an agreement. They enable the parties to the agreement to understand and express their respective roles and make them understandable to parties,
particularly the courts. A paragraph does not have to contain *whereas* to

be a recital. All that is necessary is that it precedes the text of the agreement.

Recitals do not establish the rules of the agreement or create definitions. If they introduce the reader to documents and concepts that are important to the agreement itself, these concepts and documents should be described in the agreement or appear in the definitions.

Proceeding in a logical order, break down recitals into definite and separate items. Chronological order is usually easiest and best. Common usage requires recitals to be captioned either "Recitals" or "Background."

Recitals should be used only when the background of the deal is important to understanding the agreement. They should assist in interpreting the agreement. In general, they should be drafted *after* the agreement has been prepared. Then the parties can see which factual statements, if any, are necessary to facilitate a complete understanding of the agreement. If the recitals are drafted before or even concurrently with the agreement, they can become a crutch used to avoid resolving difficult substantive issues. Also, they may be either excessively detailed or incomplete.

DEFINITIONS

Avoid unnecessary definitions. Too often, an elaborate series of definitions is added to business agreements to make the final product look more "professional." The purpose of a definition is to achieve clarity without needless repetition. For this reason, ordinary words used in their usual dictionary meaning do not need to be defined.

Never define a word in a way that conflicts with its ordinary or accepted usage. Try to use a word in a way that is consistent with its everyday commercial meaning so that you do not have to define it. Otherwise you can confuse the reader and also run the risk that the word will be used elsewhere in the agreement in its ordinary sense. This can cause serious problems in interpretation and application.

Don't write: " 'Airplane' means an airplane, helicopter, or hot air balloon."

Instead, write: " 'Aircraft' means a device that is used or intended to be used for flight."

This definition is broad enough to include any device that flies, and at the same time it does not conflict with its ordinary meaning.

A good definition excludes the word being defined. An example of this can be found in some government contracts dealing with rights in technical data and computer software. One definition provides:

Computer Data Base—a collection of data in a form capable of being processed and operated on by a computer ["computer" is also defined].

A preferable definition would omit the word *data:*

Computer Data Base—a collection of information in a form capable of being processed and operated on by a computer.

As with recitals, do not use a definition to establish a rule or condition. If you do this, future readers can easily miss the rule placed in the definitions.

Generally, define a term that is used throughout the agreement at the beginning of the agreement. If a term is used only once or in a few closely related sections, define it where it first appears to prevent the reader from having to search through the whole agreement for its definition.

It is difficult, if not impossible, to determine how many times a particular word or concept will be used in an agreement before it is drafted. If you draft definitions before you draft the agreement, you may define a word you do not use, or you may omit a definition that you need.

Whenever you use a complex or unique concept, try to develop a shorthand phrase for it. Again, formulate these phrases during the preparation of the agreement, instead of at the beginning. An example of this is a definition adapted from a government contract to define and preserve rights the government may have in computer software and related data. The definition is long, but it was evidently created to avoid needless repetition of a series of conditions each time a particular item was discussed. In addition, it uses examples to show exactly what is to be covered:

> *Technical data* means recorded information, regardless of form or characteristic, of a scientific or technical nature. It may, for example, document research, experimental, developmental or engineering work, or be used to define a design or process, or be used to procure, produce, support, maintain, or operate material. The data may be depicted in drawings or photographs, or described in specifications, related performance or design documents, or computer printouts. Examples of technical data include research and engineering data, engineering drawings and associated lists, specifications, standards, process sheets, manuals, technical reports, catalog item identifications, and related information and computer software documentation. *Technical data* does not include computer software; financial, administrative, cost and pricing, or management data; or other information incidental to contract administration.

When you have a group of definitions, it is generally appropriate to list them in alphabetical order at the beginning of the agreement. Then capitalizing the term whenever it is used lets the reader know that it has been defined. For example, "Any lien filed against the Aircraft financed under this agreement" lets everyone know that "Aircraft" has been defined.

THE PARTIES

Similar principles apply in drafting identifications of the parties to an agreement. Feel free to substitute a term for each party's proper name. The term can be generic, a commercial catch phrase, or even initials. Do not use "party of the first (or second) part," which becomes very confusing in a long agreement.

For example: "This agreement is between the Sascha Fertilizer Corporation and the Kali Distributing Company." The Sascha Fertilizer Corporation can be referred to as "the Seller," "Sascha," or "SFC." Similarly, the Kali Distributing Company can be called "the Buyer," "Kali," or "KDC." The agreement would then read: "This agreement is between the Sascha Fertilizer Corporation ("Sascha") and Kali Distributing Company ("Kali")."

Use these terms consistently throughout. Never use the lazy drafter's version: "The Sascha Fertilizer Corporation, sometimes referred to herein as Sascha or the Seller." This usually means that the drafter has not gone through the agreement with care. In fact, he may have merged two or more older agreements. Also, there is no need for the wordy and archaic "hereinafter referred to as" or any of its variations.

EACH AND *ANY*

One method of avoiding ambiguity is to write in the singular. In English a singular noun is preceded by the article. For example: "The airplane has a tail rudder." When preparing the agreement, break this rule in situations when the use of the article *a* or *an* can create ambiguity.

Don't write: "The plan administrator shall make medical services available to a person 65 years or older."

Instead, write: "The plan administrator shall make medical services available to each person 65 years old or older."

In general, if the wording could be ambiguous, follow these two rules:

1. Use *each* if you are imposing an obligation to act. For example: "Each employee shall file . . ."

2. Use *any* if you are granting a right, a power, or a privilege. For example: "Any supervisor may ask for a review of . . ."

SUCH AND *SAID*

Instead of using *such,* use the more common pronouns *the, that, those, it,* or *them* to refer to something or someone already identified. If the word you are referring to appears much earlier, consider making it a definition or a cross-reference.

Using *said* to refer to something already named disappeared from ordinary speech hundreds of years ago. It has survived only in legal writing and speaking, since lawyers are reluctant to discard old forms of speech, no matter how dated. Instead, use *the, that,* and *those* to refer to something already named. As with *such,* consider using a definition or a cross-reference.

CALCULATIONS

Do not be afraid to put calculations in an agreement. If they are needed, use them. There are two approaches to drafting calculations clearly: You can use either a list or a formula. For example, a list might read:

Section 15. Computing retirement fund withholdings. The payroll administrator shall compute the retirement fund withholdings for an employee as follows:

(a) Subtract $300 from the employee's gross pay for one year.

(b) Multiply this result by 0.16.

(c) Add $50 to the result of (b) of this section.

The same calculation in a formula would read:

Section 15. Computing retirement fund withholdings. The payroll administrator shall use the following formula to compute the retirement fund withholdings for an employee: [(employee's gross pay for one year $-\$300) \times 0.16] + \$50 =$ withholding.

CROSS-REFERENCES

Cross-references are a delight to lawyers and distressing to clients. Often cross-references are made in the formative stages of an agreement and later renumbered or renamed. The result is confusion and possible litigation. In addition, too many cross-references can make a provision hard to read and understand. Include a cross-reference only when it is essential to the meaning of the provision or when it limits or makes exceptions to the provisions.

If you must include a cross-reference, try to cite a specific section. A reference such as "as calculated under this Agreement" is substantially less helpful than "as calculated in Section 12, Payments in Advance." This example also illustrates the application of another rule—that of including a brief description of the subject matter of the cross-reference. This makes the purpose of the cross-reference understandable, and the reader will not be forced to turn to it to see what effect it has on the section he is using.

GENDER-SPECIFIC TERMINOLOGY

Avoid the use of a gender-specific pronoun when both sexes are or may be involved.

Don't write: "The Treasurer or his designee signs all notes . . ."

Instead, write: "The Treasurer or the Treasurer's designee signs all notes . . ."

The more common gender specific terms and substitutes are listed in the Appendix.

Sometimes it is not possible to avoid the third person singular, *he* or *she*. If it is not, do the following:

1. Use *she or he* or *she/he* instead of *he*
2. Use *him or her* or *him/her* instead of *him*
3. Use *his or hers* or *his/hers* instead of *his*

In recognition of the changes in the roles of women in business, avoid using gender-specific job titles such as Chairman and Chairwoman. Instead, use Chairperson.

The impact of the movement to make contracts readable can be illustrated by the comments of an expert in legal drafting analyzing a standard clause in federal mortgage documents:

When lay borrowers are addressed, technical terms should be eliminated, illustrated, or defined; conditions and exceptions should be identified in separate short sentences; and penalties, such as extra loan fees or increased interest rates, should be given in detail, rather than indirectly. Short sentences and rapid syntactic closure should be used whenever possible to increase readability.[6]

7

Preprinted and "Standard" Form Agreements

Often, after you have entered into an agreement, you will be presented with a printed form to sign. It may contain minor changes, typewritten additions, or deletions or simply include the names of the parties and other key details of the transaction. Invariably, you will be told that this is the "standard" form, or "all of our deals are made on this basis."

Those who produce and use standard form agreements argue that they have the following benefits:

1. They permit one court's interpretation of one agreement to serve as the interpretation of all similar agreements
2. They save time and money and reduce uncertainty by using well-known and accepted language
3. They simplify the planning and administration of contracts
4. They make the skill of the drafter available to everyone
5. They make risks calculable

But there are also dangers inherent in the use of standard form agreements:

1. They can help one side to impose its will on an unwilling or unknowing party
2. They permit the parties to avoid thinking through the transaction by agreeing to be bound by terms neither may understand
3. They tend to be used long after they are out of date

Remember, with the exception of those few contracts whose language is mandated by law, such as certain insurance policies, there is no such thing as a standard invariable form contract. A form is merely an agreement prepared by someone to satisfy the needs of particular clients or customers. It takes a stand on issues, and that stand may not always be to your benefit. For example, many realtors in major metropolitan areas use forms prepared by local real-estate or trade associations and designed with the interests of their members in mind. If the form is a lease, it will probably be pro landlord rather than pro tenant. If it is a listing agreement, it will favor the broker or agent over the seller of the property.

Never sign a form agreement without reviewing it first. And don't be put off by the all too frequent statements: "Oh, that's just boilerplate. Don't worry about it. I don't understand it myself." Or: "That's just something my lawyer made me put into the agreement. It's not really important." Even if you are not in a position to bargain for changes in the agreement, take the time to read and understand it. If there are any changes that you want, make them on the agreement *before* signing; do not wait for a later addition or modification. If that modification does not come through, you are stuck with what you signed.

The portions of the rental lease reprinted here are an instructive example of a standard form. This simple lease contract is adaptable either to a commercial or to a residential lease situation. When read closely, this lease is seen to be a landlord's lease, as might be expected inasmuch as it was prepared by an association of realtors, who make their commissions from the landlord. (While it is pro landlord, it is not as much so as many preprinted leases.)

To analyze this long document, use the captions. Take, for instance, Paragraph 16(a). This paragraph provides that the tenant, called the lessee, waives any legal right he has to keep the landlord, the lessor, from seizing his property and selling it to pay overdue rent. Often, a landlord, if questioned by a prospective tenant about this, may say something like, "Oh that clause doesn't apply here. See, Paragraph 37 says 'except as expressly prohibited by law.' The law would prevent me from doing that." Your response should be, "Then let's take it out."

Notice that Paragraph 11(b) provides that, if the landlord wants to change some of the conditions of the lease during its term, he can do so by issuing rules and regulations. The balance of the lease is similarly pro landlord, as can be seen by reading such Paragraphs as 14, 18, 23 and 32, where the tenant waives many of his rights. In fact, in some states the language permitting a "confession of judgment," such as that in Paragraph 20, is illegal, but it still remains in many preprinted forms.

This form is only one of several "standard" leases which can be obtained at office and legal supply stores, or from various real estate associations. When you use or receive a standard form, always keep in mind that each one differs. Today's standard form may not be the same as the one you signed yesterday.

Lessor's Rights

11. Lessee covenants and agrees that Lessor shall have the right to do the following things and matters in and about the demised premises:

Inspection of Premises

(a) At all reasonable times by himself or his duly authorized agents to go upon and inspect the demised premises and every part thereof, and/or at his option to make repairs, alterations and additions to the demised premises or the building of which the demised premises is a part.

Rules and Regulations

(b) At any time or times and from time to time to make such rules and regulations as in his judgment may from time to time be necessary for the safety, care and cleanliness of the premises, and for the preservation of good order therein. Such rules and regulations shall, when notice thereof is given to Lessee, form a part of this lease.

Sale, Rent, Signs and Prospects (11-74)

(c) To display a "For Sale" sign at any time, and also, after notice from either party of intention to determine this lease, or at any time within six months prior to the expiration of his lease, a "For Rent" sign, or both "For Rent" and "For Sale" signs; and all of said signs shall be placed upon such part of the premises as Lessor may elect and may contain such matter as Lessor shall require. Prospective purchasers or tenants authorized by Lessor may inspect the premises Monday thru Saturday between the hours of 11:00 AM and 8:00 PM.

Discontinue Service, etc.

(d) The Lessor may discontinue all facilities furnished and services rendered by Lessor or any of them, not expressly covenanted for herein, it being understood that they constitute no part of the consideration for this lease.

12. (a) In the event that the demised premises is totally destroyed or so damaged by fire or other casualty not occurring through fault or negligence of the Lessee or those employed by or acting for him, that the same cannot be repaired or restored within a reasonable time, this lease shall absolutely cease and determine, and the rent shall abate for the balance of the term.

(b) If the damage caused as above be only partial and such that the premises can be restored to their former condition within a reasonable time, the Lessor may, at his option, restore the same with reasonable promptness, reserving the right to enter upon the demised premises for that purpose. The Lessor also reserves the right to enter upon the demised premises whenever necessary to repair damage caused by fire or other casualty to the building of which the demised premises is a part, even though the effect of such entry be to render the demised premises or a part thereof untenantable. In either event the rent shall be apportioned and suspended during the time the Lessor is in possession, taking into account the proportion of the demised premises rendered untenantable and the duration of the Lessor's possession. If a dispute arises as to the amount of rent due under this clause, Lessee agrees to pay the full amount claimed by Lessor. Lessee shall, however, have the right to proceed by law to recover the excess payment, if any.

Damage for Interrupted Use

(c) Lessor shall not be liable for any damage, compensation or claim by reason of inconvenience or annoyance arising from the necessity of repairing any portion of the building, the interruption in the use of the premises, or the termination of this lease by reason of the destruction of the premises.

Representation of Condition

13. The Lessor has let the demised premises in their present condition and without any representations on the part of the Lessor, his officers, employees, servants and/or agents. It is understood and agreed that Lessor is under no duty to make repairs or alterations at the time of letting or at any time thereafter.

Miscellaneous Agreements and Conditions

14. (a) No contract entered into or that may be subsequently entered into by Lessor with Lessee, relative to any alterations, additions, improvements or repairs, nor the failure of Lessor to make such alterations, additions, improvements or repairs as required by any such contract, nor the making by Lessor or his agents or contractors of such alterations, additions, improvements or repairs shall in any way affect the payment of the rent or said other charges at the time specified in this lease.

Effect of Repairs or Rentals

(b) It is hereby covenanted and agreed, any law, usage or custom to the contrary notwithstanding, that Lessor shall have the right at all times to enforce the covenants and provisions of this lease in strict accordance with the terms hereof, notwithstanding any conduct or custom on the part of the Lessor in refraining from so doing at any time or times; and further, that the failure of Lessor at any time or times to enforce its rights under said covenants and provisions strictly in accordance with the same shall not be construed as having created a custom in any way or manner contrary to the specific terms, provisions and covenants of this lease or as having in any way or manner modified the same.

Waiver of Custom

Conduct of Lessee

(c) This lease is granted upon the express condition that Lessee and/or the occupants of the premises herein leased, shall not conduct themselves in a manner which the Lessor in his sole opinion may deem improper or objectionable, and that if at any time during the term of this lease or any extension or continuation thereof, Lessee or any occupier of the said premises shall have conducted himself, herself or themselves in a manner which Lessor in his sole opinion deems improper or objectionable, Lessee shall be taken to have broken the covenants and conditions of this lease, and Lessor will be entitled to all of the rights and remedies granted and reserved herein, for the Lessee's failure to observe any of the covenants and conditions of this lease.

Failure of Lessee to Repair

(d) In the event of the failure of Lessee promptly to perform the covenants of Par. # 8. (c) hereof, Lessor may go upon the demised premises and perform such covenants, the cost thereof, at the sole option of Lessor, to be charged to Lessee as additional and delinquent rent.

15. If the Lessee

(a) Does not pay in full when due any and all installments of rent and/or any other charge or payment herein reserved, included, or agreed to be treated or collected as rent and/or any other charge, expense, or cost herein agreed to be paid by the Lessee; or

(b) Violates or fails to perform or otherwise breaks any covenant or agreement herein contained; or

(c) Vacates the demised premises or removes or attempts to remove any goods or property therefrom otherwise than in the ordinary and usual course of business without having first paid and satisfied the Lessor in full for all rent and other charges then due or that may thereafter become due until the expiration of the then current term, above mentioned; or

Remedies of Lessor (11-74)

(d) Becomes embarrassed or insolvent, or makes an assignment for the benefit of creditors, or if a petition in bankruptcy is filed by or against the Lessee or a bill in equity or other proceeding for the appointment of a receiver for the Lessee is filed, or if proceedings for reorganization or for composition with creditors under any State or Federal law be instituted by or against Lessee, or if the real or personal property of the Lessee shall be sold or levied upon by any due process of law, then and in any or either of said events, there shall be deemed to be a breach of this lease, and thereupon ipso facto and without entry or other action by Lessor;

(d1) The rent for the entire unexpired balance of the term of this lease, as well as all other charges, payments, costs and expenses herein agreed to be paid by the Lessee, or at the option of Lessor any part thereof, and also all costs and officers' commissions including watchmen's wages and further including the five percent chargeable by Act of Assembly to the Lessor, shall, in addition to any and all installments of rent already due and payable and in arrears and/or any other charge or payment herein reserved, included or agreed to be treated or collected as rent, and/or any other charge, expense or cost herein agreed to be paid by the Lessee which may be due and payable and in arrears, be taken to be due and payable and in arrears as if by the terms and provisions of this lease, the whole balance of unpaid rent and other charges, payments, taxes, costs and expenses were on that date payable in advance; and if this lease or any part thereof is assigned, or if the premises or any part thereof is sub-let, Lessee hereby irrevocably constitutes and appoints Lessor Lessee's agent to collect the rents due by such assignee or sub-leasee and apply the same to the rent due hereunder without in any way affecting Lessee's obligation to pay any unpaid balance of rent due hereunder; or in the event of any of the forgoing at any time at the option of Lessor;

(d2) This lease and the term hereby created shall determine and become absolutely void without any right on the part of the Lessee to save the forfeiture by payment of any sum due or by other performance of any condition; term or covenant broken; whereupon, Lessor shall be entitled to recover damages for such breach in an amount equal to the amount of rent reserved for the balance of the term of this lease, less the fair rental value of the said demised premises, for the residue of said term.

16. In the event of any default as aforesaid, the Lessor, or anyone acting on Lessor's behalf, at Lessor's option:

(a) May without notice or demand enter the demised premises, breaking open locked doors if necessary to effect entrance, without liability to action for prosecution or damages for such entry or for the matter thereof, for the purpose of distraining or levying and for any other purposes, and take possession of and sell all goods and chattels at auction, on three days notice served in person or in the Lessee, or left on the premises, and pay the said Lessor out of the proceeds, and even if the rent be not due and unpaid, should the Lessee at any time remove or attempt to remove goods and chattels from the premises without leaving enough thereon to meet the next periodical payment, Lessee authorizes the Lessor to follow for a period of ninety days after such removal, take possession of and sell at auction, upon like notice, sufficient of such goods to meet the proportion of rent accrued at the time of such removal; and the Lessee hereby releases and discharges the Lessor, and his agents from all claims, actions, suits, damages and penalties, for or by reason or on account of any entry, distraint, levy, appraisement or sale; and/or

(b) May enter the premises, and without demand proceed by distress and sale of the goods there found to levy the rent and/or other charges herein payable as rent, and all costs and officers' commissions, including watchmen's wages and sums chargeable to Lessor, and further including a sum equal to 5% of the amount of the levy as commissions to the constable or other person making the levy, shall be paid by the Lessee, and in such case all costs, officers' commission and other charges shall immediately attach and become part of the claim of Lessor for rent, and any tender of rent without said costs commission and charges made after the issue of a warrant of distress shall not be sufficient to satisfy the claim of the Lessor. Lessee hereby expressly waivers in favor of Lessor the benefit of all laws now made or which may hereafter be made regarding any limitation as to the goods upon which, or the time within which, distress is to be made after removal of goods, and further relieves the Lessor of the obligations of proving or identifying such goods, it being the purpose and intent of this provision that all goods of Lessee, whether upon the demised premises or not, shall be liable to distress for rent. Lessee waives in favor of Lessor all rights under the Act of Assembly of April 6, 1951, P.L. 69, and all supplements and amendments thereto that have been or may hereafter be passed, and authorizes the sale of any goods distrained for rent at any time after five days from said distraint without any appraisement and/or condemnation thereof. The Lessee further waives the right to issue a Writ of Replevin under the Pennsylvania Rules of Civil Procedure, No. 1071 &c. and Laws of the Commonwealth of Pennsylvania, or under any other law previously enacted and now in force, or which may be hereafter enacted, for the recovery of any articles, household goods, furniture, etc., seized under a distress for rent or levy upon an execution for rent, damages or otherwise; all waivers hereinbefore mentioned are hereby extended to apply to any such action; and/or

(c) May lease said premises or any part or parts thereof to such person or persons as may in Lessor's discretion seem best and the Lessee shall be liable for any loss of rent for the balance of the then current term.

(d) Any re-entry or re-letting by Lessor under the terms hereof shall be without prejudice to Lessor's claim for damages and shall under no circumstances release Lessee from liability for such damages arising out of the breach of any of the covenants, terms and conditions of this lease.

17. It is understood and agreed that the Lessor hereof does not warrant or undertake that the Lessee shall be able to obtain a permit under any Zoning Ordinance or Regulation for such use as Lessee intends to make of the said premises, and nothing in this lease contained shall obligate the Lessor to assist Lessee in obtaining said permit; the Lessee further agrees that in the event a permit cannot be obtained by Lessee under any Zoning Ordinance, or Regulation, this lease shall not terminate without Lessor's consent, and the Lessee shall use the premises only in a manner permitted under such Zoning Ordinance or Regulation.

18. Lessee agrees to be responsible for and to relieve and hereby relieves the Lessor from all liability by reason of any injury or damage to any person or property in the demised premises, whether belonging to the Lessee or any other person, caused by any fire, breakage or leakage in any part or portion of the demised premises, or any part or portion of the building of which the demised premises is a part, or from water, rain or snow that may leak into, issue or flow from any part of the said premises, or of the building of which the demised premises is a part, from the drains, pipes, or plumbing work of the same, or from any place or quarter, whether such breakage, leakage, injury or damage be caused by or result from the negligence of Lessor or his servants or agents or any person or persons whatsoever.

Further Remedies of Lessor

Zoning

Responsibility of Lessee

(11-74)

Additional Responsibility of Lessee (11-74)

19. Lessee also agrees to be responsible for and to relieve and hereby relieves Lessor from all liability by reason of any damage or injury to any person or thing which may arise from or be due to the use, misuse or abuse of all or any of the elevators, hatches, openings, stairways, hallways of any kind whatsoever which may exist or hereafter be erected or constructed on the said premises, or from any kind of injury which may arise from any other cause whatsoever on the said premises or the building of which the demised premises is a part, whether such damage, injury, use, misuse or abuse be caused by or result from the negligence of Lessor, his servants or agents or any other person or persons whatsoever.

Confession of Judgment

20. If rent and/or charges hereby reserved as rent shall remain unpaid on any day when the same should be paid Lessee hereby empowers any Prothonotary or attorney of any Court of Record to appear for Lessee in any and all actions which may be brought for rent and/or for the charges, payments, costs and expenses reserved as rent, or agreed to be paid by the Lessee and/or to sign for Lessee an agreement for entering in any competent Court an amicable action or actions for the recovery of rent or other charges or expenses, and in said suits or in said amicable action or actions to confess judgment against Lessee for all or any part of the rent specified in this lease and then unpaid including, at Lessor's option, the rent for the entire unexpired balance of the term of this lease, and/or other charges, payments, costs and expenses reserved as rent or agreed to be paid by the Lessee, and for interest and costs together with an attorney's commission of 15%. Such authority shall not be exhausted by any one exercise thereof, but judgment may be confessed as aforesaid from time to time as often as any of said rent and/or other charges reserved as rent shall fall due or be in arrears, and such powers may be exercised as well after the expiration of the original term and/or during any extension or renewal of this lease.

Ejectment

21. When this lease shall be determined by condition broken, either during the original term of this lease or any renewal or extension thereof, and also when and as soon as the term hereby created or any extension thereof shall have expired, it shall be lawful for any attorney as attorney for Lessee to file an agreement for entering in any competent Court an amicable action and judgment in ejection against Lessee and all persons claiming under Lessee for the recovery by Lessor of possession of the herein demised premises, for which this lease shall be his sufficient warrant, whereupon, if Lessor so desires, a writ of habere facias possessionem may issue forthwith, without any prior writ or proceedings whatsoever, and provided that if for any reason after such action shall have been commenced the same shall be determined and the possession of the premises hereby demised remain in or be restored to Lessee. Lessor shall have the right upon any subsequent default or defaults, or upon the termination of this lease as hereinbefore set forth, to bring one or more amicable action or actions as hereinbefore set forth to recover possession of the said premises.

Affidavit of Default

22. In any amicable action of ejectment and/or for rent in arrears, Lessor shall first cause to be filed in such action an affidavit made by him or someone acting for him setting forth the facts necessary to authorize the entry of judgment, of which facts such affidavit shall be conclusive evidence, and if a true copy of this lease (and of the truth of the copy such affidavit shall be sufficient evidence) be filed in such action, it shall not be necessary to file the original as a warrant of attorney, any rule of Court, custom or practice to the contrary notwithstanding.

Waivers by Lessee of Errors, Right of Appeal, Stay, Exemption Inquisition

23. Lessee expressly agrees that any judgment, order or decree entered against him by or in any Court or Magistrate by virtue of the powers of attorney contained in this lease, or otherwise, shall be final, and that he will not take an appeal, certiorari, writ of error, exception or objection to the same, or file a motion or rule to strike off or open or to stay execution of the same, and releases to Lessor and to any and all attorneys who may appear for Lessee all errors in the said proceedings, and all liability therefor. Lessee expressly waives the benefits of all laws, now or hereafter in force, exempting any goods on the demised premises, or elsewhere from distraint, levy or sale in any legal proceedings taken by the Lessor to enforce any rights under this lease. Lessee further waives the right of inquisition on any real estate that may be levied upon to collect any amount which may become due under the terms and conditions of this lease, and does hereby voluntarily condemn the same and authorizes the Prothonotary to enter a fieri facias or other process upon Lessee's voluntary condemnation, and further agrees that the said real estate may be sold on a fieri facias or other process. If proceedings shall be commenced by Lessor to recover possession under the Acts of Assembly, either at the end of the term or sooner termination of this lease, or for nonpayment of rent or any other reason, Lessee specifically waives the right to the three months notice and/or the fifteen or thirty days notice required by the Act of April 6, 1951, P.L. 69, and agrees that five days notice shall be sufficient in either or any such case.

Right to Enforce

32. The Lessor shall have the right, at all times, to enforce any or all the covenants and provisions of this lease, notwithstanding the failure of the Lessor at any previous time, or times, to enforce his rights under any of the covenants and provisions of this lease.

Definition of Lessor and Lessee

33. The word "Lessor" as used herein, shall include the Owner and the Landlord, whether Person, Firm or Corporation, as well as the Heirs, Executors, Administrators, Successors and Assigns each of whom shall have the same rights, remedies, powers, privileges and obligations as though he, she, it or they had originally signed this lease as Lessor, including the right to proceed in his, her, its, or their own name to enter judgment by confession, or otherwise. The word "Lessee" as used herein, shall include the Tenant, whether Person, Firm or Corporation, as well as the Heirs, Executors, Administrators, Successors and Assigns, each of whom shall have the same rights, remedies, powers, privileges, and shall have no other liabilities, rights, privileges or powers than he, she, it or they would have been under or possessed had he, she, it or they originally signed this lease as Lessee.

Agent

34. It is expressly understood and agreed between the parties hereto that the herein named agent, his salesmen and employees or any officer or partner of agent and any cooperating broker and his salesmen and employees and any officer or partner of the cooperating broker are acting as agent only and will in no case whatsoever be held liable either jointly or severally to either party for the performance of any term of covenant of this agreement or for damages for the nonperformance thereof.

Heirs and Assignees

35. All rights and liabilities herein given to, or imposed upon, or waivers of the respective parties hereto shall extend to and bind the several and respective heirs, executors, administrators, successors and assigns of said parties; and if there shall be more than one Lessee, they shall all be bound jointly and severally by the terms, covenants and agreements herein, and the word "Lessee" shall be deemed and taken to mean each and every person or party mentioned as a Lessee herein, be the same one or more; and if there shall be more than one Lessee, any notice required or permitted by the terms of this lease may be given by or to any one thereof, and shall have the same force and effect as if given by or to all thereof. No rights, however, shall inure to the benefit of any assignee of Lessee unless the assignment of such assignee has been approved by Lessor in writing as aforesaid.

Lease Contains Entire Agreement

36. The Lessor and Lessee hereby agree that this lease sets forth all the promises, agreements, conditions and understandings between the Lessor, or his Agent, and the Lessee relative to the demised premises, and that there are no promises, agreements, conditions or understandings, either oral or written, between them other than as are herein set forth, and any subsequent alteration, amendment, change or addition to this lease shall not be binding upon the Lessor or Lessee unless reduced to writing and signed by them.

Severability (11-74)

37. If any section, subsection, sentence, clause phrase or requirement of this lease is contrary to law or laws subsequently enacted, or should be found contrary to laws during the term or any renewal or extension thereof, the validity of the remaining portions shall not be affected thereby. The parties hereby agree that they would have agreed to each section, subsection, clause sentence, phrase or requirement herein irrespective of the fact that one or more section, subsection sentence, clause, phrase or requirement was contrary to law or during the term or any renewal or extension thereof or are found to be contrary to the law.

Descriptive Heading

38. The descriptive headings used herein are for convenience only and they are not intended to indicate all of the matter in the sections which follow them. Accordingly, they shall have no effect whatsoever in determining the rights or obligations of the parties.

Approval (1-78)

IN WITNESS WHEREOF, the parties hereto, including to be legally bound hereby, have hereunder set their hands and seals the day and year first above written.

WITNESS AS
TO LESSEE . . . . LESSEE . . . . (SEAL)

WITNESS AS
TO LESSEE . . . . LESSEE . . . . (SEAL)

WITNESS AS
TO LESSEE . . . . LESSEE . . . . (SEAL)

The Lessor hereby approves this contract on this . . . . day of . . . . 19 . . . . . . and in consideration of the services rendered in procuring the herein named Lessee and/or collection of rents as agreed and specified in part one of this lease, the Lessor agrees to pay the herein named agent a fee and/or commission in the amount of $ . . . . for obtaining Lessee together with a commission of . . . .% for the collection of rents during the term, renewal or extention of this lease or additional lease with the herein named Lessee. Should the Lessee purchase the demised premises from the Lessor during the term of this lease, or during a renewal, extention or any additional lease between said parties for the demised premises, or within a reasonable period of time after the expiration of any such lease, the Lessor agrees to pay to the agent, at the time of settlement, a sales commission of . . . .% based on the purchase price.

LESSOR . . . . (SEAL)

WITNESS AS
TO LESSOR . . . .

LESSOR . . . . (SEAL)

WITNESS AS
TO LESSOR . . . .

AGENT BY . . . .

Challenges to Form Agreements

Standard form agreements are constantly under attack. A 1981 ruling by a federal appeals court shows that you can and should question any provision of a standard form agreement, no matter who prepared it.

In Texas, the state bar issued two legal forms, a real-estate note and a builder's and mechanic's lien. Each provided for attorney's fees of 10 percent of the unpaid balance to be added to any amount due in case of a default on the debt covered by the form. This would be paid to the lawyer of the party holding the note. The forms were challenged on the grounds that they constituted price fixing by the bar. The reasoning was that, by preparing these forms, the state bar was fixing how much lawyers would be paid for particular services.

The courts rejected this challenge on the basis that the state bar did not require its members to use these forms. Also, the state bar had never even suggested that the 10-percent-fee provision must be followed.

The lesson here bears repeating. A standard form, no matter how "official," is almost never mandatory. Virtually any provision can be modified. Don't accept the frequently heard argument that a form or a provision is "standard" and that "we cannot change it." What they mean is that they *won't* change it. If that is so, have that fact clearly established. If they are willing to change it but lack the authority to do so, go to the person who has that authority. There is a critical difference between "I cannot" and "I will not." People don't want to seem stubborn, so they hide behind the false front of a lack of power. Don't be misled.

PRINTED DISCLAIMERS

Attorney Gilbert N. Kruger, from Newport Beach, California, in *Boardroom Reports,* a highly regarded management magazine, suggests that corporations undergo a "legal audit" to identify potential problems and correct them before they become problems. Significantly, two of his three examples involved form agreements. These examples illustrate how much under attack form agreements are and how careful the company that relies on boilerplate language must be in using its forms. Kruger points out that common problems disclosed by a legal audit include:

Lack of notations on the front of sales order forms regarding additional information on the back. *Problem:* Customers may claim the material on the back doesn't apply since they weren't informed of it.
Failure to print warranty disclaimer language in boldface type, as required by the Uniform Commercial Code. *Problem:* This negates the disclaimers.[1]

Printed form disclaimers are perpetually under attack. In general, a disclaimer that an item is sold "as is" or "with all faults" prevents a buyer from being able to sue a seller on the grounds that an implied warranty existed. The law provides that, to be valid, this disclaimer must be printed so that it is clearly visible to the buyer. In a recent case, one court concluded that because this type of clause was buried inconspicuously in the body of a contract it provided no protection to the seller.

The mounting attack on disclaimers extends even to those that had previously been accepted without question by the general public. One such disclaimer is often found on the receipt you receive when you take film to a processor for developing and printing. Typically, it provides that the developer and the manufacturer of the film are obligated to replace only lost or damaged film. In a case before the Indiana Court of Appeals, the Carr family was suing the developer because four rolls of exposed film containing pictures of the family's vacation in Europe were lost. The Carrs were awarded $1,013.60 for the loss. The court ruled that the pictures "in almost every case" were more valuable than the film, so the disclaimer of liability was unfair.

Responding to Form Agreements

Even if a company you are dealing with has its own form agreement, you should draw up an outline of your considerations, needs, and limitations and negotiate. Negotiating on the basis of the company's form alone will put you at a disadvantage. After all, the company no doubt spent a lot of time preparing the agreement, and it knows its language and priorities better than you do. You will be much better off stating what you need, agreeing on that language, and then modifying the form to conform to your mutual agreement.

THE BATTLE OF THE FORMS

Manufacturers use their own purchase order forms when they buy or sell goods. Blanks are to be filled in for each transaction and a number of printed sections cover shipping, cancellation, insurance, disputes, and so on. To get the seller to agree to the buyer's terms, the buyer uses an acknowledgment form or has a place for the seller to sign, marked "acceptance." If the seller signs, he is bound by these terms. Even if the seller does not sign but ships the goods without doing anything else, such as calling and accepting orally, the seller is regarded as having accepted the buyer's terms.

Some sellers try to avoid this by sending their own "acknowledgment" or "sales order" form, which contain different terms from the purchase order. The seller may also print these terms on the invoice that accompanies the goods shipped. The courts treat this as a counter-offer. If the buyer, with knowledge of this counter-offer, accepts the goods sent by the seller, he has accepted the seller's terms.

Another situation can arise when price quotations are given. A price quotation is not by itself an offer, and accepting it cannot form the basis for a contract. But price quotations can contain preprinted detailed terms that are similar to a contract. They may then be regarded as offers, which, when accepted, create a contract.

If a potential buyer asks for a quotation, receives one of these forms, and responds with a purchase order, he risks having the purchase order treated as an acceptance. This acceptance binds him to the terms of the seller's quotation. The buyer can protect himself by making it clear that the purchase order is merely an offer to purchase. He would do this by adding a conspicuous notice on the front of the order, in type larger than the rest of the form. For example:

This is an offer to purchase on our terms and conditions. Your acceptance must exactly conform to these terms and conditions.

COMPUTER SERVICES AND SOFTWARE: CASE STUDIES

Many businesses are considering the purchase of a minicomputer system, or updating their current system. The sellers of these systems of course have their own standard forms, and these forms have several defects. Whether or not you can negotiate necessary changes depends on the competitive environment in which the sale is made and the extent to which the seller feels that you have already committed yourself to his product or system.

Among the defects that could be corrected:

1. The contract disclaims traditional warranties that are available to the buyer under the Uniform Commercial Code. The buyer should seek a statement that the product meets at least minimum standards of serviceability. Also, he should ask that the contract state that he has relied on the seller's expertise in deciding what to buy. This will give him substantial protection in case the product does not perform.

2. The contract expressly negates all the promises, claims, and technical descriptions made by the seller, either when talking to you or showing you advertising literature. If the claims of performance, service, capacity, and so forth are important to you, try and get them back in the agreement for your own protection.

3. The agreement describes in very general terms what you are buying, including its model number. It will not include any of the performance standards or descriptions that have been shown to you. If the performance level of the system is important—for example, that it is capable of printing 200 one-page invoices per hour—the agreement should include this standard.

4. The agreement does not include performance or quality standards of any kind against which the systems operation can be measured. Again, if these standards were the reason for the purchase of a

particular system, get them into the agreement. Also state how it will be determined that these standards have been met.

5. The agreement is vague about delivery, training, and so on. If it is important to you, specify clearly the delivery, installation, training, and maintenance schedules applicable to this equipment.

6. The agreement includes a lot of technical terms and phrases. If they are important to you, particularly from the performance end, ask that they be defined. For example, if the language to be used is compatible with COBOL, a computer language, you must define exactly what *compatible* means. Will you have to buy additional software to use COBOL or not?

Many long-term computer services and software agreements also provide that rates for some services or products specified during the term of the agreement will be increased to reflect increased costs to the supplier. These are "standard" clauses that the supplier is stuck with. Among the more common would be a provision providing for a pass through of increases in direct costs, such as the charges for service on particular dedicated equipment imposed by the manufacturer or distributor. ("Dedicated" equipment is designed exclusively for a particular system and is available only from the manufacturer.) Another common provision permits the supplier to pass through increases in material prices as they occur.

Realistically, the customer can do little in trying to negotiate away the pass through of such cost increases because the supplier cannot go back to the manufacturer and get this removed from his contract. In agreeing to them, however, the customer should consider the following:

1. Is the current price of the product or service subject to escalation?

2. How frequently have the prices changed recently?

3. How is the supplier notified of price increases? If he is given 90 days' notice of these increases in the cost of the service contract, you could ask to receive 60 days' notice of the pending change. This will give you a chance to budget for it or to consider alternative sources for the services.

4. If the price increases are on products, consider retaining the option of supplying the product yourself, if you can get a more stable or even a guaranteed price.

5. Are the prices subject to change potentially so important that you may prefer to terminate the agreement if they are too frequent or too high? If so, have this clarified in writing at the beginning in the contract itself.

6. When costs do increase, you may want to have the amount and effective date of the change verified in the form of invoices to the supplier or new price lists.

A more troublesome clause is one that permits the supplier to raise his rates for services under the agreement to reflect increases in his related expenses. For example, if an agreement provides for printing services or printed output, changes in the contract price may be keyed to annual increases in incurred printing expenses. The difference from the earlier clause is that this is a pass through of indirect, not direct, costs. In an era of rapidly changing costs, this clause invites trouble. No agreement containing such a clause should be signed without additional clarification and protections. The major problem is one of definition: Exactly what are the base expenses, how are they determined, how are changes passed through, and in what proportion? This clause has all of the problems that the direct-cost clause has, and the comments on that clause are appropriate here as well.

The critical issue is that indirect costs cannot be passed through on a dollar-for-dollar basis. They can be passed through only indirectly. There are several ways to accomplish this:

1. The parties can specifically agree upon the impact of changes in direct costs. This includes what costs are affected, what they are now, how changes in them are measured, how only increases in these costs can be passed through, and what formula should be applied in passing them through.

2. The parties should consider using a mutually agreed upon index of costs, prices, wages, or products as a surrogate for the actual costs

of the supplier. One way would be to permit a certain increase in the supplier's costs, say 1 percent for every 5-percent increase in the price of an indirect cost, such as printing inks. An alternative is to use a published government index. The main drawback here is that they are often several months behind the actual changes in costs.

3. The parties can agree to set a ceiling on the increases that are able to be passed through during each year. When the ceiling is reached, any excess, if the parties agree, can be carried forward to the next year.

Given the difficulties in providing for fair handling of such price changes, the customer should find out from the supplier why such a clause is desired. Every business faces cost increases, but every business does not try to obtain an automatic pass through of changes in its indirect costs. By their very nature, indirect costs cannot be allocated to a particular client or project. If a supplier is concerned that radical changes in his indirect costs will make a long-term contract unprofitable, he may have alternatives. Permitting a supplier to increase his prices by a fixed percentage, say 30 percent over the term of a five-year contract, with no more than 7 percent in any one year, provides protection for the supplier and relative predictability for the purchaser.

In general, pass-through clauses should not be dismissed. Their impact should be understood and protections or alternatives considered.

How to Fill Out a Form

The General Release on page 165 is designed to be a part of the settlement of a dispute between two parties. As drafted, it settles all disputes which these two parties might have had.

Assume that the release is being given to the Doe Corporation by Mr. Richard Roe. Fill out the form according to the numbers:

1. The name of the person giving the release, "Richard Roe."
2. The person receiving the release, "The Doe Corporation."

3. The subject of the dispute. For example, "Claims arising from Richard Roe's purchase of typewriters from the Doe Corporation on April 2, 1982."

4. The same as number 1.

5. Add "his." The pronoun must match the number of persons giving the release.

6. This space is used when the release is limited to a specific transaction.

7. Add "he" and change "have" to "has."

8. Add "his."

9, 10. Add an *s* if two persons are giving the release to one person. Otherwise, leave it blank.

11. The day of the month.

12. The month.

13. The year.

Note that this form has to be signed only by the party giving the release.

To adapt this form to your own needs, suppose that you are being paid to give the release, and the party getting the release wants that to be acknowledged. You can change entry number 1 as follows:

in consideration of the sum of ____ dollars paid to it by [the party getting the release], [your name].

Now, suppose that you want to limit the release to settling a dispute arising from a particular transaction, say the shipment of goods that arrived on a particular day on a particular ship. The form as printed gives a release for everything "from the beginning of the world to the date of these presents"—that is, *every* dispute, whether or not there has been a lawsuit, or even if the parties have not yet found out about the problem. To limit the release:

Item 3. Delete ", of and from all" and the first "and all" after the blank spaces.

KNOW ALL MEN BY THESE PRESENTS THAT (1) _____

_____

do hereby remise, release and forever discharge (2) _____

_____

and   heirs, executors and administrators, of and from all (3) _____

_____

and all manner of actions and causes of action, suits, debts, accounts,

dues, bonds, covenants, contracts, agreements, judgments, demands and

claims whatsoever in law or in equity, which against the said (4) _____

_____

ever had, now have   , or which (5) heirs, executors, administrators or

assigns, or any of them hereafter can, shall or may have, for or by

reason of any cause, matter or thing whatsoever, from the beginning of

the world to the date of these presents (6)

IN WITNESS WHEREOF, (7) have hereunto set (8) hand (9) and seal (10) the

___(11)___ day of ___(12)___ in the year one thousand nine hundred

and eighty ___(13)___

Signed, Sealed And Delivered)
    In the Presence of Us   )
)   _____ (Seal)
_____   )
)
)   _____ (Seal)
_____   )
)

Item 6. Delete everything from "cause, matter" to "these presents" and add: "Claims arising from the shipment of goods by [one party] from New Orleans, Louisiana, on the S.S. Jones, which arrived at Valparaiso, Chile, on or about August 28, 1982."

Finally, make sure that all the blanks are completely filled in so that the release cannot be changed later. Any changes that are made should be initialed by the signatories.

Another General Release form has been completed for the following situation:

A release from John McGonagle to the Doe Corporation, for which Doe pays $10,000. McGonagle is giving up his right to sue for damages resulting from the Doe Corporation's alleged failure to ship McGonagle's order for copiers on time. The copiers were ordered by McGonagle on January 1, 1982.

For this transaction, note how much the form had to be adapted. In this case, it would be easier and faster to type the entire release on plain paper and have it signed.

Using Your Own Form Agreements

When should you have your own form agreement and why? If you find that you are engaged in the same or similar transactions time and time again, and you prepare a new agreement for each one, or if you tend to use a prior form as a model for drafting, it may be time to make up your own form.

Additionally, using a form agreement has management benefits beyond the time saved in preparing essentially the same contract over and over. By having your own form, you can exercise some control over the terms and conditions under which these common transactions are negotiated. In fact, the use of a form can limit the ability of officers and employees to commit the company. For example, if you have a form agreement for the sale of advertising space, you can require that all

KNOW ALL MEN BY THESE PRESENTS THAT *John McGonagle, in consideration of the sum of $10,000 paid to him by the Doe Corporation*

do**es** hereby remise, release and forever discharge *the Doe Corporation*

and *its* heirs, executors and administrators, of and from all

and all manner of actions and causes of action, suits, debts, accounts, dues, bonds, covenants, contracts, agreements, judgments, demands and claims whatsoever in law or in equity, which against the said *John McGonagle*

ever had, now have , or which *his* heirs, executors, administrators or assigns, or any of them hereafter can, shall or may have, for or by reason of any ~~cause, matter or thing whatsoever, from the beginning of the world to the date of these presents~~ *claim arising out of John McGonagle's order of copiers from the Doe Corporation on or about January 1, 1982.*

JM

IN WITNESS WHEREOF, *he* ~~have~~ *has* hereunto set *his* hand and seal the *15th* day of *March* in the year one thousand nine hundred and eighty *two*

Signed, Sealed And Delivered)
)
In the Presence of Us)
A. Witness)
  A. Witness)
)
)

John McGonagle (Seal)
John McGonagle

_____(Seal)

sales be made on this agreement, even if there are major changes in it. Then, to limit who can accept these agreements, you can require that no such agreement for an amount in excess of $5,000 can be made without being cosigned by, say, the vice president. This provision keeps employees and officers who lack authority from obligating the company to large expenditures.

To be effective, a form should reflect your own needs and circumstances. It should not require additional language in order to be usable; in other words, you should be able to complete it and have a deal. This requires you to consider it carefully, and you should review it from time to time to make sure it is not out of date and ineffective. If you find that you constantly have to add or delete material to accommodate each deal, it is time to make up a new one. Finally, the form should not be so elaborate or so rigid in terms of the conditions it establishes that it will alienate potential customers.

You can use your own form agreements in one of two ways:

1. As the printed form on which a final agreement between you and the other party is prepared.
2. As an aid in negotiating a contract between you and the other party, particularly in negotiating changes on his own form. This is more likely if his form was developed by an association or taken from a form book than if he made up his own.

Using your own form in negotiations has several advantages:

1. The discussion will focus on your terms and the way you propose to structure the transaction.
2. You set forth all the important conditions, so the person representing you is not likely to exclude something important.
3. If each party has his own form, you can see immediately where you differ.
4. Some people accept the form without serious discussion.
5. Your instructions on using the form, whether simple or elaborate,

guide your personnel in making the deal. The instructions outline what you want, what you will give up, and the point beyond which they will not be permitted to make concessions.

Many agreements are made on printed forms prepared by the parties to the agreement, trade associations, or form book printers. With any form, provisions will have to be inserted or completed. Remember, regardless of its source, almost any form can be changed by individual agreement, using deletions and revisions to reflect the negotiations. If you use your form as the basis for negotiations, you will quickly be able to see the impact of changes requested by the other party. Even if the other party refuses to use your form as the basis of an agreement, the form can still help you to evaluate his proposal and negotiate changes. Whether used with or without instructions, it permits a clause-by-clause comparison between your needs, as set forth in your form, and the other party's form.

Your instructions should explain the form's provisions and options and recommend terms that must be inserted in various clauses. They should also cover clauses that either you or the other party may seek to delete as well as additional clauses that the other party may want to add and your response. The instructions can also suggest alternatives for certain clauses, particularly those most likely to be resisted by the other party. For ease of use, the various sections of the contract should be numbered and the comments and instructions numbered in the same order as the corresponding section of the agreement. The basic instructions should include coverage of the following technical points:

Insertions: Dates, amounts, names, and figures should be made in clearly identified spaces.

Deletions: Every word, number, phrase, line, or section to be deleted should be crossed out in ink or by typewriter. In general, deletions should be initialed by each party.

Additions: Any new clauses or language should be typed on the last page and extra pages added if necessary. Each new clause should be numbered separately. If it supplements or replaces a section in

the body of the agreement, add the phrase "see section _____"
next to the material in the margin. If the signature line appears
above the new material, this should also be initialed.

Blanks: Never sign an agreement if any blank is unfilled. Sign it only
after the blanks have been completed. Think of it this way: A
blank contract is the same as a blank check. If the blank does
not apply, either put a line through it or insert "n/a" or "not applicable." Some cautious attorneys advise that you draw a line from
the last word on a page to the bottom of the page on any multipage
agreement so that nothing can be added later.

When using your form or anyone else's, remember that no form is
ever complete. You can always find something to add or delete. Always
review changes in a form carefully. To effect a change, you may have to
modify more than one portion of the agreement. In fact, some forms are
intentionally complex just to make it difficult to make a change without
having to revise a number of other clauses and sections.

8

Special Problems

While all business agreements are governed by the same basic contract law doctrines, and all are subject to the same rules of interpretation, there are a few commercial situations in which the context is as important as the agreement. This chapter covers several of those special cases: copyrights, bankruptcy, restraints on trade, land sales, and requirement and output contracts. Each case involves a special body of law that determines whether or not the contract should be written, and exactly what it must or must not contain.

Copyrights

By copyrighting a work, you create a tangible asset that can then be rented, sold, or leased. The copyright law is designed to allow the creator to benefit from the creative process financially as well as emotionally. To do this, it provides that certain classes of things can be copyrighted and ownership assigned to the creator, unless there is a specific agreement to the contrary or the creator is a full-time employee.

Many kinds of items can be copyrighted, some of which are often created in a business situation:

1. Literary Works
   Books, pamphlets, leaflets, nonfiction writings, catalogues, directories, compilations, computer programs, data bases, newsletters, bulletins, advertisements, lectures, addresses, speeches, and panel discussions

2. Pictorial, Graphic and Sculptural Works
   Drawings, prints, filmstrips, fabric designs, postcards, greeting cards, advertising artwork, labels, engineering diagrams, mechanical and architectural drawings, models, and maps

3. Motion Pictures and Audiovisual Works
   Slide series and series of images with accompanying sound

4. Sound Recordings
   Spoken sounds and sound effects as well as music

By working full time for you, an employee may have given up his right to copyright his work for you. However, if that person is not working full time for any one employer, you may want to obtain the rights to the copyrightable work in an employment or consulting agreement.

The basis for this distinction is that if an employee is required, as a part of his job, to produce works that can be copyrighted, he has lost his status as owner of those works. This is because that employee is presumed to be paid a salary to produce the copyrightable works for someone else, the employer. Thus, the employer can copyright it himself.

However, if that person is working for you on a free-lance, consulting, or independent contractor basis, be certain to specify in your contract with him who has the right to copyright the work he produces for you, because if you do not, then he owns it. The way to make sure that the client is the owner is to have the contract state that the contractor is preparing a "work made for hire." Another option is for the individual (contractor) to license back the work to you after it has been copyrighted. You may want to provide for this as well if ownership of the work is not clear.

Bankruptcy

Usually, if you have sold goods to a company that later goes bankrupt, you become a general creditor. This means that all you have is a claim for a share of its assets after all secured creditors and government tax collectors are paid. There are several situations under which the terms of your agreement may provide additional protection for you.

First, the United States Bankruptcy law provides that if you relied on inaccurate financial information submitted by the bankrupt and extended him credit, you may have a claim that takes priority over those of the other general creditors. However, you will have to prove that you relied on the false statements. Here written records surrounding the negotiation and administration of the contract may enable you to salvage more from the bankruptcy proceedings.

If you shipped goods to a company shortly before it declared bankruptcy, you may still be able to protect yourself. As soon as you know of the insolvency, you should contact the company, rescind the agreement, and demand the return of the goods. Your claim to the goods will take precedence over the claims of the general creditors. If the goods will lose value during this period, such as Christmas ornaments returned on December 26, you will be stuck, for your entire claim on the bankrupt will have been disposed of by the return of these goods. From a contract point of view, this means that you should provide a method for rapid communication of notices. Certified mail may be certain, but it is slow. Consider permitting mailgrams, confirmed by a certified letter. Also, you may want the contract to provide that all your goods be clearly marked so that they can be identified and recovered promptly in case of bankruptcy.

Restraints on Trade

When lawyers speak of restraints on trade, they mean contracts or actions that violate antitrust laws. Compliance with these laws is a complex subject and beyond the scope of this book. However, one author has formulated a series of rules, based on antitrust laws, which should be referred to as a part of the analysis of the legality of any business agreement. If an agreement seems to transgress one of these rules, you may have an antitrust problem:

The application of the antitrust laws to the so-called horizontal relationships of a corporation with its competitors may be roughly summarized as follows:

First: A corporation may meet with its competitors. . . .

Second: A corporation should not control its competitors. . . .

Third: A corporation should not conspire with its competitors. . . .

Fourth: A corporation should not unfairly compete with its competitors. . . .

The application of the antitrust laws to what is termed the vertical relationships of a corporation, that is to say with its customers, has resulted in a comparable set of rules:

First: A corporation may select its customers. . . .

Second: A corporation should not dominate its customers. . . .

Third: A corporation should not unduly discriminate between its customers. . . .

Fourth: A corporation should not deceive its customers. . . .

The application of the antitrust laws to the internal corporate relationships of a business organization is not as clearly defined . . . as is the impact of these laws upon the relationships just discussed.

The corporate rules currently [1975] evolving, however, would seem to be approximately as follows:

First: A corporation may manage its corporate family. . . .

Second: A corporation should not monopolize the markets of its corporate family. . . .

Third: A corporation should not misuse the muscle of its corporate family. . . .

Fourth: A corporation should not indiscriminately multiply, through mergers with others, its corporate family.[1]

Land Sales

Any transaction that pertains to land requires a written agreement. The law demands this because ownership of land and rights in land can be protected only by recording a written agreement, making it part of the history of that land. If no documents are recorded, a third party may be able to purchase the land without regard to any agreements that the former owner may have made before his sale.

When purchasing property, be very careful before you sign any document. Make sure that all the details of the deal are included in the very first paper you sign, regardless of its title. The sale of land and the documents involved in the sale vary widely from one part of the country to another. The first document goes by many names: deposit receipt, contract of sale, sales agreement, offer, purchase agreement, binder, preliminary sales agreement, or earnest-money agreement. No matter how it is labeled, it should contain certain key elements, because this paper is generally a binding contract, even if the parties intend to sign other papers later. Even if the papers you sign seem to be incomplete, they may still constitute a binding contract. Always treat them as such.

The key elements that every real-estate agreement should contain at minimum are:

1. The purchase price.

2. The date the money is due and under what terms (interest, conditioned on the sale of another building, and so forth).

3. The name of the property being sold and a full legal description of it. If anything other than the property is being sold, such as a building or its contents, list that as well.

4. The type of deed and evidence of title that the buyer will receive.

5. The conditions, if any, under which the buyer can withdraw and get some or all of his deposit back. How much of the deposit will be returned?

6. The conditions, if any, under which the seller can withdraw and the penalty for cancellation.

7. Any guarantee that the seller makes about the condition of the building and the kinds of uses that it can be put to.

8. The date when the buyer can take possession of the land and building.

9. How any outstanding obligations pertaining to the property, such as taxes and utility bills, will be allocated.

10. The signature of the legal owner or owners of the property, not just that of an agent or attorney.

As with almost every other agreement, there is no such thing as a "standard" agreement for the sale of property. All have been prepared commercially, and they reflect the needs of the drafter. Because it may not fit your needs, don't be afraid to change the form that is offered to you. A checklist for real property agreements is included in the Appendix.

Even though you think you have an agreement to sell land or property, the transaction still is not complete. You must meet six minimum requirements in any effective transfer of land or of any interest in land:

1. A document in writing.

2. A document that has been effectively executed. Effective execution includes:

a. *Signing.* State law requires that the person giving up the interest in land sign the document.

b. *Sealing.* In the early days of English and American law, land transfers could be made only under a document that carried both the owner's signature and his personal seal. This requirement has been eliminated in most states, but printed deed forms still recite that they are "made under seal."

c. *Attestation.* There must be signing witnesses to the transfer. Some states require this, but only to record the deed. The lack of witnesses to a deed between two parties does not make the deed invalid.

d. *Acknowledgment.* Commonly, a swearing before a notary public or similar official that you are the person named in the deed and that you made the deed. It is usually an alternative to attestation and necessary only to record the deed.

e. *Delivery.* Signing and delivery are universally required. The requirements of attestation and acknowledgment are usually necessary only to record the deed in a public office.

3. The document must contain language that shows an intent to convey; that is, to transfer some interest in the land.

4. The person transferring the interest, the grantor, and the person acquiring the interest, the grantee, must be identified.

5. What is being transferred must be identified in the document, meaning that there must be a full and accurate description of the property.

6. The document must state the nature of the interest being transferred: for example, full ownership, drilling rights, or a lease.

One item that is not required in the document transferring land, the conveyance, is a recital of the payment of consideration—that is, the value for the interest acquired. For historical reasons many deeds, even if they represent the transfer of land without payment, such as a gift, include a recital of some nominal consideration. Typically, the transfer is made for "one dollar and other good and valuable consideration." Some people actually exchange a dollar, but this is not necessary to make the transfer valid.

Requirement and Output Contracts

A requirement contract between two parties provides that the quantity of goods covered by the contract is to be measured by the requirements of the buyer during a predetermined period, rather than providing a specific number. The quantity may also be established in terms of the output of the seller during a predetermined period. This is known as an output contract.

The major problem in these contracts is that one party can control the quantity ultimately covered by the contract. This can be done through decisions to close a business, contract it, expand it, leave it the same, or make changes in related functions, such as in available storage space.

In early times these agreements were not considered to be enforceable. As the law developed, the courts permitted the contracts to stand under certain stated conditions so that they were not faced with a speculative agreement:

1. One party had an existing output (or need) or had specific and immediate plans to operate a business that would generate that output (or need).

2. In an output contract, the seller did not reserve the right to dispose of its output to another source. In a requirements contract, the buyer did not reserve the right to fill its requirements from another source.

This does not mean that the party operating the business generating the output or using the requirements cannot close the business. That party can retire, sell the business, close part of the business for good cause, or take similar business actions that end the requirements or the output, so long as that action is taken in good faith.

9
Disputes

Although the parties to a business agreement may intend never to have a dispute and, in fact, may expect that their agreement covers every possible question that could arise between them, disputes are inevitable. The parties to an agreement may differ as to their particular rights or obligations under the agreement, no matter how carefully the document is written and no matter how detailed the specifications of the performance required by each side. These disputes may lead to delays in performance and complaints about the quality or quantity of goods or services. They may arise out of the contentions that one party has not cooperated with the other, thereby making his or her own job more difficult, or similar operational misunderstandings. It is an unfortunate fact that even with the best of intentions parties to the agreement may deliver less than they have promised in writing.

Handling Disputes

When the parties to an agreement face a dispute, the first question is whether or not the agreement already covers the subject of the dispute. This, in turn, requires the parties to determine what constitutes their agreement. A business agreement can be memorialized on a single sheet of paper, or it can be made up of a combination of written documents, oral agreements, trade practices, and the behavior of the parties. If the parties have thought through the relationship thoroughly, it is likely that their agreement has some provision dealing with the subject of the dispute, or the agreement may provide a way to settle the dispute, such as by arbitration. If so, the parties should be able to arrive at a quick and amiable conclusion.

A dispute may have to be settled by negotiation when a contract requires some evidence of good faith. If the contract states that the performance of one party must be satisfactory to the other, and the second party's determination of whether or not the work produced is satisfactory must be made in good faith, it still may not resolve the dispute. The courts have held that the existence of good faith necessitates an examination not only of the parties' own statements but also of how they behave. This means that a clause requires both good faith and a demonstration of good faith. For example, if a corporation asserts that it cannot use a report prepared by a consultant and does not in fact use it, a court would probably rule that the corporation acted in good faith, even if the consultant could show that some other corporation could use the report. But if the court finds that officers of the corporation were concerned about the high cost of the contract (even if the cost is as originally estimated) and then rejected the report, it will probably rule that the corporation acted in bad faith. Of course, good faith is in the eye of the beholder; a demonstration of good faith can still result in a breakdown in negotiations and ultimately in charges of breach of contract.

Whether the injured party is the purchaser or the seller, before seeking to use any of the remedies available—suits for breach of contract, specific performance, rescission, restitution, enforcement of liquidated damage clauses, or resort to arbitration or mediation—there are several key steps to follow. The first is that any party who feels it has been damaged by the other party should reread the contract, any amendments made to it, and any instructions that were exchanged between the parties to see if the disputed points are covered. A surprising number of disputes in the business world arise between parties who have not taken this first step. If the agreement does not cover the dispute, the parties should look at their past relationship and course of conduct. The courts will often look to the course of conduct to determine the rights of the parties.

If a party to an agreement believes there has been a breach of contract, he should begin immediately to document that breach and any damages he is suffering, including delays, difficulties in obtaining replacement parts or services, default on related contracts, and other impacts on his own customers and suppliers. For example, if the sale of land is involved and the seller refuses to conclude the sale, selling the land to someone else, the potential buyer may suffer various damages. The buyer may already have spent money searching the title or surveying the land for development. The parcel of land may be integral to a planned residential development, which now cannot go forward. The buyer will now never realize the profits he expected from that development. The seller may be liable to the buyer for all of these damages.

Communication between the parties in the case of a possible breach of contract should be cautious and careful. Communication should be in writing to make sure that there is a clear understanding between the parties regarding the grievance. In fact, the parties should make sure that all communications to date that relate to the contract are in writing. Written communication protects the parties from violating the statute of frauds, mentioned in Chapter 2, and protects their positions when a contract dispute arises. Although language can be ambiguous, a written record is substantially easier to review than the incomplete recollection of the parties after a falling out.

When two parties disagree on the terms of a contract, each party must take care to preserve his rights from the moment of the dispute. A case in point arose in Bucks County, Pennsylvania, in 1981. Mr. Fazio had agreed to sell a golf course to Mr. Kane. Their signed agreement set the closing date for December 20, unless "the time of closing is extended in writing by the parties." Kane put $50,000 of the purchase price in escrow. The buyer, Kane, as a condition of the closing, was to file an application for a liquor license for the golf club "as soon as reasonably possible." About a week before the closing, Kane, the buyer, met with the attorneys for both sides and signed a written agreement to extend the closing date to December 31. The seller's consent was to be obtained later because Fazio was out of the state, but his attorney confirmed the meeting by a letter to Kane dated December 17. Mr. Kane did not respond to that letter, and on December 22 he filed the application for a liquor license.

On December 27, Kane's attorney called Fazio's attorney and told him that Kane would not settle and take the land. In a letter dated the next day, the buyer stated that there had been no written or oral extension of the time agreed on for the settlement and that, in the buyer's opinion, the conditions to settlement set out in the agreement had not been met. The closing was not held.

Kane later sued to get his $50,000 escrow deposit back. The court ruled that the buyer had waived the seller's defaults in the agreement because the buyer, by filing for the liquor license, had proceeded as though the agreement were still in force. The court also noted that the buyer had waited for a week after the original closing date to terminate the agreement.

This case illustrates an important point: If you feel that a contract has been breached by the other party, you must think seriously about what steps you will take, if any, at that point. Although your agreement may provide that if you waive one breach you still have the right to sue for another breach, the courts will look at the conduct of the parties to determine if this is fair and equitable under the facts. In this case the court ruled that, since both parties to the agreement had permitted the time agreed on for performance to pass, neither could terminate the agreement suddenly without giving the other an opportunity to perform under it.

In addition, the court ruled that Kane's failure to contradict or deny the assertion in the seller's letter confirming the extension of the closing date—particularly when viewed in the context of Kane's actions after receiving it, that is, filing for the license—was his admission that there was a valid agreement to extend the closing date. This points out another key element in handling disputes: Don't let damaging assertions go unchallenged, in light of any actions you plan to take, if they could later be regarded as an admission. If you plan to take steps to minimize your losses that could be interpreted as actions fulfilling the very agreement you think has been breached, protect the record. It is the record of the actions and documents that will ultimately determine how a court will interpret an agreement and what relief it will give when relief is sought. It is not enough to be right; you must be able to *show* that you are right.

Should You Sue?

The first step in any lawsuit is not the bringing of the lawsuit, but the decision of whether or not to sue at all. To make an intelligent decision, you must consider several different matters.

First, you must feel that you have been wronged. But the wrong must be one for which the law can furnish some relief. For many losses the law provides no relief. For example, you may expend a great deal of effort trying to sell a product to a customer, but the customer then buys from your competitor. Your loss here cannot be remedied by the courts. If your injury is one that the courts cannot remedy, a lawsuit is a useless and costly exercise.

If your grievance is one for which the courts will grant relief, consider honestly your chances of winning that lawsuit. Just because you have been wronged does not mean that you will win. Consider the following:

Can you locate the party who breached the contract and bring him to court?

Can you produce the documents and witnesses that will prove your case?

Can the other party justify his conduct, or can he establish any defenses to your action, such as that you may have waited too long to sue?

How strong is the law on the point in dispute?

After you have considered these factors carefully, then consider whether what you can win is worth the time, money, and effort to achieve it. This includes the benefits and costs of alternatives to the lawsuit, such as a negotiated settlement, arbitration, mediation, self-help, or just walking away from the problem. Decide what relief the courts can give you if you win. For example, usually a breach-of-contract action seeks money damages. If this is true in your case, will money satisfy you? Can you show how much you have been injured?

Assuming that you get this far, you then have to decide if the defendant is able to pay a judgment. How difficult and expensive will it be to collect from him? When you finish with the costs of collecting, will you have enough to pay your lawyer and the other expenses incurred in the lawsuit? If so, how much will you have left?

If you are seeking something other than money, such as specific performance, will the defendant be able to comply with that judgment? For example, if the defendant promised to sell you a piece of land and he did not, does he still own it? If he has sold it to someone else, specific performance—that is, an order to sell it to you—is meaningless. If the defendant can comply with such an order, will that compliance be sufficient for you? The passage of time may diminish the value of specific performance.

Once you have decided that you should and can sue and that the potential defendant can satisfy a judgment, look at the courts where you will have to bring your case. In most major metropolitan areas the civil courts have backlogs of up to seven years. Unless your case is special, you may have to wait this long for a jury trial. If you are willing to have the case tried before a judge, the waiting time may be less. Keep in mind, though, that the judicial system is inherently cold and impersonal. Just because the case is important to you does not mean it is important or special to the courts.

In nonurban areas the case backlog is less severe. In federal district (trial) courts the backlog on civil cases currently stands at four to five years. One key reason for this is the constitutional right that criminal defendants have to a speedy trial. Since most civil judges are also criminal judges, and since the two types of trials use the same court rooms, court stenographers, and administrative services, a crowded criminal docket usually means the civil docket will be slow. You can check on the state of a court's docket by calling the court clerk or by actually attending a trial to see how old the case being tried is.

Some people believe that their case will be heard if the damages being sought are vital; for example, without the contract payment they will go bankrupt. This is not enough. The judicial system regards the right to damages and interest as sufficient in most ordinary contract cases to compensate for the delay in receiving justice. In fact, if you are not paid and sue and then go bankrupt, your breach-of-contract suit will not be moved up for this reason. The trustee of the bankrupt estate will manage the case because now it is treated as any other asset of the bankrupt. When damages can be collected, they will be divided among the creditors.

Because of the delay in civil cases, particularly in metropolitan areas, both potential plaintiffs and the courts have encouraged access to other methods of dispute resolution. One is to use small claims court, which is fast but limited in other respects in comparison with regular courts. The other is voluntary or mandatory arbitration of all civil cases under a certain amount. In Philadelphia, for example, civil cases demanding less than $15,000 are candidates for mandatory arbitration by lawyers selected by the court and the parties to the case.

The following sections discuss ordinary civil cases, small claims court, and nonlitigation approaches to resolving disputes. Consider their benefits and detriments carefully before selecting one or the other. At the end of the chapter is a decision chart, illustrating the key decisions to be made in handling any contract dispute.

Lawsuits

PLEADINGS

To understand what is involved in a lawsuit for breach of contract, you should first understand what the pleadings, the papers filed to begin it, have to contain and what you will have to prove at the trial, if there is one. If you cannot establish the facts necessary to show these items, either from your own records and witnesses or from documents held by the other party, you will not be able to win. That means that you have no case, even though you may have been wronged. This is a difficult distinction to keep in mind. If you can do so, you will avoid bringing lawsuits that you cannot win.

There are three basic elements in an action for breach of contract:

1. There must be a contract or agreement that is supported by consideration (or by the existence of some other factor that the law says can also make the agreement binding).
2. The party bringing the suit, the plaintiff, has performed all of the conditions that he has to perform before the other party, the defendant, was required to perform.
3. The defendant has breached the contract. The exact damages suffered because of the breach generally do not have to be included in the pleadings. Even so, at a trial you will have to prove that there was damage and that it was related to the breach by the defendant. You must also state the amount of the damage.

Before you sue, look at the potential remedies that are available. These are discussed later in the chapter. When a pleading, or a complaint, is filed in a breach-of-contract case, the court rules permit the plaintiff to use as many theories as he or she can in the pleading. This is because the courts are not overly strict in reviewing the pleadings. Today, the pleadings are designed to give the defendant notice of the plaintiff's grievances. Using a variety of theories in the pleadings permits the party seeking relief to improve his chances of winning. If you, as plaintiff, are unable to prove one theory that entitles you to one form of relief, you may be more successful on another. For example, if you had a contract to buy a certain piece of property and the seller did not transfer it to you, you may have the following different claims against the seller, each of which will have to appear in the pleadings in order to be awarded:

1. Specific performance (seeking to get the land transferred)
2. Return of the deposit
3. Damages resulting from the inconvenience of not closing on the property, such as temporary lodging
4. Punitive damages resulting from the seller's bad faith in failing to transfer the land
5. Out-of-pocket losses, such as title-search fees already paid
6. Lost profits if the land was ready to be resold or developed at a profit

If a theory is not in the pleadings, you may be barred from introducing evidence under that theory and obtaining the proper relief. Conversely, you cannot go into court with a shotgun assortment of claims and theories. Some theories or remedies are so inconsistent that the courts have developed a rule called "election of remedies." For example, if you sue on the ground that there was no valid contract with another person because of some fraudulent act, you are in essence suing under the assumption that there is a contract that should now be disaffirmed. On the other hand, if you seek rescission of the contract, you are viewed as disaffirming the contract. In some states you cannot have it both ways. You will have to decide at the outset whether your suit assumes that the contract exists or that one never existed.

POTENTIAL REMEDIES

The remedies available in contract disputes are varied. Each has its special benefits as well as its limitations. The most common remedy is an action seeking cash damages for losses that result from the alleged breach. Others include an action for restitution, or an action for specific performance, rescission, or liquidated damages.

Damages

The basic legal doctrine surrounding breach of contract says that if one party breaches an agreement, the other party may collect monetary damages proximately caused by the breach—that is, as the result of the breach. This is intended to make the party who did not breach the contract whole, by placing him in the same position he would have been in had the contract been performed in accord with its terms. Lawyers describe this as getting the "benefit of his bargain."

Several types of damages can be obtained in an action for breach of contract:

1. *Liquidated damages:* This is a contract provision specifying fixed cash damages for a potential breach and is discussed later in the chapter.

2. *Compensatory damages:* As the name implies, these compensate for the breach. The party breaching the contract must pay the difference between the cost of performance and the cost in the contract.

3. *Consequential damages:* These make up the lost profit that results from, or is a consequence of, the breach and resulting nonperformance.

4. *Other damages:* Those proximately caused by the breach, or losses incurred as a result of bad-faith bargaining.

5. *Reliance damages:* After a contract has been breached, the breaching party pays the innocent party the money that the innocent party actually spent by relying on the terms of performance in the contract. Generally the injured party has the obligation to reduce the damages that he suffers from the breach. This is known as a *duty to mitigate.* If the party does not do this, in an action for damages a court can reduce the amount of money he received by the amount that could have been saved by appropriate actions taken to mitigate.

Damages may not always be appropriate, particularly under agreements that require the breaching party to provide services, such as a consulting agreement. A problem with the consulting relationship is that often the employer purchases the consultant's expertise and services to solve an unknown problem or come up with new concepts. Thus it is difficult to determine the value of the work if it was not performed. The employer may not be able to sue for breach of contract because he cannot show how he was damaged. If there was a breach of contract, the consultant faces the same problem. If he was to be paid a fixed fee, clearly the fee can be a measure of damages. If he was to be paid on an hourly basis or on a percentage of the money saved, the damages may be too speculative to award. This means that both parties may have a right to sue, but they may not be able to prove any money damages.

Restitution

The remedy of restitution is a variation of damages but with a different legal tradition. In restitution, the courts try to restore to each party the monies expended and attempt to exchange additional money to compensate the parties for expenses incurred. The effort here is to dissolve the contract and to restore parties to their original positions, rather than to restore the contract or pay for losses caused by a breach.

Related to this are equitable remedies, in which a party to a broken contract sues for value. For example, an investment adviser sues a corporation to collect the value of services to the corporation. An alternative is to sue for the value of the services rendered by the adviser in terms of lost time, if he bills by the hour. There can be a significant difference between the value of the services rendered from the points of view of the adviser and the client. The rules regarding which remedy is available were made to allow the courts to reach the fairest and most equitable solution to a disputed agreement. From the point of view of the client, the same choice of remedies applies—that is, to achieve a return of monies expended or some return of value.

Rescission

Rescission of an agreement is an effort to eliminate the agreement and return the parties to the state they would have occupied if the agreement had never existed. The parties wash their hands of the whole affair. In many cases rescission may yield a result similar to restitution, particularly when the dispute involves the purchase and sale of goods. One of the major limitations on the availability of rescission as a remedy is that the grounds for rescission must have existed at or before the time the agreement was entered into by the parties. In addition, the party seeking rescission must show that mere money damages would be inadequate to compensate him and that the only way he can obtain a fair remedy is to have the agreement voided by a court. There are four bases for rescission:

1. *Mutual mistake:* Each party to the agreement made a mistake of fact, the fact being so important that it goes to the very essence of the agreement. Such a fact is called a material fact.
2. *Unilateral mistake:* A court may order rescission only if the nonmistaken party knew of or should have known of the mistaken party's major error.
3. *Innocent misrepresentation of a material fact.*
4. *Fraudulent misrepresentation of a material fact with the knowledge that it is false.* The misrepresentation must have been done with the intent to deceive the innocent party, and that party must have relied on that misrepresentation to its detriment.

In the case of agreement where services are exchanged for money, rescission is a difficult remedy to obtain from the courts because there is no real physical commodity to transfer and return. For example, rescission easily can be obtained in the sale of a car; the court can force one party to return the car and the other to return the money, with some adjustment for wear and tear on the car. In the case of services, although one party can return the money, the services themselves cannot be returned. It is difficult, if not impossible, for a court to force a party to disgorge the benefits of services completely, for once they have been rendered they can never be returned.

Specific Performance

In agreements to provide a unique good or service, one remedy to the injured party is specific performance. One party sues the other and asks an intervening court to force the defending party to live up to the terms of the contract.

A good example of specific performance of services might be enforcing a contract to repair a parking lot. In the case of the sale of goods, specific performance can be ordered when the goods are unique. In the past, *unique* was limited to items such as specific works of art. Now specific performance may be available in the case of an output or requirements contract involving a particular or peculiarly available source or market. The availability of specific performance is enhanced when the buyer is unable to get comparable goods on the open market. If he could get the goods on the open market, he could then sue for the difference between the price he paid on the market and the price he would have paid under the contract.

In specific performance, if the buyer is sued by the seller and the seller wins, the buyer is required to cooperate in the performance of the seller's services. The buyer is forced to pay the seller under the terms and conditions agreed on, and the parties generally restore relations as though they had never broken down. If the seller is sued by the buyer, the court will order the seller to perform the services or provide the goods promised in the agreement under the standards of care, good faith, and timeliness required by the contract or in that trade or business.

When a contract requires services to be performed by one or more specifically designated individuals, it can be regarded as one for personal services. This is an old notion in which the party seeking performance entered into a contract with an individual only on the condition that all the services are performed by that individual, who, presumably, possesses unique skills. The more unusual the skills, the more difficult it is for the courts to secure performance. In the past the courts refused to enforce personal-services contracts because they had no way to assure adequate compliance with an order. They reasoned that any means at the court's disposal to force a person to perform, including monetary penalties and the threat of prison, would take away the "spirit" of the performance.

The oldest cases go back to those brought by theater owners who wished opera singers to honor their contracts and appear. The courts said that they were unable to enforce the agreement, not because they couldn't force the singers to show up, but because both parties clearly had intended the singers to perform in a skillful, professional manner and the courts had no way to judge the quality of the performance; and even if they had, they had no way to insist that the performance be done properly.

Later, the courts arrived at a compromise in such cases. When services are regarded as personal and unique, the courts hold that they cannot force a person of high skills to perform under such a contract. Under the proper circumstances, however, they can keep the skilled individual from entering into a contract to perform the same services for another person, usually a competitor. The courts have noted slyly that if the effect of such an order is to bring the two disputing parties together again, then they are all for it.

There are signs that the courts, particularly in employment agreements, may be inclined to veer away from granting even this limited injunctive relief. In a recent case before the New York Court of Appeals, the American Broadcasting Companies sought an injunction to bar a sportscaster, Warner Wolf, from working for a competing network, CBS. Wolf's employment contract with ABC had expired and he signed with CBS, fulfilling an oral agreement he had made during the term of the ABC agreement. The court found that Wolf had violated the terms of his employment agreement with ABC by failing to negotiate a renewal of that contract with ABC in good faith, as required by his agreement.

The court did not find that Wolf was working for CBS while still under contract with ABC, nor did it find any anticompetitive agreement or trade-secrets restriction that was applicable to Wolf's job with CBS. The court concluded that to enjoin Wolf from working for CBS under those circumstances would unduly interfere with his livelihood and inhibit free competition. However, the court's decision did not stop ABC from suing Wolf for money damages because of his breach of contract.

Given the current limits on specific performance, the parties to any agreement should be extremely careful when specifying that only one individual can perform the services under the agreement. It is clear today that while a request for specific performance of a business agreement will not be refused by the courts solely on the grounds that the performance requires the personal involvement of the defendant, the courts are still reluctant to grant specific performance if it means supervising the day-to-day performance of highly skilled and talented individuals.

DEFENSES

Just as the plaintiff must determine what he must prove to win a breach-of-contract action, he must also consider the defendant's defense. (If you are the one being sued, you should go through the same analysis as the plaintiff to see if you want to go to court and with what probable results.)

If a contract has been breached, some reasons may still keep the plaintiff from collecting any damages for the breach. These defenses range from the very technical to the very obvious, but they should always be kept in mind:

1. Statute of limitations
2. Laches
3. Misleading conduct
4. Misunderstanding and mistake
5. Fraud or duress
6. Impossibility of performance
7. Failure of consideration
8. Illegality of the contract

The Statute of Limitations and Laches

The statute of limitations restricts a party to the contract from suing to collect damages for a wrong to a certain period of time. You must start the suit within the applicable statute of limitations, which for contracts ranges from three to ten years from the date of the breach.

The exception to this rule is in the case of an old debt. If the debtor admits that the debt exists and is valid, his admission, in essence, creates a new agreement to pay the debt. In most states this admission has to be in writing, but in nine states—Connecticut, Delaware, Hawaii, Kentucky, Maryland, New Hampshire, Pennsylvania, Rhode Island, and Tennessee—it can be verbal. This exception shows that even discussing matters in dispute can result in a new agreement.

Laches is a name given to the defense that "the plaintiff waited too long to sue." Usually it is used in actions for injunctions or for specific performance. It differs from the statute of limitations in that in some cases the time period can be very short. When the courts decide that the party suing waited too long to sue, they rule that the other party would be unfairly hurt if the suit were allowed to proceed. For example, suppose you hired a contractor to build a garage onto your home, with an opening to the side. The contractor's architect made a mistake and prepared plans for a front-opening garage, which was built while you watched. One year later, you sue the contractor for breach of contract. The contractor may be able to stop the action on the basis of laches. That is, you stood by and said nothing about the mistake at a time when the contractor could have corrected it. Now, you cannot sue for a breach of contract, even though you have brought the action within the statute of limitations.

Misleading Conduct

Your own conduct may deprive you of the right to collect for a breach of contract by someone else. For example, if you misled the other party as to the quality of goods that you were selling, the courts may disallow your suit for breach of contract if the other party refuses to take the goods. The courts take the position that one party cannot benefit from its own wrongdoing.

Misunderstanding and Mistake

A misunderstanding or mistake by both parties to an agreement is also a defense to an action for breach of contract. This is because the existence of the misunderstanding or mistake means that there was no real "meeting of the minds" in the first place, and without that there was no contract.

A classic illustration of this arose almost a century ago in Michigan.

Mr. Walker, a cattle breeder, sold a prize cow, Rose 2d of Aberlone, to Mr. Sherwood, a banker. Rose was sold for $80 because both parties thought she was sterile. After the sale, but before Mr. Sherwood took possession, Mr. Walker found out that Rose was pregnant and therefore worth ten times the sale price. He refused to hand Rose over to Mr. Sherwood, who then sued. The Michigan State Supreme Court ruled that no contract existed because there was a difference between the item sold and that bargained for. The difference was not merely one of quality or degree. In essence, the parties agreed to the transfer of a sterile cow. In the words of the court, "[a] barren cow is substantially a different creature than a breeding one."

This concept does not mean, however, that one party can take advantage of the other's mistake to get the upper hand. The mistake or misunderstanding that enables one of the parties to the agreement to avoid that agreement must concern the subject matter of the agreement itself, the nature of the agreement, or the identity of the parties. The mistake must go to the heart of the deal in order for a court to rule that a contract can be avoided.

Fraud or Duress

If a contract is entered into as the result of fraud, it is not enforceable. But fraud is not the same as "puffing" or a salesperson's overemphasis on the good points of a product or service. The courts expect a certain amount of puffing. For example, the owners of a thirty-year-old building may tell a prospective buyer that it is a "good" building. After the sale the buyer finds substantial termite damage. So long as the seller did not know of the damage and actively conceal it, the buyer cannot rely on such a general statement. It is merely opinion or puffing.

The use of force or a threat of force to make a party sign an agreement similarly is a defense to an action for breach of contract. The technical reason: As with fraud and mistake, there was no "meeting of the minds," because the consent was not voluntary but secured by duress.

Impossibility of Performance

If, after the agreement has been signed, it becomes impossible for one party to perform because of circumstances beyond his control, there may be a defense to the suit for breach of contract. (However, the courts may permit rescission of the agreement on the grounds of impossibility: The party willing to perform should not be damaged by the inability of the other to perform.)

For example, impossibility would apply in a case where one party leases space in a particular building for a trade show. If the building burns down, the contract cannot be enforced against the landlord.

A different situation arises when the impossibility is considered either as being within the party's control or the party has accepted the risk of impossibility. Here impossibility is not a defense. For example, in the 1950s a major defense contractor signed a government research and development contract to design and build an instrument meeting specifications that no previous instruments had met. The contractor did not deliver the instrument and was sued for breach of contract. His defense was that the research and development contract was impossible to perform. The defense was rejected on the basis that either the contractor was aware of this risk of failure and accepted it or that he was reckless in accepting the contract.

Failure of Consideration

Failure of consideration is a more technical defense that goes to the heart of the agreement. Most often this occurs in an exchange of services. If the performance of one service is contingent on the prior performance of another service, the failure of that prior performance eliminates the agreement. The failure of the one, without an adequate excuse, excuses the failure of the other to perform. If this situation arises, you should protect your rights by indicating your willingness and ability to perform your part of the agreement. If you are not ready, willing, and able to perform, it may be you who later is accused of failure of consideration.

Illegality of the Contract

If a contract is illegal, it cannot be enforced. For example, a contract to lend money at a rate higher than the maximum legal limit for that kind of loan is usurious and therefore illegal.

A more complex problem can occur when the agreement is legal when signed but afterwards becomes illegal. Here the courts must decide on whom the risk of any loss will fall. If one party can be deemed to have assumed the risk that the agreement could become illegal, that party bears any losses resulting from its illegality. Otherwise, the courts will try as best they can to restore the parties to their positions before the contract.

WHEN PAROL EVIDENCE IS PERMITTED

The parol evidence rule is discussed in Chapter 5. Basically, this rule prevents a party from introducing oral evidence at a trial to alter the terms of a written agreement. A key exception to this rule is that such evidence can be offered to prove either that no contract was ever entered into or that the contract was admittedly entered into, but it was the result of one of the following:

1. Fraud
2. Mistake
3. Duress
4. Undue influence
5. Legal incapacity of one or both of the parties
6. Illegality of the object of the contract

Without these exceptions, no party would be able to raise these contract defenses in a case involving a written contract.

DISCOVERY

Once a lawsuit has started, the parties have a right to discovery, a procedure to obtain information from the opposing party in the case and from witnesses. The scope of discovery is quite broad. Basically, discovery can sweep the field, seeking any information that might be relevant to the case, including information that could lead to the production of evidence. The grounds on which you can object to discovery demands are limited and vary from state to state. The two most common are that the information is privileged or that the demand is overly broad and burdensome. That is, the other side is seeking to cause you vast amounts of work and costs with no real aim in mind other than to harass you. An example of privileged information would be communications between a lawyer and his client.

Discovery is usually broken down into four types:

1. Depositions
2. Written interrogatories
3. Orders for production of documents
4. Requests for admissions

Depositions

Depositions are generally regarded as the major and most effective form of discovery. In a deposition a person is questioned by lawyers from both sides. The questions and answers are transcribed and then signed by the party who was questioned under oath. Depositions are useful in finding information relevant to the case; in particular, they give leads to important witnesses and documents. They also may prevent a witness from attempting to change his or her story at the trial. The deposition can be read and the witness challenged as to the reason for a change in the evidence or testimony. The deposition of one party can be used to obtain admissions, which can be used as evidence in the trial. In the case of witnesses who are not parties to the suit, it can be used to replace their testimony of witnesses if they are unavailable for the trial.

Depositions are expensive and time-consuming. Since many actions for breach of contract involve documentary evidence rather than testimony alone, some lawyers prefer to use other discovery tools first.

Written Interrogatories

Written interrogatories are questions from one party to the other, but they are not asked of persons who are witnesses only. The questions must be answered in writing by the party to whom they were sent, and the assistance and review of a lawyer is permitted. Of course, these answers will not be spontaneous, as in a deposition. However, in answering interrogatories the party must supply information that he can obtain, even if he cannot recall it from memory. Thus the answering party is obligated to review the facts and records in order to answer completely.

Orders for Production of Documents

Requests for specific documents can be made by one party and turned over to the other side. The orders may be lists of particular documents or description of documents by type and class. The other types of discovery may produce leads to these documents.

Requests for Admissions

After a case has proceeded through other types of discovery, one party may want to clear the air and request that the other make certain admissions. Basically, this is to simplify the case. If the party requested to make the admission does so, the first party does not have to introduce evidence on the point; the admissions are enough. If the requested party refuses to make an admission and the other party introduces evidence on the point, at the end of the trial the judge may penalize the requested party if he feels that the refusal to admit was in bad faith and imposed additional costs on the requesting party.

TRIAL

Many courts have instituted pretrial proceedings in an effort to narrow the issues in pending cases or to encourage settlements. In these meetings the parties may be asked to agree on which facts are no longer in dispute and to estimate how long the trial will take so that the court can schedule it. Very often these meetings result in a partial or complete settlement of the dispute.

At a trial, if there is a jury, the lawyers for each side participate in its selection by questioning a group of prospective jurors brought in by the court clerk. Each side can reject a number of jurors without giving any reason. They can also ask the court to reject any juror whose answers indicate that he or she will not be impartial. This is called "excusing a juror." After the jury has been selected, or at the opening of the trial if there is no jury, each lawyer makes a brief opening statement. This statement outlines the client's version of the facts and explains the theory of the case so that the court and jury will understand the significance of evidence as it is presented. The party bringing the action always has the obligation to convince the court and jury of the merits of his case. This is what is meant by the plaintiff bearing the burden of proof. In the trial of a commercial dispute, this burden means the plaintiff must establish the truth of his claim by a preponderance of the evidence. Thus the plaintiff must present evidence that has a more convincing effect on the judge or jury than does the defendant's evidence.

Evidence is presented both through documents or exhibits and through the testimony of witnesses. The plaintiff's attorney calls his witnesses to the stand to testify and be cross-examined by the defendant. When all of the plaintiff's evidence has been presented, he rests his case. The defendant can then ask the court to dismiss the case because the plaintiff has failed to show evidence that he has a "cause of action"—that is, a reason to bring suit against the defendant. If this motion is denied, and it usually is, the defendant then brings its own witnesses, who can be cross-examined by the plaintiff.

A lawyer can object to a question asked of a witness for a number of reasons. If the objection is sustained, the witness is not allowed to answer. The lawyer whose position was not upheld may note an exception to the ruling, meaning that he reserves the right to attack the validity of the ruling in an appeal on the basis that the ruling was wrong and led to an erroneous result in the case.

After all the evidence has been presented, each side has the right to make a brief closing statement. In a jury trial, the judge instructs the jury on the law. The jury decides on the disputed facts, applies the law, and renders a verdict. If there is no jury, the judge renders the verdict. The verdict may dismiss the plaintiff's case, award the plaintiff some or all of the damages he sought, or order the defendant to do something or stop doing something, depending on the plaintiff's complaint.

APPEAL

Either party may appeal a verdict. Appeals are expensive primarily because of the time involved and because the appealing party must file a printed record on appeal together with an appeal brief. The brief analyzes the facts and law and asks the reviewing court to overturn the verdict.

An appeal is made only on the basis that the trial court committed errors of law, usually in allowing or disallowing evidence to be presented or in the instructions to the jury. The appeals court does not review the factual conclusions made at the trial level, unless it can be shown that these conclusions cannot be supported by *any* reasonable interpretation of the evidence presented. Appeals must be filed soon after the original trial verdict or they cannot be filed at all. Usually the party appealing the verdict will ask that the verdict be stayed—that is, not enforced—while the appeal is pending. After the appeal briefs have been filed, the appeals court may ask for an oral argument before it by the lawyers for both sides. Today, oral arguments are not requested in every case. An oral argument is an argument on the record of evidence introduced before the trial court. No new evidence is introduced in an appeal.

ENFORCING JUDGMENTS

When a trial is over, unless there is an appeal, you will have a verdict or a judgment. If the plaintiff won, he will probably be awarded money, or an order will require or prohibit some action by the defendant. If the defendant won, the plaintiff wins nothing from his complaint.

If you are awarded a sum of money, it is up to you to collect it from the defendant. If the defendant does not pay voluntarily, the most common way to collect is to get an execution. The court issues a document commanding an officer, usually a sheriff or constable, to seize some asset owned by the losing party. The property can be salary, a bank account, a car, or personal property. If necessary, the officer is ordered to sell that property at a public sale and use the proceeds to pay the winning party's judgment. But first, you have to tell the sheriff where the losing party's property or money is. If you do not know, you can file a "supplemental proceeding," which requires that party to appear in court and answer your questions about the location of his property. Or you may be able to serve a subpoena on any other person who might know about the loser's financial status.

If the plaintiff's judgment is an order forcing the defendant to do something, the judgment (sometimes called a decree) is aimed at the defendant personally. If the defendant fails to obey it, he may be held in contempt of court and punished by a fine or imprisonment.

Most judgments award "costs" to the winning party, but this does not mean that all of the costs associated with the lawsuit are paid for by the loser. Only certain costs provided by statute or court rule are paid, generally out-of-pocket disbursements related to the service of process and the costs of the trial. They do not include the attorney's fees of the winning party. The costs awarded by the court are usually nominal when compared with the total costs of the lawsuit.

A judgment may also provide for interest, if the judgment is for money. The rate of interest is set by local law and generally begins from the date the case was filed, although sometimes it can extend back to the date the agreement was breached. In a case that takes a long time to reach trial, this can be a significant item.

Small Claims Court

Resorting to small claims courts to resolve money disputes arising from business agreements is becoming more and more common. If you think the payment terms in an agreement have been violated, you should consider using these courts, particularly if the amount involved is small and you want to resolve it quickly. The maximum amount of money you can collect in a small claims court is limited, for example, to $750. The amount varies from state to state. If your claim is larger, you can either sue in a higher court, or you can decide to accept only this amount and give up any claim to the balance. You cannot divide one claim and file several suits, each less than $750, to collect all of it.

In some states small claims court is known by another name, such as Magistrate's Court, Justice Court, or the Justice of the Peace. What they have in common is that you can begin an action for breach of contract and seek money damages on your own and at a moderate cost. Information on small claims courts and their rules can be obtained from state consumer-protection agencies, from the courts themselves, or from state and local bar associations.

The rules of evidence used in regular civil courts are not strictly applied in small claims court. However, do not assume that you can go to the court, tell your story, and win. You must review your case and be just as prepared as though you were going into a regular court. You cannot, for example, count on repeating what a third party said; you should ask that witness to testify. When the case comes before a judge, you explain why you feel that the defendant owes you money, presenting any evidence or witnesses you have to help prove the case. After hearing the two sides, the judge will decide who is right. Usually all you can get in a small claims court is money; the court cannot give restitution or specific performance, for example. If you lose your case, in some states you cannot appeal that decision.

Some small claims courts are so much "people's courts" that they do not permit parties bringing an action or defending one to use a lawyer. However, that does not usually prevent either side from having an attorney who is a regular employee of the company appear and run the case. In some states you can have a lawyer represent you. In others, such as California, you can consult with a lawyer before trial, but neither party can have a lawyer represent him in court.

A small-claims action can be particularly effective when you have a contract dispute with a large business. The case is heard quickly and informally, which is to the advantage of the smaller businessperson. Some businesses will not even send a representative to defend itself in small claims court because the costs to them are so high compared with the amount at stake. Instead, they will default, meaning that they will not put on a case. After you make your case to the presiding judge, including showing how much you have lost, the judge can enter a judgment against the absent party. Remember that you must be able to prove your case, even if your opponent fails to show up. Also remember that the court cannot award you more money than you said you were owed in your complaint. Once you have a judgment, you must still enforce it. In some states this may mean recording it in another court if the defendant does not pay promptly. The operations of small claims courts vary from state to state, but the following sections outline fairly typical practices and procedures.

WHERE TO FILE THE SUIT

The judges of small claims courts may also be members of other courts. If they are, they set aside certain days and times to hold small claims court hearings. Usually, you file your suit at the court located in the district where the defendant lives or where the business involved is located. For example, if you live in Sacramento, California, but you bought a defective tool from a store in San Francisco, you would have to sue in San Francisco. If the person you are suing owes money under a contract, you may be able to file the suit in the district where the contract was entered into, rather than in the district where the person lives. If the defendant is a corporation, you may be able to sue wherever it does a substantial amount of business. If you are not sure where to file, ask the clerk at the local court.

The next step is to obtain the proper form for filing the suit from the court clerk in the district where you are going to file. On the form, along with your name and address, give the name and address of each person you are suing. You may sue more than one person if you are not sure who is responsible. If you are suing a business, you must find out the full legal name of the individual or individuals responsible for the business and sue them. If the business is a corporation, you have to use its full and correct name. This information may be available from a city license bureau, a Better Business Bureau, or the Secretary of State's office in the case of a corporation.

You also have to fill in the amount of money you claim and a brief statement about the nature of the claim. The clerk then prepares an order to be served on the defendants, telling them that they are being sued and that they must appear in court if they want to defend themselves against your claim. There are several alternatives for serving the order, but you do not serve it yourself. Usually the clerk sends the order by certified mail and requests a return receipt. You pay the clerk a mailing fee for each defendant. You can also have a marshal, sheriff, or constable serve the order, but this requires a larger fee. In some states any person over the age of eighteen who is not involved in the case may serve the order by delivering it to the defendant personally. The person serving signs a proof of service, which the clerk will give him, stating that the order was delivered. This form has to be returned to the clerk well before the trial.

PREPARING FOR THE TRIAL

When you file the claim, the clerk may be able to tell you when the trial is scheduled. Otherwise, he will notify you later. In the meantime, gather together all important papers and documents, including contracts, correspondence, bills, receipts, and cancelled checks. Bring the originals of these to the court on the day of the trial. Also, bring any witnesses who can testify on your behalf. For example, a friend who was with you when you bought the new tool and saw that it was defective could be a witness, if you are suing the store where you bought the tool. If witnesses will come to court voluntarily, all you have to do is tell them the date and time of the trial and make sure that they appear. If they do not come, you cannot merely tell the court what they would have said and expect a ruling in your favor.

In a few small claims courts you may be able to skip the use of an expert witness to establish the value of merchandise and repairs. This can be done in New York City, for example, by getting an itemized paid bill or invoice certified and verified by the person who did the work and gave the bill. To have the bill certified that person makes a sworn statement in front of a notary public in a form prepared by the small claims court. This is not the practice everywhere, so check with the court clerk before you decide to use this method.

If you believe that a person could be a witness but may not testify voluntarily, ask the clerk how to get a subpoena. A subpoena is an order by the court demanding that the witness appear at the trial. This must be served on the witness in person, not by mail. Witnesses may demand a set fee and mileage for attending the hearing. If they do, you must pay this, sometimes in advance. If you win the case, the judge may add these costs to the amount the defendant must pay you.

Once the defendant receives the order notifying him that you are suing, he may decide to settle out of court. If you agree, you must arrange with the clerk for a dismissal of the case. You will still probably have to pay the fees associated with serving the original complaint.

In some major metropolitan areas, such as New York City, the small claims court may ask if the parties will agree to arbitration. This can usually be done with less waiting than would be involved in a trial. In those states the arbitration may be final, and there may be no right to appeal. If one or both of the parties objects to arbitration, the case will proceed to trial.

A few days before trial, check with the clerk to make sure that everything for the trial is in order, particularly that he has all the papers in his file to permit the judge to hear the case. If you cannot attend the trial on the day set, notify the clerk at once to arrange for a postponement. If there is an emergency, have someone go to the court and ask for a continuance. If you do not do this, the court will proceed and, in your absence, dismiss the case.

THE DAY OF THE TRIAL

Come to the court early and check with the clerk to see where the case will be heard. In busy courts a calendar may be posted outside each courtroom or the clerk's office listing the cases to be heard in each courtroom that day. The cases are not always heard in the order listed. If your case is not listed as it should be, check with the clerk or an officer of the court.

The judge usually explains the court's procedures to those present for all cases. If you do not understand them, ask questions before your case begins. The court clerk will announce your case when it is ready to be heard. You and the other parties will then come forward and be sworn in by the clerk. If you are the plaintiff, you begin first. Tell why you are suing the defendant. The judge may ask questions to obtain more information. You should not argue the case unless and until the judge asks you to do so. Your witnesses will also be sworn in to tell their story. You and the other party may have a chance to ask questions of the witness, and the judge may also do so. Keep your testimony brief and to the point. If you have documents or papers that you think the judge should know about and are part of the case, mention them in your testimony and give them to the judge.

After hearing both sides, the judge often will give his decision right there. Sometimes he will want to think it over, examine a particular law, and review the documents more carefully. He will then take the case "under submission" or "advisement." The court will tell the parties later in writing about the judge's decision. Most courts must give their decisions within a week.

If the judge rules in your favor, he will either award you what you asked for, or he will award you less if he thinks your request was too high. The judge cannot give you more than you requested. You should ask that you receive your court costs if you win. The judge decides this; it is not automatic. In some states you must make this request in the papers beginning the lawsuit.

If the plaintiff does not appear, the judge may dismiss the case; no money is awarded. If the defendant does not appear, the judge will still take your testimony. At the close of your testimony, the judge may rule that the defendant is in default and award you the money you asked for.

Before trial, you may receive a notice from the defendant that he has filed a cross-claim against you. This means he believes that you owe him money as a result of the same incident or contract, and he will try to collect it at the same trial. The judge will hear both cases at the same time.

IF YOU ARE THE DEFENDANT

If you get an order to appear in small claims court, you probably already know the nature of the claim being filed against you. If you do not, find out about it immediately. If you think the claim is justified or want to avoid a trial, you can settle it out of court to minimize court costs. Even if there is some merit to the claim, you may prefer to go to trial to challenge any part of the plaintiff's complaint that you feel is unjustified.

If the plaintiff's case is unjustified, attend the trial and bring any evidence or witnesses to help in your defense. If you have a claim against the plaintiff arising from the same incident or contract, file a cross-claim. The cross-claim is filed with the same court where the plaintiff began his action. It must be served on the plaintiff well before the trial date. How far in advance is a matter of local law. Your cross-claim cannot be larger than the amount you could sue for as a plaintiff.

Whether or not you file a cross-claim, you have the same rights as the plaintiff to bring evidence to support your side of the case, to bring witnesses with you, and to subpoena a witness who will not come voluntarily.

IF YOU LOSE

If you are the defendant and lose the lawsuit, usually you have a right to appeal the decision to a higher court within a short time from the entry of the judgment. While the case is on appeal, you do not have to make any payments on the judgment against you. If you are the plaintiff and you lose the suit, in some states, such as California, you can go no further. In others, such as Pennsylvania, you also have a right to appeal the suit to a higher court. In that court, whether you are appealing the decision against the plaintiff or the defendant, the case is usually heard again from the beginning. This appeal results in a new trial. In the higher court each side may be represented by counsel. Since that court is a regular civil trial court and does not apply the rules of a small claims court, you should have a lawyer represent you.

HOW DO YOU COLLECT AFTER THE TRIAL?

If the judge decides that you were right and awards you some or all of the money you asked for, the clerk enters a judgment against the losing party. This judgment may specify whether this money is to be paid all at once or in installments. The small claims court, like any other court, is not a collection agency. It does not obtain the money for the winning party, but it will supply documents and orders to help a winning party collect. If the defendant did not appear in court, or if he refuses to pay, you can go to the court for help. The clerk will give you a "writ of execution," which operates just like one obtained after a regular trial.

As the winning party, you may ask the court to order the loser to pay your court costs and all related fees before and after the hearing. You may have to file a memorandum listing the costs you incurred with the clerk. Be sure to list all costs in bringing the action and also the costs incurred in trying to collect the judgment.

Resolving Disputes Without Litigation

In a business agreement the parties can handle potential disputes in two ways. They can insert a liquidated-damages clause in the contract, or provide that any unresolved disputes will be settled by arbitration.

LIQUIDATED DAMAGES

If a liquidated-damages clause has been inserted in the contract, and one party breaches the contract, he agrees to pay a set amount of damages to the other party. The original purpose of this clause was to solve the problem when the court was unable to decide how much a party had been injured by the breach of the other party.

Liquidated-damages clauses often spawn more litigation than they prevent, however. After these clauses were generally accepted, some parties to business agreements went to the extreme and inserted liquidated-damages clauses of high amounts to prevent the other party from breaching the contract by the threat of an onerous fine. The courts decided they would not enforce what they regarded as penalty clauses, but only "true" liquidated-damages clauses. In general, the courts will seek to determine whether, at the signing of the contract, the damages agreed on were reasonably related to the foreseeable losses that could be incurred by each party. They will not enforce damages clauses that may constitute a penalty or a direct threat to the livelihood of one of the parties. In practice, this means that the parties must review the major potential breaches of contract in advance and assign a dollar value to them during contract negotiations. Because this is difficult to do in negotiations, these clauses are few and far between. They are more common in commercial agreements where commodities or financial options are involved because the parties can more easily estimate potential losses in good faith at the beginning of the contract. These good-faith estimates are generally upheld.

The courts are reluctant to enforce liquidated-damages clauses for a personal services agreement for some of the reasons given in the older specific-performance cases; they will not participate in what they see as coercion through contracts. Some courts state that they will not engage in violations of the constitutional amendment against slavery by forcing people to perform contracts against their will. This overstates the law, but it should clearly indicate to the parties that there are limits to the use of penalties such as liquidated-damages clauses.

ARBITRATION

Controversies arising from commercial agreements seldom involve major legal issues; usually they concern evaluation of facts and interpretation of contract terms. Consequently, when differences arise from day-to-day commercial relations, the parties may prefer to settle them privately and informally in order to encourage a continuing relationship. This is why many businesses use commercial arbitration.

In arbitration, disputes are submitted for decision by a panel of individuals instead of by a judge. Arbitration usually occurs in two situations: (1) the parties agree in the contract to submit any future disputes to arbitration, and (2) the parties involved in a current dispute agree to avoid a lawsuit and submit that dispute to arbitration. The kinds of disputes that can go to arbitration are limited only by the terms of the arbitration agreement between the parties.

If the parties have an arbitration clause in their business agreement they will probably use the American Arbitration Association (AAA) to carry out the arbitration, although this is not necessary. Some contract clauses specifically provide for arbitration by the AAA under its rules. If the parties want to provide for this in advance, they should use the arbitration clause included in Forms in the Appendixes.

Arbitration has been used increasingly in recent years for several reasons. First, crowded court calendars make it profitable to find quick ways to resolve disputes without resorting to the judicial process. Second, the AAA has undertaken major efforts to educate businesspeople about arbitration's benefits and effectiveness. Third, arbitration provides a decision by experts in the area in dispute. Finally, more than three-fourths of the states have passed specific laws recognizing arbitration by upholding arbitration agreements as valid and enforceable, whether the agreements were entered into before or at the time a dispute arose.

Parties also may provide by special agreement that, so long as they fulfill the terms of the agreement, the results of the arbitration and its award will be kept confidential. Arbitration proceedings usually are held in private and are not a matter of public record. Thus arbitration provides an additional level of flexibility, particularly when the parties may be disclosing sensitive commercial or business information.

How Arbitration Works

The rules and procedures of the AAA's Commercial Arbitration Tribunal, which administers a large part of all commercial arbitrations, provide a good model for understanding how arbitration works. If arbitration is not conducted by the AAA, the parties may have to adopt rules on how disputes will be handled in the arbitration. For that reason alone, many parties will refer all disputes to the AAA, if they are not of major financial significance, and if they agree to its rules in advance.

The first step in beginning arbitration is to see if the agreement has a future-disputes arbitration clause, or, if arbitration was not provided for in advance, if there is an agreement to submit a current dispute to arbitration. Included in the Appendix is a copy of the AAA's Demand for Arbitration form, based on a typical contract clause to submit all future disputes to arbitration. Also included is a Submission to Arbitration form, prepared by the AAA as a model. This agreement is used for contracts that do not include an arbitration clause; the parties may agree nonetheless to submit their dispute to arbitration under the AAA rules. The AAA supplies these forms on request.

Regardless of the form of the agreement to arbitrate, notifying the AAA and the other party of the claim is all that is required to begin arbitration. On receiving the initiating papers, the AAA assigns the case to its tribunal administrator, who assists both sides in all procedural matters until an award is made. The AAA charges an administrative fee based on the amount of any claim and counterclaim. The fee is payable at the time of the filing, and it is paid by both parties under the AAA rules.

Unless the parties request another method, the AAA follows its basic system for selecting the arbitrator. On receiving the demand for arbitration or a submission agreement, the tribunal administrator gives each party seven days to review a list of proposed arbitrators. They may cross out any names they object to and number the remaining names in order of preference. Information about potential arbitrators is given on request. The tribunal administrator selects the arbitrator from the mutual choices. If the parties do not have a mutual choice, additional lists may be requested. If the parties cannot agree on an arbitrator, the AAA will appoint one. In no case will an arbitrator be chosen whose name was crossed out by either party.

Under some arbitration clauses, each party to a dispute appoints one arbitrator, and the two select a third arbitrator from AAA panels according to the same procedure. To avoid the danger that a compromise award may have to be rendered for the sake of a majority, the parties sometimes provide—and the AAA recommends—that the third arbitrator be permitted to render the award alone when a unanimous award is not possible. This may be done by the parties in their agreement to arbitrate or in a later written agreement.

Arbitration hearings are less formal than court trials, and they do not follow strict rules of evidence. They hear all the material evidence but determine what is relevant. Thus arbitrators accept evidence that judges may not allow.

The complaining party usually proceeds first at the hearing, but the burden of proof is not on one side more than on another. After both sides present all their evidence, the arbitrator closes the hearing. He must rule on each claim and counterclaim submitted and render an award within thirty days, unless the arbitration agreement provides for a different time period. If the arbitration board consists of more than one arbitrator, the decision of a majority is binding. Once an arbitration award is made, either party can ask a court to confirm the award. Confirmation means that the arbitration award has the same effect as any court decision and can be enforced just as a court's judgment can.

The parties can appeal the award only on the grounds that the arbitrator exceeded his authority. This means, in practice, that the arbitrator ruled on an issue that was not actually before the panel.

MEDIATION

Mediation usually is not regarded as a true remedy for breach of contract because when it is over, there is no guarantee that the dispute is resolved. Mediation brings in another party to attempt to work out an amicable settlement between the two parties of the dispute. The mediator should be someone who is trusted by each party, but not someone who is aligned too closely with one or the other.

Although mediation is often confused with arbitration, it is not the same because the recommendations of the mediator are not binding. It gives the parties a chance to review their cases and communicate their differences to a detached third party who has not participated in the transaction. It permits each party to a dispute to make his case and air his grievances without souring an important commercial relationship by resorting to more formal procedures. If the parties use a mediator properly, they may be able to solve their problems by entering into a new or amended agreement, perhaps making some adjustment in the terms of compensation or performance.

MINITRIALS

The minitrial is a new and as yet relatively untried procedure that may be useful in solving business agreement disputes. It falls somewhere between mediation and arbitration. As currently envisioned, a panel of three individuals—a management representative from each side and a neutral adviser—would hear the dispute. The management representatives must come with settlement authority. The neutral adviser is usually a judge, chosen by mutual agreement of the parties. The parties agree in advance to the ground rules for the hearing. These rules may be custom designed for each dispute.

THE DISPUTES DECISION TREE

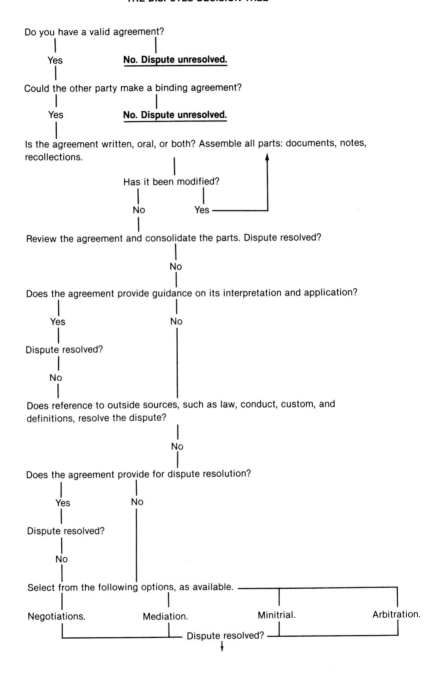

Do you have a valid agreement?

Yes   **No. Dispute unresolved.**

Could the other party make a binding agreement?

Yes   **No. Dispute unresolved.**

Is the agreement written, oral, or both? Assemble all parts: documents, notes, recollections.

Has it been modified?

No   Yes

Review the agreement and consolidate the parts. Dispute resolved?

No

Does the agreement provide guidance on its interpretation and application?

Yes   No

Dispute resolved?

No

Does reference to outside sources, such as law, conduct, custom, and definitions, resolve the dispute?

No

Does the agreement provide for dispute resolution?

Yes   No

Dispute resolved?

No

Select from the following options, as available.

Negotiations.   Mediation.   Minitrial.   Arbitration.

Dispute resolved?

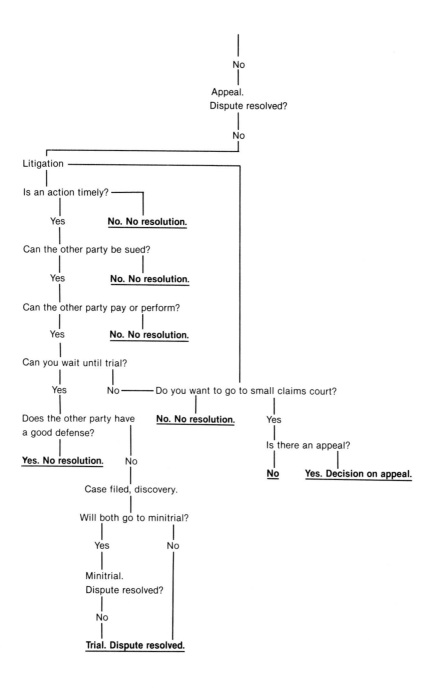

At the minitrial, lawyers for each side present a concise version of the case. To keep the proceedings short, as much of the case as possible is prepared on paper and submitted to the panel before the hearing. Typically, the majority of the witnesses will not be present; their testimony will be presented through depositions or affidavits. After the presentations the two managers meet privately and try to work out a settlement. If they cannot reach one, the neutral adviser must write an opinion on how he or she believes the case would be decided in court. The rules may provide that the neutral adviser will give a verbal opinion at the end of the hearing and/or after the negotiations. The opinion of the neutral adviser is not binding as in a trial or arbitration hearing.

Advocates of minitrials argue that after the parties to the disputes see how the case may be resolved, they have a greater incentive to settle and a fairly narrow target to aim for. An additional argument has been made that, if a company advocates a lawsuit after hearing from the neutral adviser that it will probably lose in court, it may well face difficulties with its stockholders.

The advocates of the minitrial argue that it has certain benefits over traditional trials:

It is fast

It brings matters in dispute to the attention of senior management in a large company, which may not be the same in a routine case

It is less expensive than a full-scale trial

It provides a confrontation between the parties that may be necessary to break the deadlock

It can be completely confidential

It is effective in resolving disputes where there are predominately questions of fact, or questions of fact and law, such as patent infringement or product liability

By enhancing negotiations, the final result may better serve each party, unlike a trial, where the judgment ends the dispute but may not resolve the underlying cause of the problem

The disadvantages of minitrials lie both in the lack of experience in their use and with the circumstances under which they are used. To date, only one minitrial has been reported in which the neutral adviser was required to write a formal opinion. In all others reported the parties worked out a settlement. Thus it is unknown how it will work in practice in a wide variety of cases.

Because a minitrial is inexpensive only relative to the costs of a trial, it is probably useful only in complex, expensive lawsuits. Further, the decision of the neutral adviser is not binding. One party can dig in his heels after receiving the decision, even though he sees a probable defeat. In fact, he may do so *because* he sees a defeat.

If the parties are able to agree to a minitrial, it would seem that they could either negotiate a settlement or submit to binding arbitration. A minitrial can occur only if both parties agree.

Finally, there is the question of obtaining a neutral adviser with a judicial background. Clearly, you cannot expect to hire a judge from the same court where the case is pending or might be tried. In some states, and in the case of federal judges, it may be improper for a current judge to accept such an assignment. This leaves you with retired judges. The odds are that they are with law firms, so their services will be costly. Thus a minitrial may be a costly proceeding, particularly when the lawyer's preparatory time and stenographic services are included.

Appendixes

Checklists

Action Verbs to Be Used for Passive Verb Forms

Don't Write	*Write*
give consideration to	consider
give recognition to	recognize
have knowledge of	know
have need of	need
in the determination of	to determine
is applicable	applies
is dependent on	depends on
is in attendance at	attends
make application	apply
make payment	pay
make provision for	provide for

Words and Expressions to Avoid

above (as an adjective)
above-mentioned
afore-mentioned
aforementioned
afore-granted
aforesaid
before-mentioned
henceforth
herein
hereinafter
hereinbefore
hereinunto
hereunto
premises (in the sense of "matters
    previously stated or set forth")
said (as a substitute for *the, that,* or
    those)

same (as a substitute for *it, he,*
    him, and so forth)
thenceforth
thereunto
therewith
to wit
under-mentioned
unto
whatsoever
whensoever
whereof
wheresoever
whosoever
within-named
witnesseth

Preferred Expressions

Don't Write	*Write*
accorded	given
adequate number of	enough
admit of	allow
afforded	given
all of the	all the
along the lines of	like
ameliorate	improve
approximately	about
attempt (as a verb)	try
at the time	when
by means of	by
calculate	compute
category	kind, class, group
cause it to be done	have it done, do it
cease	stop
commence	begin, start
complete (as a verb)	finish
consequence	result
contiguous to	next to
corporation organized and existing under the laws of New York	New York Corporation
deem	consider
does not operate to	does not
during such times as	while
during the course of	during
effectuate	carry out
encourage	urge
endeavor (as a verb)	try
enter into a contract with	contract with
evince	show

Don't Write	Write
excessive number of	too many
expedite	hasten, speed up
expend	spend
expiration	end
facilitate	ease
feasible	possible
for the duration of	during
for the purpose of	for
for the reason that	because
forthwith	immediately
hereafter	after this . . . takes effect
heretofore	before this . . . takes effect
in case	if
in cases which	when, where
indicate	show
inform	tell
initial	first
in lieu of	instead of, in place of
in order to	to
inquire	ask
in sections 2034 to 2044 inclusive	in sections 2034–2044
institute	begin
interrogate	question
in the event that	if
in the interest of	for
in the neighborhood of	about
is able to	can
is authorized	may
is binding upon	binds
is empowered	may
is unable to	cannot
it is directed	shall

Don't Write	Write
necessitate	require
no later than May 1, 1982	before May 1, 1982
obtain	get
occasion (as a verb)	cause
of a technical nature	technical
on his own application	at his request
on the part of	by
party of the first part	(the party's name)
preserve	keep
prior	earlier
prior to	before
proceed	go, go ahead
prosecute its business	carry on its business
provision of law	law
pursuant to	under
remainder	rest
render (in the sense of "cause to be")	make
render (in the sense of "give")	give
retain	keep
subsequent to	after
suffer (in the sense of "permit")	permit
summon	send for, call
supplement	add to
the manner in which	how
to the effect that	how
until such time as	until
with reference to	for, about
with the result that	so that

Pairs of Words That Have the Same Effect

any and all

authorized and empowered

by and with

each and all

each and every

final and conclusive

from and after

full and complete

full force and effect

null and void

order and direct

over and above

sole and exclusive

type and kind

unless and until

Gender-Specific Terms

Don't Write	*Write*
businessman	business person, executive, member of the business community, business manager
crewman	crew member
draftsman	drafter
female, male	person, individual
foreman	supervisor
man	person, human, human being
manhours	hours worked
manmade	artificial, of human origin, synthetic, manufactured
manpower	personnel, workforce, worker, human resources
per man	per person
six-man commission	six-member commission
to man (as in "operate")	to staff
trained manpower	trained workforce, staff, personnel
wife, wives, husband, husbands	spouse, spouses
workman's compensation	worker's compensation

Computer Equipment and Services Contracts

I. Service Agreement
  a. Warranty period
  b. Coverage options
  c. Pricing/payment alternatives
  d. Response time
  e. Backup equipment
  f. Major versus minor malfunctions: definitions, coverage

II. Hardware Equipment Agreement
  a. Purchase options
  b. Tax credits
  c. Delivery
  d. Support and installation
  e. Criteria for acceptance

III. Turnkey Computer Agreement
  a. Expansion of equipment
  b. Upgrading of the system
  c. Computer languages
  d. Degradation

IV. General Considerations
  a. Future attachment of third-party equipment
  b. Rights to source codes
  c. Modification of programs
  d. Maintenance of hardware and software
  e. Backup provisions
  f. Telecommunications
  g. Enhancing software
  h. Schedule for installation
  i. Testing and acceptance
  j. Terms for payment

Partnership Contracts

The answers to the following questions will influence the contents of any partnership agreement:

A. The parties
1. Full names and addresses.
2. Financial position of each partner.
B. Proposed name of the partnership
1. What name will the business use?
2. What if that name cannot be used?
C. The nature of the business
1. What will the partnership be doing?
2. Will there be a distinction in business activities of the partners within the partnership?
D. New or existing business
1. Is the partnership formed to carry on an existing business or to serve a new one?
2. If the former, will the partnership assume the liabilities of the old business?
E. Location of the business
1. Will the partnership have offices in a state other than the one where it will be created?
2. Will it do any business in that state or any other state?
F. Term of the partnership
1. Most partnerships are indefinite in terms of their duration. Does the nature of the business require a fixed period of existence?
2. When will the partnership begin its business?
G. Capital contributions
1. Will the contributions be in money or in property? If the latter, what is it and what is it worth?
2. Will service contributions be made? If so, what? When?
3. Is any property being loaned to the partnership by a partner?
4. When will the capital contributions take place?
5. What percent of the total capital will each partner own?

6. Can a partner make additional contributions or withdraw a part of his initial contribution?

H. Distributions and salaries
1. Will any partner receive a salary for services to the partnership?
2. Will any partner be guaranteed a minimum return of a share of the gross or net profits?
3. Will any partner receive interest on his contribution?
4. What is the percentage distribution of net or gross profits to each partner?
5. When and how will the distribution be made?

I. Time devoted to the business
1. Will all partners devote full time to the business?
2. Is there a limit on the amount and nature of outside activities and employment?

J. Management and control
1. Will the partners have an equal voice in management? Will one or more have a preferred position?
2. Will there be an executive partner to oversee the business?
3. Should the partners be prohibited from or limited in their power to perform certain acts, such as mortgaging property, lending money, or entering into any transaction involving more than a certain percentage of the partnership assets?
4. Will there be regular meetings of the partnership? Where and when?

K. Accounting and banking
1. What will be the partnership's fiscal year?
2. Will there be a drawing account for each partner?
3. How are checks to be signed?
4. What bank will have the partnership accounts? What kinds of accounts?
5. Where are the books to be kept? Who will keep them?

L. Voting and disputes
1. Should voting be by a majority of partners, a majority of interest, or a majority of capital contribution?
2. What happens in the case of a deadlock? Should there be arbitration?

M. New partners
   1. Can new partners be admitted to the partnership?
   2. If so, when and under what terms?
N. Termination on a partner's death, resignation, disability, or expulsion
   1. Should provision be made for expulsion of a partner?
   2. Should a stated time period of disability be grounds for expulsion?
   3. Should notification be required of a partner's intention to withdraw? How long and of what kind?
   4. Should there be a penalty for a partner who withdraws from the partnership in violation of the agreement?
   5. Will the partnership continue following the death, resignation, disability, or expulsion of a partner? If so, will the remaining partners have the option to buy the interest of that partner? In what shares?
   6. How is the value of the interest of a departing partner to be determined?
   7. Should a departing partner be subject to a noncompetition agreement or a trade-secrets agreement?
O. Dissolution of the partnership
   1. The partnership will continue until its affairs are completed. Which partner should act as the liquidator of the business during that time?
   2. Most statutes provide a procedure for winding up affairs on dissolution of a partnership. Do you want something different?

Distributor's Contract with a Manufacturer

1. *What products are covered?* The parties should clearly identify the specific products covered or if all are to be covered. What about products that are later withdrawn and for which there is no identified replacement? Does the distributor get a replacement product of a different type?

2. *Manufacturer's price.* What notice must the manufacturer give when it changes prices? How far in advance? Is there any limit on the number or range of changes in any one year? Who pays for freight and taxes on the goods?

3. *Distributor's price.* The manufacturer cannot dictate or control the distributor's resale price. Are there any suggested prices? Are the goods premarked? What about special price promotions advertised by the manufacturer? Does the distributor have to go along?

4. *Territory.* The manufacturers will seek to define the sales territory and restrict the distributor from selling outside of that area. Does the distributor have an exclusive in that territory? How many other distributors may be appointed, and for what parts of the area?

5. *Excluded accounts.* Some manufacturers reserve certain accounts for themselves and retain the right to sell directly to them, even if they are within the distributor's territory. The rule now is that the manufacturer can do this for certain categories of accounts, but not for named accounts.

6. *Term of the agreement.* How long is the agreement? What happens after it expires? For example, will the manufacturer continue to service the distributor's customers, and can the distributor return the goods it has on hand? Under what terms can it be cancelled by either party?

7. *Warranties and product liability.* How are these responsibilities allocated between the two parties? Does either have to obtain and keep insurance? What happens if the distributor modifies the product? Who is responsible in the event of a recall situation?

8. *Governing law.* The parties may want to specify what law applies to the contract if they are in different states.

Real Property Sale

A. The purchase price
B. When that price is due and under what conditions
   1. Interest rate
   2. Contingent on availability of financing?
C. The property being sold
   1. Name and address
   2. Full legal description. You cannot assume that a person owns all the property that he seems to own. Some of it may be rented. Also, other persons may have a special legal interest in the property.
   3. List of all fixtures and personal property being transferred
D. The type of deed and evidence of title that the buyer will receive. This can be important for financing.
E. The conditions, if any, under which the buyer can withdraw and get some or all of the deposit back
   1. The conditions
   2. The amount returned
F. Any guarantee made about the condition of the buildings or use that can be made of them
   1. Insurability of buildings affected
   2. Zoning restrictions may prevent you from using the building for something new or even from expanding its present use
G. The date when the buyer can take possession of the land and building
   1. Penalty clauses for late delivery
   2. Removal of all of previous owner's possessions
H. The manner in which outstanding obligations pertaining to the property will be allocated
   1. Taxes
   2. Utility bills
   3. Fuel stored on the premises
   4. Liens
 I. The signature of the legal owner(s). This should include both spouses, even if the land is in one name only. If signed by a corporate officer, get a certified copy of the directors' resolution giving him authority to sign this.

Small Claims Court

1. Determine the full legal name and address of the person or business you want to sue. This will help you to determine where you can sue them.

2. Visit the clerk of the small claims court, fill out the form he will give you and pay the fee.

3. Arrange for the papers to be served on the defendant. For a fee, the clerk can arrange for mailing or can arrange personal service. The fee for this will vary.

4. While waiting for the trial date, prepare the case. Get originals of all important documents and plan the testimony. Contact all potential witnesses and arrange for them to come with you to the trial, or get a subpoena from the clerk for any witnesses who will not come voluntarily.

5. Go to the court house early and ask the clerk where the case will be heard. When you arrive at the courtroom, check the calendar to see if the case is listed.

6. Give your testimony, presenting only the facts. Be brief. Submit to the judge all papers and documents you think will help your case.

7. If you win, ask the defendant for the money awarded in the judgment.

8. If you have difficulty in collecting the judgment, ask the clerk to assist you.

Forms

Hourly-Fee Retainer Letter (including terms of representation and fees)

[Letterhead]

Mr. Adam Smith
14 Main Street
Client, Pennsylvania 19000

Dear Mr. Smith:

Confirming our meeting today, I am pleased that your company, Smith Supply Corporation, has retained our firm to represent it in matters pertaining to the formation of a subsidiary to provide repair services.

As we discussed, there are several areas in which our firm will assist your company. First, we will review the lease you have given us. Second, we will incorporate the new subsidiary under a name to be chosen by you. Please send us this name as soon as you have chosen it so that we can file the necessary papers. Finally, we will draft contract forms to be used by this new company and its customers.

As we agreed, our firm will not handle the tax aspects of your business or of its subsidiary, since you have already retained the services of a tax accountant. We will contact your accountant to obtain her directions as to the final details of the incorporation.

Our fee is $50 per hour for services performed by me or by any other partner in the firm. You will be billed $35 per hour for the time of any associate of the firm, and $20 per hour for the time of any paralegal. Our expenses on your behalf will also be billed. It is the firm's policy to send itemized statements monthly. Thank you for your retainer check of $250 representing the estimated incorporation expenses. It will be applied toward your first statement.

Please contact me if you have any questions. On behalf of the firm, we are pleased to be representing you.

Sincerely yours,

[Firm name]

by_____
                [a partner]

Contingent-Fee Retainer Letter (including terms of representation and fees)

[Letterhead]

Mr. Adam Smith
14 Main Street
Client, Pennsylvania 19000

Dear Mr. Smith:

Confirming our meeting today, I am pleased that you have retained our firm to represent you in matters relating to your recent accident.

As we discussed, there are several areas in which our firm will assist you. First, we will investigate the circumstances surrounding the accident, including reviewing insurance, police, fire, doctor, and hospital reports, interviewing witnesses, and ascertaining if other persons were injured at the same time. Second, the firm will make a tentative recommendation as to the value of your losses, and at your direction, we will begin negotiations to see if this claim can be settled. Third, if the firm is able to secure a settlement offer, we will discuss it with you and evaluate the merits of the offer and the need for additional action. Finally, if there is no settlement offer, or if the offer is unacceptable to you, we will represent you in litigating your claim.

Our fee will be one-third of any recovery prior to litigation, and one-half of any recovery that results after litigation has begun. Expenses incurred by the firm on your behalf must be paid even if there is no recovery. It is our policy to send itemized statements monthly.

If this is in accord with your understanding of our meeting, please sign the original of this letter and return it to me in the enclosed envelope. I have enclosed a copy for your files.

If you have any questions, please contact me. On behalf of the firm, we are pleased to be representing you.

Sincerely yours,

[Firm name]

by_____
            [a partner]

Accepted and agreed to
_____ , 1982

_____
Adam Smith

Employment Agreement

EMPLOYMENT AGREEMENT made this 1st day of January, 1983, between _____, a New Jersey corporation and _____ (the "Executive").

The parties hereto hereby agree as follows:

1. *Employment and Term.*

1.1 The word "Company" as used herein shall include _____ and its subsidiaries, affiliates, and other related companies.

1.2 The Company agrees to employ the Executive, and the Executive agrees to work for the Company for a term commencing with the date hereof and continuing through December 31, 1983, unless employment is sooner terminated as provided herein.

2. *Salary, Bonus, and Employee Benefits.*

2.1 The Board of Directors of the Company, in reasonable exercise of its discretion, shall annually set or adjust the salary of or grant bonuses to the Executive during the term hereof, taking into consideration the performance of the Executive, the success of the Company, increases in salaries paid to other executives, and bonuses paid to such executives and other relevant factors.

2.2 The Executive shall be entitled to participate in all insurance and fringe benefits applicable to other executives of the Company.

3. *Positions and Duties.*

3.1 Subject to the power of the Board of Directors of the Company to elect and remove officers, the Executive shall serve as President of the Company. The Executive shall perform, faithfully and diligently, such executive duties on behalf of the Company and/or any subsidiary of the Company as may be assigned to him from time to time by the Board of Directors. Without limiting the generality of the foregoing, the Executive recognizes that the variety and responsibilities of his duties on behalf of the Company's subsidiary, _____, a New York corporation, will be materially increased in comparison with those, if any, heretofore performed by the Executive for such subsidiary and that the increase in such duties will be effected without diminution of the variety and responsibilities of his duties on behalf of the Company. The

Executive shall devote his full time and best efforts (reasonable vacation time and reasonable absence for sickness or similar disability excepted) to the performance of his duties hereunder. The Executive shall conduct himself at all times in such manner as to maintain the good reputation of the Company, its shareholders, and its subsidiaries. The Executive shall not accept or undertake, directly or indirectly, any other employment without first having obtained the prior approval of the Board of Directors of the Company. This shall not be construed as preventing the Executive from investing his assets in such forms or manner as will not require significant service on the part of the Executive in the operation or affairs of the business in which such investments are made, and it shall not be construed as requiring the Executive to divest himself of ownership in or management of any investments or businesses that he may now have.

3.2 Subject to the power of the shareholders to elect and remove directors, the Executive shall be a member of the Board of Directors of the Company.

4. *Termination by Company for Cause.* If the Executive violates any of his obligations under this Agreement, the employment hereunder may be terminated by the Company, at its option at any time upon not less than thirty (30) days' written notice, provided that such notice shall specify the alleged violation or violations and the Executive shall have failed for thirty (30) days after receipt of such notice to comply with such obligations. If the employment of the Executive under this Agreement is terminated for cause as hereinabove provided, the Executive shall be entitled to (i) his salary to the date of termination, (ii) any bonus declared but not yet paid by the Company, and (iii) those benefits, if any, that may be due him under the Company's pension, profit-sharing, stock option, or other similar plans.

5. *Termination at Option of Company.* The Company shall have the right to terminate the employment of the Executive under this Agreement at any time, at its option and without cause, upon its giving not less than sixty (60) days' written notice to the Executive, provided that in the event of termination pursuant to this paragraph the Company shall be obligated to pay the Executive (i) the remaining salary that would have become due and payable hereunder from the date of termination to the end of the term of employment hereunder, calculated at the annual rate

then being paid to the Executive, (ii) any bonus declared but not yet paid by the Company, and (iii) those benefits, if any, that may be due him under the Company's pension, profit-sharing, stock option, or other similar plans. The amounts payable to the Executive under clauses (i) and (ii) of this paragraph shall be payable in substantially equal monthly installments (without interest) over the period from the date of termination to the end of the term of employment hereunder.

6. *Termination by Executive for Cause.* If the Company violates any of its obligations under this Agreement, the employment of the Executive under this Agreement may be terminated by the Executive for cause, at his option at any time, upon his giving to the Company not less than sixty (60) days' written notice, provided that such notice shall be given within sixty (60) days of the occurrence of such violation and the Company shall have failed for thirty (30) days after receipt of such notice to comply with such obligations. If the employment of the Executive is terminated for cause as provided above in this paragraph, the Executive shall have the same rights and benefits that are set forth in paragraph 5 with respect to termination at the option of the Company.

7. *Disability.*

7.1 If the Executive shall have been incapacitated from sickness, accident, or other disability and unable to perform his normal duties hereunder for a cumulative period of six (6) months in any period of twelve (12) consecutive months, the employment of the Executive hereunder may be terminated by the Company or the Executive upon giving the other party not less than thirty (30) days' written notice. Such notice may be given at any time during such period of twelve (12) consecutive months or reasonably promptly thereafter. In the event of such termination, the Executive shall be entitled to (i) all benefits under any accident, sickness, disability, health or hospitalization plan, or insurance policy of the Company then in effect to the extent that the Executive has participated therein, (ii) his salary to the date of termination, (iii) severance pay equal to six (6) months' salary, (iv) any bonus declared but not yet paid by the Company, and (v) those benefits, if any, that may be due him under the Company's pension, profit-sharing, stock option, or similar plans. The Company will continue in force or pay the premiums upon all accident, sickness, disability, health and hospitalization plans, or insurance policies then in effect in which the Executive has participated until the Executive reaches the age of sixty-five (65) years or dies, whichever is first.

7.2 The Board of Directors of the Company shall determine whether the Executive shall have been incapacitated and unable to perform his duties hereunder for the period set forth in paragraph 7.1. In each instance the determination of the Board of Directors of the Company shall be final and binding upon the Executive and the Company, subject only to such determination having been made in good faith.

8. *Death.*

8.1 This Agreement shall, in any event, terminate upon the death of the Executive. In the event of the Executive's death, his estate shall be entitled to any bonus declared but not yet paid by the Company.

8.2 In consideration of the services that the Executive has heretofore rendered to the Company and in consideration of the services to be rendered by the Executive pursuant to this Agreement, if the Executive dies during the term of his employment, the Company shall pay two-and-one-half times the Executive's "total annual compensation" as follows:

(a) The "total annual compensation" as used herein shall be the average of all compensation (including bonuses) paid to the Executive by the Company, and by any of its subsidiaries, affiliates, or other related companies during the three (3) calendar years immediately preceding his death.

(b) The payments shall be made monthly (without interest) and shall continue for a period of five (5) years from the Executive's date of death.

(c) The payments shall be made to the Executive's surviving spouse, or, if his spouse predeceased him or having survived him dies prior to the expiration of the five (5) year period, to the Executive's surviving spouse's estate. Any amounts that are to be paid under this subparagraph to Executive's surviving spouse's estate may, at the option of the Board of Directors of the Company, be paid in a lump sum.

9. *Confidential Information.* The Executive agrees that during his employment hereunder and until December 31, 1985, he will not disclose to any person, firm, or corporation any confidential information regarding the Company or its subsidiaries or affiliates, whether related to their

finances, personnel, sources of supply, prices, customers, or otherwise.

10. *Assignment, Successors, Etc.* Neither the rights nor obligations under this Agreement may be assigned by any party, except that it shall be binding upon and inure to the benefit of any successor of the Company, whether by merger, sale of assets, reorganization, or otherwise.

11. *Insurance on Executive.*

11.1 The Company now owns the following paid-up insurance policy on the Executive: _____ [company and policy number].

The Company agrees that it will continue to hold said policy and that, on the Executive's termination, retirement, death, or when he shall have reached the age of sixty-five (65) years, whichever is sooner, the Company will pay the then applicable proceeds of the said policy monthly for ten (10) years certain to the Executive, or if he should die before all proceeds have been paid out, then to his surviving spouse, or if the spouse shall not survive him or shall die before all proceeds have been paid out, to the Executive's personal representative.

11.2 The Company is now the owner of a policy on the Executive's life issued by [company and policy number]. The Company will pay the annual premiums on the said policy so long as the Executive is employed by the Company. The said policy is and will continue to be payable to the Executive's surviving spouse at approximately Five Thousand ($5,000.00) Dollars per year for ten (10) years.

In the event that the Executive's employment is terminated by the Company under either paragraph 5 or paragraph 7.1 of this Agreement, the Company will continue the said policy in force for three (3) years from the date of termination. Thereafter, the Executive may acquire the said policy from the Company or may continue it in force by paying the then applicable premiums.

11.3 Except as otherwise provided for above, the Executive agrees that the Company may continue or terminate and may, from time to time, apply for and take out, in the Company's own name and at the Company's own expense, life, health, accident, or other insurance upon the Executive in any sum or sums that the Company may deem to be necessary to protect its interests. The Executive also agrees to aid the Company in procuring any and all such insurance by submitting to the usual and customary medical examinations and by filling out, executing, and delivering such application and other instruments in writing as may be reasonably required by any insurance company or companies to which any application or applications for insurance may be made by or for the Company. The Executive further agrees that he shall have no right, title, or interest in or to any such insurance.

12. *Notices.* Any notice hereunder shall be sufficient if in writing and sent by registered mail addressed as follows:

(a) If to the Company, to
Corporate Secretary

_____

_____

_____

(b) If to the Executive, to

_____

_____

_____

Either party may change the address herein specified by giving to the other written notice of such change as herein provided.

13. *Year-to-Year Extension.* This Agreement shall continue in effect on a year-to-year basis beyond the expiration of the initial term on December 31, 1983, unless either party gives to the other party notice of intention to terminate the contract in effect not less than one hundred and twenty (120) days prior to the end of the calendar year 1983 and not less than sixty (60) days prior to the end of any subsequent calendar year. With each such annual extension, the date referred to in paragraph 9 shall be extended one year.

14. *Arbitration.* Any controversy or claim arising out of or relating to this Agreement or the breach thereof shall be settled by arbitration in New Jersey, in accordance with the rules then obtaining of the American Arbitration Association. The party initiating arbitration shall give notice to the other party of his or its intention to arbitrate. Such notice shall set forth the nature of the dispute, the amount (if any) involved, the remedy sought, and the name and address of the initiating party's arbitrator. The other party shall, within fifteen (15) days of the receipt of such notice,

give the initiating party notice of the name and address of his or its arbitrator; and, upon his failure to do so within such fifteen (15) days, the American Arbitration Association at the request of the party or parties initiating arbitration shall select a second arbitrator. Within fifteen (15) days after the date of the selection of the second arbitrator, the two arbitrators so chosen shall select a third arbitrator. If the two arbitrators, however chosen, shall be unable to agree upon a third arbitrator within fifteen (15) days after the selection of the second arbitrator, the American Arbitration Association, at the request of the party initiating arbitration, shall select a third arbitrator. The arbitration shall commence twenty (20) days after the selection of the third arbitrator. Judgment upon the award rendered by the arbitrators may be entered in any court having jurisdiction thereof. The costs and expenses of the arbitration (including, without limitation, reasonable compensation to each arbitrator and counsel fees) shall be paid by the party against whom or which the award is made.

15. *Other Agreements.* This instrument supersedes all other agreements by and between the parties hereto (or their predecessors) that have or would apply to the subjects covered within this Agreement.

16. *Governing Law.* This Agreement is made and shall be construed and performed under the laws of New Jersey.

17. *Entire Agreement.* This instrument contains the entire agreement of the parties. It may not be changed orally, but only by an agreement signed by the party against whom enforcement of any waiver, change, modification, extension, or discharge is sought.

IN WITNESS WHEREOF, the parties have hereunto set their hands and seals and caused these presents to be executed by their appropriate corporate officers as of the date first above written.

_____ COMPANY

Attest:

_____ By_____

Secretary   President

Witness:

_____   _____

Consulting Agreement

1. Appointment: We are pleased to confirm your appointment as a team member to serve in conjunction with a contract to be issued by _____ _____ pursuant to _____ _____ .

2. Services: You shall perform the work as set forth in Exhibit A, attached to and made a part of this agreement. You will keep Helicon informed of your progress on any work being performed under this agreement.

3. Compensation: You will be paid at the rate of $_____ per hour for work done under this agreement. Payment will be based on the time record forms (enclosed). You will submit these time records every _____ . It is anticipated that you will be required to work between _____ and _____ hours total. No compensation for time in excess of this will be made without prior written consent.

4. Reports: Any and all reports, manuscripts and any other work produced, whether completed or not, prepared or developed by you as a part of the work under this agreement are Helicon's property and shall be turned over to us promptly at our request or at the termination of this agreement, whichever is earlier.

5. Independent Contractor: You will exercise control over the means and manner in which you perform any work requested under this agreement and, in all respects, your relationship to Helicon shall be that of an independent contractor, not an employee.

6. Government Contract: This agreement is subject to and incorporates by reference all terms and conditions included or to be included in the government contract.

7. **Noncompetition; Credit:** You agree that you will not, directly or indirectly, compete with Helicon for any contracts or proposals arising from Helicon's performance under the contract for a period of two years after the termination of this agreement. If you publish any articles or give any speeches related to your work under this agreement, you agree to give Helicon appropriate credit and to provide Helicon with a copy of the article or speech.

8. **Term:** This agreement runs concurrently with the term of the contract held by Helicon, unless terminated by Helicon on thirty days' written notice.

9. **Entire Agreement:** This letter, Exhibit A, and the contract contain the entire agreement of the parties. It may not be changed orally, but only by an agreement signed by both parties.

10. **Approval:** We trust that the terms of this appointment meet with your approval. If so, please indicate by signing a copy of this letter and returning it to Helicon. An additional copy of this letter is enclosed for your records.

Very truly yours,
the Helicon group, ltd.
by _____
          President

Accepted and agreed to this
_____ day of _____ ,
198_____ .
_____

Source: the Helicon group, ltd., © 1981.

Share Transfers

(1) No shareholder shall during his lifetime sell, mortgage, hypothecate, transfer, pledge, create a security interest in or lien on, encumber, give, place in trust (voting or other), or otherwise dispose of all or any portion of his shares in the Corporation now owned or hereafter acquired, except that if a shareholder should desire to so dispose of any of his shares in the Corporation during his lifetime, he shall first offer to sell all of his shares to the Corporation at the price hereafter provided. Any shares not purchased by the Corporation within thirty (30) days after receipt of such offer in writing shall be offered at the same price to the other shareholders, each of whom shall have the right to purchase such portion of the remaining shares offered for sale as the number of shares owned by him at such date shall bear to the total number of shares owned by all the other shareholders excluding the selling shareholder, provided, however, that if any shareholder does not purchase his full proportionate share of the shares, the balance thereof may be purchased by the other shareholders equally. If his shares are not purchased by the remaining shareholders within sixty (60) days of the receipt of the offer to them, the shareholder desiring to sell his shares may sell them to any other person but shall not sell them without giving the Corporation and the remaining shareholders the right to purchase such remaining shares at the price and on the terms offered to such other person.

(2) Any person who becomes the holder or possessor of any shares, or share certificates, of this Corporation by virtue of any judicial process, attachment, bankruptcy, receivership, execution, or judicial sale shall immediately offer all of said shares to the Corporation, whenever requested by the Corporation so to do, at the price herein fixed, and none of said shares shall be entitled to any vote, nor shall any dividend be paid or allowed upon any of such shares, after failure to comply with such request.

(3) Upon the death of any shareholder party to this agreement, the Corporation shall purchase, and the estate of the decedent shall sell, all the decedent's shares in the Corporation, and the parties hereto and the

Corporation shall take such action as may be necessary to permit it to make such purchase. Title to all said shares shall be deemed to vest in the Corporation immediately upon the death of any such shareholder. The purchase price of such shares shall be computed as hereinafter provided.

(4) In the event that any shareholder becomes entitled to payment of the fair value of his shares under Chapter 11 of the New Jersey Business Corporation Act, or any amendment thereto, or related or similar statute, the fair value of his shares for all purposes thereunder shall be conclusively presumed to be the price hereinafter fixed, and the shareholder shall be bound to accept any offer of the Corporation to pay said amount in exchange for his shares.

(5) No purported sale, assignment, mortgage, hypothecation, transfer, pledge, creation of a security interest in or lien on, encumbrance of, gift of, trust (voting or other) of, or other disposition of any of the shares of this Corporation by any shareholder in violation of the provisions of this agreement, the certificate of incorporation or the bylaws shall be valid, and the Corporation shall not transfer any of said shares on the books of the Corporation, nor shall any of said shares be entitled to vote, nor shall any dividends be paid thereon, during the period of any such violation. Such disqualifications shall be in addition to and not instead of any other remedies legal or equitable to enforce said provisions.

Further, the parties hereto expressly waive any voting, dividend, or appraisal rights to which they would otherwise be entitled, except as herein provided.

(6) Nothing herein contained shall be construed to limit or render ineffective any other provisions of this agreement, or of the certificate of incorporation or bylaws of this Corporation consented to by all the parties hereto, further restricting or conditioning the transfer of shares of this Corporation, or providing penalties or disqualifications for violations of said restrictions or conditions.

(7) The value of each share of this Corporation is for all purposes fixed at fifty dollars ($50) per share. Such value includes an amount representing the goodwill of the Corporation as a going concern. Within thirty (30) days following the end of each fiscal year of the Corporation,

the shareholders shall by unanimous mutual agreement redetermine the value of each of said shares, for the next fiscal year, and endorse said value in the Schedule to this agreement, which is made a part thereof.

In the event that, for any reason whatsoever, no such advance redetermination is made for any fiscal year, the value of each of said shares shall be the value as last fixed under this agreement, increased or decreased as the case may be, by the proportionate amount, allocable to the shares whose value is being determined, of the algebraic sum of the net earnings and net losses, before all federal corporate income, state franchise, income, business personal property, and municipal (including, but without limitation thereto, real property taxes) taxes, of the Corporation from the date of such last value until the date of the death of the shareholder, offer, on request, as the case may be.

The determination of the net earnings and losses shall be made by the Corporation's regular accountant, in accordance with generally accepted accounting principles, on a basis consistent with that normally used in determining the Corporation's net earnings and losses.

(8) The Corporation shall purchase insurance on the life of each of the parties hereto, payable to the Corporation as beneficiary, and shall pay the premiums thereon, in the respective amounts hereafter shown:

_____ Face Amount of Policy $_____
_____ Face Amount of Policy $_____
_____ Face Amount of Policy $_____

(9) All certificates for shares of this Corporation shall, in addition to any notice thereon required by the certificate of incorporation or bylaws of this Corporation, bear the following notice conspicuously on the face or back thereof:

Sale, assignment, mortgage, hypothecation, transfer, pledge, creation of a security interest in or lien on, encumbrance of, gift of, trust (voting or other) of, or other disposition of these shares is restricted by the terms of a shareholder agreement dated _____, 1982, which may be examined at the office of the Corporation.

No shares of the Corporation shall be deemed properly issued, and no shares shall be transferred upon the books of the Corporation, nor shall any dividends be paid thereon, nor shall the holder thereof be entitled to any voting or other rights of a shareholder, unless the certificate evidencing such shares contains said legend.

(10) Failure of the Corporation or of the shareholders to exercise any option to purchase given under this agreement, and any waiver of any rights hereunder as to any transfer, shall not, as to any future transfer of said shares (either voluntary or by operation of law) discharge such shares from any of the restrictions herein contained.

(11) Payment for all shares purchased under this agreement shall, except where the seller is a party to this agreement or the estate, executor, administrator, committee, guardian, heir, next of kin, legatee, or other legal representative of a party to this agreement, be in cash upon delivery of the share certificate or certificates properly endorsed.

Where the purchase is made from a party to this agreement, or the estate, executor, administrator, committee, guardian, heir, next of kin, legatee, or other legal representative of a party to this agreement, instead of payment solely in cash, payment may be made, at the election of the purchaser or purchasers as the case may be, in the following manner:

(a) a down payment of ten (10) percent of the purchase price in cash, together with

(b) a note or notes providing for payment of the balance in equal monthly installments without interest over a period of twenty-four (24) months, with acceleration of the entire obligation in the event of nonpayment of any installment when due. The seller shall be bound to deliver the certificate or certificates properly endorsed for all shares to be purchased, upon tender by the purchaser or purchasers as the case may be of the down payment and note or notes as above provided.

Nothing herein shall be construed to validate a sale or other disposition of shares otherwise prohibited by this agreement.

American Arbitration Association

SUBMISSION TO ARBITRATION

Date:

The named Parties hereby submit the following dispute to arbitration under the COMMERCIAL ARBITRATION RULES of the American Arbitration Association:

Amount of money involved: ....

Number of Arbitrators desired: one ☐   three ☐

Place of Hearing: ....

We agree that we will abide by and perform any Award rendered hereunder and that a judgment may be entered upon the Award.

Name of Party ....

Telephone ....

Address ....

Signed by ....

Name of Party ....

Telephone ....

Address ....

Signed by ....

PLEASE FILE TWO COPIES
Consult counsel about valid execution

COMMERCIAL ARBITRATION RULES
DEMAND FOR ARBITRATION

DATE:_____

TO: (Name) _____
(of party upon whom the Demand is made)

(Address) _____

(City and State) _____ (Zip Code)_____

(Telephone)_____

Named claimant, a party to an arbitration agreement contained in a written contract,

dated _____, providing for arbitration, hereby demands arbitration thereunder.
(attach arbitration clause or quote hereunder)

NATURE OF DISPUTE:

CLAIM OR RELIEF SOUGHT: (amount, if any)

TYPE OF BUSINESS:

Claimant _____ Respondent _____

HEARING LOCALE REQUESTED:_____
(City and State)

You are hereby notified that copies of our arbitration agreement and of this demand are being filed with the American Arbitration Association at its _____
Regional Office, with the request that it commence the administration of the arbitration. Under Section 7 of the Commercial Arbitration Rules, you may file an answering statement within seven days after notice from the Administrator.

Signed_____ Title_____
(May Be Signed by Attorney)

Name of Claimant_____

Home or Business Address of Claimant_____

City and State_____ Zip Code _____

Telephone_____

Name of Attorney_____

Attorney's Address_____

City and State_____ Zip Code _____

Telephone_____

To institute proceedings, please send two copies of the Demand and the arbitration agreement, with the administrative fee, as provided in Section 48 of the Rules to the AAA. Send original Demand to Respondent.

Proposal

FROM

Proposal No.

Sheet No.

Date

Proposal Submitted To	Work To Be Performed At
Name_____	Street_____
Street_____	City_____State_____
City_____	Date of Plans_____
State_____	Architect_____
Telephone Number_____	

We hereby propose to furnish all the materials and perform all the labor necessary for the completion of

_____

_____

_____

_____

_____

_____

_____

_____

_____

_____

_____

All material is guaranteed to be as specified, and the above work to be performed in accordance with the drawings and specifications submitted for above work and completed in a substantial workmanlike manner for the sum of

Dollars ($).

with payments to be made as follows:

_____

_____

Any alteration or deviation from above specifications involving extra costs, will be executed only upon written orders, and will become an extra charge over and above the estimate. All agreements contingent upon strikes, accidents or delays beyond our control. Owner to carry fire, tornado and other necessary insurance upon above work. Workmen's Compensation and Public Liability Insurance on above work to be taken out by_____

Respectfully submitted_____

Per_____

Note — This proposal may be withdrawn by us if not accepted within   days

ACCEPTANCE OF PROPOSAL

The above prices, specifications and conditions are satisfactory and are hereby accepted. You are authorized to do the work as specified. Payment will be made as outlined above.

_____

Accepted _____ Signature_____

Date _____ Signature_____

Notes

CHAPTER 2

1. Professionals Risk Management and Service Company, *Avoiding Legal Malpractice Claims,* p. 3.

CHAPTER 3

1. Adapted from U.S. Department of Commerce, Office of Minority Business Enterprise, *Federal Procurement and Contracting Training Manual for Minority Enterprises* (May 1975), pp. 107–9.
2. The American Institute of Architects, *Architect's Handbook of Professional Practice,* Chapter 9, p. 3 (1970).
3. Mike Major, "A Simple Business Contract for Writers," *Writer's Digest* (September 1981), p. 39.
4. See Carolyn M. Vella, "Employment at Will: A Dying Concept," *Supervision* (August 1982), p. 3.

5. Murray Schumach, *The Diamond People* (New York, W. W. Norton and Co., Inc., 1981), p. 57.

CHAPTER 5

1. Peter S. Vogel, "Computer Wars: Vendor vs. Lawyer," *The National Law Journal* (November 2, 1981), p. 19.
2. H. Denenberg, R. Eilers, J. Melone, and R. Zelten, *Risk and Insurance* (2d. ed., Englewood Cliffs, N.J., Prentice-Hall, Inc., 1974), pp. 232–33.

CHAPTER 6

1. Lynn B. Squires, "A Comprehensible Due-on-Sale Clause," *ALI-ABA CLE Review* 12, no. 41 (October 2, 1981), p. 6.
2. *Report to The House of Delegates by the American Bar Association Standing Committee on Legal Drafting* (August 1981).
3. Michael H. Cardozo, Notes on "A Comprehensible Due-on-Sale Clause," *ALI-ABA CLE Review* 12, no. 41 (October 2, 1981), pp. 1–2.
4. David W. Maxey, "Fundamentals of Draftsmanship: A Guide for the Apprentice in Preparing Agreements," *Pennsylvania Bar Quarterly* (January 1980), pp. 47, 58.
5. Theodore M. Bernstein, *Do's, Don'ts & Maybes of English Usage* (New York, Times Books, 1977), p. 126.
6. Squires, "A Comprehensible Due-on-Sale Clause."

CHAPTER 7

1. *Boardroom Reports* 10, no. 5 (March 9, 1981), p. 12.

CHAPTER 8

1. Jerrold G. Van Cise, *The Federal Antitrust Laws* (3d ed. rev., Washington, D.C., American Enterprise Institute for Public Policy Research, 1975), pp. 26–37.

Glossary

ACCEPTANCE: Receiving something offered with the intent of keeping it. This receipt is generally considered as an unspoken agreement to some earlier act or understanding. Acceptance of an offer is essential to the formation of a contract.

ACCORD AND SATISFACTION: An agreement between two parties for the delivery and acceptance of something, usually worth less than the amount legally owed or enforceable, to settle a debt or as damages for a wrong.

ACCOUNT STATED: The settlement of an account between two parties, with a balance struck in favor of one of them. Also, an account rendered by a creditor and assented to as correct by a debtor, either expressly or by implication of law from a failure to object.

ACKNOWLEDGMENT: A formal declaration by a person before a competent authority, such as a notary public, that his or her signature on a legal document is a free act and deed.

ACTION: A lawsuit or the right to bring a lawsuit.

ADHESION CONTRACT: A standard form contract given to someone on a take-it-or-leave-it basis, such as a rental agreement or insurance policy.

AFFIDAVIT: A written declaration or statement of fact made voluntarily and taken under oath before a competent authority, such as a notary public.

AGENCY: The relationship of one person acting for or representing another, who is called the principal, by the authority given by the principal.

AGREEMENT: A contract. The meeting of two minds, that is, an understanding between two parties with a common purpose, such as transferring property, or a right or benefit conferred on one by the other.

ALLEGATION: A formal written statement by a party in a legal action stating what he expects to prove in the action.

ANNUL: To cancel, make void, or destroy.

ANSWER: In pleadings, a pleading setting up matters of fact as a defense to an action.

APPEAL: The moving of a case from one court to a higher court for the purpose of obtaining a review and reversal of the lower court's judgment.

ARBITRATION: Resolving a contractual conflict or dispute by employing a third party selected by the two parties.

ASSIGNMENT: The act of transferring property or an interest in property. Also, the transfer of title or ownership of something not yet owned, but to which a person has a right under a contract or claim.

ASSUMPTION OF RISK: The act of one party to a contract assuming the consequences of any injury or loss to another, no matter who may be responsible for that injury or loss.

ATTACHMENT: The act or process of taking a person's property, by virtue of a court order, and bringing it into the custody of the court to be used either to bring the owner into court or to provide assets which can be used to satisfy a judgment against their owner.

ATTESTATION: The act of bearing witness to the execution of a document and signing the document as testimony to that fact.

BAILEE: The party to whom personal property is delivered under a contract of bailment.

BAILMENT: Delivery of personal property by one person (the bailor) to another (the bailee) in trust for a special purpose, with a contract that the trust will be performed and the property returned or accounted for when the special purpose is accomplished.

BAILOR: The party who delivers goods to another in a contract of bailment.

BID: An offer to purchase at a designated price property that is about to be sold, usually at an auction.

BILL OF LADING: A written document, signed by a carrier or the carrier's agent, identifying and describing freight, stating the name of the consigner, the terms of the contract to carry the goods, and agreeing or directing that the freight be delivered to the order or assignees of a specified person at a specified place.

BILL OF SALE: A written agreement by which one person assigns or transfers his right or interest in goods and personal property to another.

BONA FIDE: Latin for "in good faith."

BREACH OF CONTRACT: Violation of or a failure to perform any or all parts of a contract without a valid legal excuse.

BROKER: A person employed as an agent to negotiate contracts or sales, or to make purchases and sales, for an agreed commission.

CAPITAL: In a partnership, the aggregate of the sums of money and value of the goods contributed by its members to create or continue the business.

CARRIER: One who carries passengers or another's goods. This usually refers to a common carrier, which is a carrier that holds itself out to carry goods or people for a fee.

CAUSE OF ACTION: The grounds for a legal action. It is made up of those facts that if alleged and proved in the lawsuit, in the absence of an effective defense, would enable a plaintiff to obtain judgment against a defendant.

CIVIL: The private rights and remedies of individuals as members of the community.

COLLATERAL: Additional or auxilliary.

COMPLAINT: In civil cases, the document setting forth the cause of action alleged by the plaintiff.

CONDITIONAL SALE: A sale where the passage of title is made to depend on the performance of a condition. Usually the condition for the passing of title is payment of the purchase price by the purchaser.

CONSIDERATION: The inducement offered and accepted in forming a contract. It is a thing given or done, or to be done or abstained from by one party to the contract, which is accepted by the other party as an inducement to perform his part of the agreement.

CONSTRUCTIVE: Inferred, implied, or made to exist by legal interpretation of the facts.

CONTRACT: An enforceable agreement between two parties to do or not to do a particular thing. It can be oral, written, or implied.

COSTS: An award to the successful party in a lawsuit, payable by the losing party, for the expenses incurred in bringing or defending the lawsuit. These are fairly small and limited by statute. Generally, attorneys' fees are not included in the costs.

COUNTER-CLAIM: A claim presented by a defendant in opposition to or as a deduction from the claim of the plaintiff.

COVENANT: (1) A written agreement between two parties made under seal; (2) A specific stipulation or agreement within a contract or a deed.

CUSTODY: The care and keeping of property.

DAMAGES: An indemnity or reparation in money that may be recovered by a person who has suffered an injury to his person, property, or rights because of the unlawful act, default, or negligence of another person.

DEBT: A fixed sum of money due under an explicit agreement.

DECEIT: A trick, false statement, secret device, or pretense by which one person misleads another. That person, being ignorant of the fraud, suffers damage or injury as a result.

DECREE: The judgment of a court in equity, akin to a judgment in law.

DEED: A written instrument, signed and usually sealed and delivered, containing some contract, bargain, or transfer. It usually refers to an instrument transferring land or an interest in land.

DEFAULT: A failure or neglect to fulfill a legal obligation or requirement, such as the failure to pay money due.

DEFENDANT: The person against whom a legal claim is brought; the party defending or denying a claim in a legal action.

DEFRAUD: To trick, cheat, or swindle. To deprive a person of property by fraud, not by force or intimidation.

DELIVERY: The actual or constructive transfer of an instrument or goods from the hands of one person to those of another.

DISCHARGE: To pay a debt or to satisfy an obligation or claim. Also, the release of a bankrupt from the obligations of his debts following a bankruptcy proceeding.

DISCOVERY: In civil actions, the disclosure of facts, documents, and similar evidence by one party at the request of the other for use by the second party as evidence in a case being prepared for trial.

DURESS: Unlawful constraint exercised on a person whereby he or she is forced to do some act against his or her will.

EARNEST: Something done or given in advance as a pledge or other indication of good faith. Earnest money: a partial payment of the purchase price of goods sold or a delivery of part of the goods themselves to bind an agreement.

ENDORSE: To sign your name on the back of a document.

EQUITABLE: Just, fair, and right; available in a court of equity.

EQUITY: A body of law and legal traditions awarding relief in lawsuits other than with money.

ESCROW: A condition when a deed or money is held conditionally by a third person, to be released or returned as previously agreed upon.

ESTOPPEL: A condition when a person is prevented by law either from contradicting what he had previously said or written, or from stating or claiming what he had previously denied. Estoppel arises from a person's conduct and from written or oral statements.

ET AL.: Abbreviation of the Latin phrase "and others."

EVIDENCE: Proof legally presented at the trial of an issue to convince the judge and jury as to the truth of the contentions of each party.

EXECUTED: Completed; now in existence or in possession. The opposite of executory.

EXECUTION: (1) Signing a contract not under seal, or the signing, sealing, and delivering of a contract under seal; (2) Accomplishing the things stipulated to be done in the contract.

EXECUTORY: Designed to be executed or put into effect in the future; becoming operative on the occurrence of some future event. An executory contract between two parties requires one to perform a service for the other at a future date.

EX PARTE: One-sided; done by one party only.

EXPRESS: Explicitly set forth in words; not implied or stated.

FAILURE OF CONSIDERATION: In contract law, a situation when the consideration, event or thing on which the contract was based, fails to take place or ceases to exist.

FORFEIT: To lose or surrender money, property, a right, or a privilege because of a fault, omission, misconduct, or a crime.

FRAUD: An act of trickery, deceit, or misrepresentation deliberately performed to deprive someone of a right, to do that person harm, or to induce that person to part with something of value.

GARNISHMENT: A notice to a person holding money or property belonging to a defendant not to turn over the money or property to the defendant, but to appear and answer the plaintiff's action. Usually designed to collect a judgment against a defendant from a creditor or an employer.

GUARANTY: A promise or pledge to be responsible for the contract, debt, or duty of another in case of that person's default or miscarriage.

IMPLIED: Intended but not directly or explicitly stated; deduced from circumstances, language, or conduct; suggested or understood.

INDEMNITY: An agreement by which one party agrees to pay another for an anticipated loss. To protect one party from the legal consequences of an act or omission by the other party or by a third person, whose actions were beyond the control of the contracting parties.

INDENTURE: A legal document, such as a deed or contract, to which two or more persons are parties and which is executed by all the parties involved.

INDEPENDENT CONTRACTOR: A person who contracts to do certain work according to his or her own methods, without control by the hiring party, except as to the result or product of the work.

INJUNCTION: An order issued by a court directing the person named in it to take or refrain from taking some specified action.

IN LIEU OF: In place of; instead of.

INSTRUMENT: A formal written document having legal effect, such as a will, a lease, a promissory note, or a contract.

INTERROGATORIES: Series of written questions used in the examination of a party or witness during discovery.

JUDGMENT: The final determination by a court of the rights and claims of the parties to an action.

LACHES: Such a neglect, omission, or unreasonable delay in asserting a right or claiming a privilege that it warrants or justifies the withholding of relief by a court.

LAPSE: Termination of a privilege or right; forfeiture caused by a failure to perform some act or by the failure of some contingency.

LEASE: A transfer of land—or the right to use land—to a person for life, for a set period, or at will, in consideration of the payment of rent or other payments or services.

LESSEE: The person who receives the leased property.

LESSOR: The person who grants the lease.

LETTER OF INTENT; LETTER OF UNDERSTANDING: It usually contemplates the preparation and execution of additional agreements; it is a contract only if it meets all legal requirements.

LIABLE: (1) Subject to or exposed to some probable event, damage, penalty, or burden; (2) Bound or obliged; responsible.

L.S.: An abbreviation for the Latin *locus sigilli*—the place of the seal, meaning the place where a seal is to be affixed. It is also used to signify that the document is one under seal.

MALFEASANCE: Doing an act that the doer has no right to perform, and doing that act in a wrongful or unjust manner. Also, doing an act that the doer has agreed by contract not to do.

MALICE: The intention or desire to injure another by deliberately doing some wrongful act without legal justification or excuse.

MEDIATION: Bringing about an agreement between two parties by using a third party to help resolve the dispute.

MEMO OF INTENT; MEMO OF UNDERSTANDING: See Letter of Intent.

MERGER: A fusion. In contracts, the absorbtion of oral negotiations into a written document.

MISFEASANCE: Doing a lawful act in an unlawful or improper way.

MISREPRESENTATION: An intentionally false statement made by a party to a contract about a matter of fact that is material to the contract and was influential in producing it.

MISTAKE: An omission or act caused by a misunderstanding of fact or law.

MITIGATE: To make less severe or to lessen.

MORTGAGE: A lien on land or property as security for the performance of some obligation, usually the repayment of a loan.

NEGLIGENCE: The omission to do something that a reasonable person would do, guided by the considerations that usually control the conduct of human affairs; or to do something that a prudent and reasonable person would not do.

NOMINAL: Existing in name only. Nominal damages are trivial in amount, indicating the violation of a legal right without any important damage or loss to the plaintiff.

NONFEASANCE: A failure to perform some act that one party should or is required to perform.

NOTE: A signed promise by one party to another to pay a certain sum of money at a set time and place, as in "promissory note."

NOTICE: Information about or knowledge of the existence of some fact or condition. Constructive notice is knowledge imputed to a party by law, regardless of actual knowledge, because the party could have obtained that knowledge and should have done so because of the particular situation.

OFFER: A proposal to make a contract, having within it all the terms of the contract. Acceptance of such a proposal creates a contract.

PAROL EVIDENCE RULE: A rule that prohibits the change or modification of a written agreement by any oral agreements made by the parties prior to the writing of the agreement, in the absence of a plea of mistake, ambiguity, or fraud in the writing.

PER SE: Latin for "by itself" or "inherently."

PLEDGE: A security consisting of personal property for some debt or obligation.

PRESUMPTION OF FACT: An inference that affirms or denies the existence of an unknown fact, based on the existence of some other fact that is already known or proven.

PRESUMPTION OF LAW: An inference based on a rule of law that courts are compelled to draw a particular inference from a particular fact or evidence, unless and until contradictory evidence is offered that disproves the truth of that inference.

PUNITIVE DAMAGES: Damages awarded to a plaintiff above those to which he is entitled because the defendant has violated a legal right. They are awarded either because of the special nature of the wrong of the defendant (violence, malice, fraud) or to punish the defendant and thus deter others from acting in the same way.

QUASI: Latin for "appearing as if." Used with English words to suggest a lack of reality.

QUASI-CONTRACT: A contractual agreement arising from transactions between the parties that gives them mutual rights and obligations but does not involve a specific and express agreement between them.

RATIFICATION: The act of approving, confirming, or sanctioning.

REBUT: To contradict, refute, oppose, or deny.

RECEIPT: The written acknowledgment of receiving money or a thing of value, without containing any affirmative obligation on either party to it.

RELEASE: The giving up by someone of something or some right that was theirs.

REMEDY: A legal method for enforcing a right or for redressing or preventing a wrong. It includes money damages, restitution, injunction, and specific performance.

RESCIND: To make void, abrogate, annul, or cancel.

RESCISSION: To abrogate a contract from its beginning, restoring the parties to the positions they occupied before the contract was made.

RESTITUTION: (1) Restoration of the parties to a rescinded contract to the positions they occupied before making the contract; (2) Restoration of property to the person entitled to it.

REVOCATION: The recall of some power, authority, or thing granted, or the destroying or making void of some deed that existed until the act of revocation made it void.

SALE: A contract under which property is transferred from one person (the seller or vendor) to another (the buyer or purchaser). This is in return for the buyer's payment or promise of payment of a fixed price in money or property.

SATISFACTION: Extinguishment of an obligation or claim, by, for example, payment, performance, restitution, or the rendering of an equivalent of these.

SEAL: An impression on wax or some other substance, usually used to attest to the execution of a document. *See* L.S.

SET-OFF: A counter-claim or cross-demand in an action in which the defendant sets off against the plaintiff's claim, as being due the defendant, by which the defendant can lessen or eliminate the plaintiff's demand.

SPECIFIC PERFORMANCE: The actual carrying out of, or a legal proceeding to force the carrying out of, the terms of an agreement; for example, the transfer of real property.

STATUTE OF FRAUDS: A law requiring that certain classes of contracts and certain memoranda of sales be in writing and signed by the party in order to be enforceable.

STATUTE OF LIMITATIONS: A law that imposes time limits on the right to sue in certain cases.

SUBPOENA: A writ or order commanding a person to appear in court to give written testimony.

SUBSCRIBE: It usually refers to writing one's signature at the end of a written or printed document.

SUMMONS: A writ or order, directed to the sheriff or similar officer, requiring him to notify the person named that an action has been commenced against him in the court issuing the summons, and that the person named is required to appear on the day named and answer the complaint filed against him in that action.

SURETY: One who agrees to be responsible for the obligation, default, or wrongdoing of another.

TENDER: The formal offer of money or property, in satisfaction of some claim or demand held against the one making the tender.

THIRD PARTY: A person not a party to a contract; someone other than the buyer and seller, employer and employee, etc.

TORT: A wrong or wrongful act for which an action can be brought. It is independent of contract.

TRANSFER: An act by which a right, title, or interest in real or personal property is conveyed from one person to another.

UNDERTAKING: A promise, engagement, or stipulation. Each of the promises made by the parties to a contract, considered independently and not as mutual, may, in this sense, be labeled as an "undertaking."

UNLIQUIDATED: Not ascertained as to amount.

USAGE: Customary or habitual practice that is lawful, reasonable, and either (1) known to the involved parties, or (2) so well established that it is presumed that the parties have acted in accord with it.

VENDEE: A purchase or buyer; one to whom something is sold.

VENDOR: The seller; one who transfers property by sale.

VERIFICATION: A sworn statement attesting to the truth of a pleading, a petition, or any other document.

VOID: Without force or validity; invalid; incapable of confirmation or ratification.

VOIDABLE: Capable of being made void, but not necessarily void in itself.

WAIVER: The renunciation, repudiation, abandonment, or surrender of some right, claim, or privilege or of the opportunity to take advantage of some defect, irregularity, or wrong.

WARRANTY: An undertaking or stipulation, in writing or orally, that a certain fact in relation to the subject of the contract is or shall be as it is stated or promised to be. It is given contemporaneously with the contract and as a part of it.

References

Basic Legal and Contract Law References

The Attorney's Pocket Dictionary (1981). Includes definitions as well as citations for further research.

Black's Law Dictionary (5th edition, 1979). A basic reference for lawyers and nonlawyers on the meaning of legal words and expressions. It is particularly useful in discerning the meanings of foreign and Latin phrases in agreements. Found in most public libraries.

William C. Burton. *Legal Thesaurus* (1980). This first legal thesaurus is useful both in analyzing and drafting legal documents.

Morris L. Cohen. *Legal Research in a Nutshell* (3d edition, 1978). A basic book designed for law students, but it is useful for anyone doing legal research.

Stephen Elias. *Legal Research: How to Find and Understand the Law* (1982). A paperback book designed for those who want to do basic legal research. The author explains basic research, outlines a research strategy, describes how to use legal research tools, and shows how to analyze statutes and cases.

Deborah E. Larbalestrier. *Paralegal Practice and Procedure* (1977). A basic reference for paralegals, but it is useful for anyone dealing regularly with civil litigation or real-estate transactions. The problems are presented step by step.

Martin J. Ross. *New Encyclopedic Dictionary of Business Law: With Forms* (1975). A basic business law dictionary as well as general legal reference. The author cautions that this is "not a do-it-yourself book."

Gordon D. Schaber and Claude D. Rohwer. *Contracts in a Nutshell* (1975). A short summary of basic contract law designed for the law student and for the lawyer who wants a quick pocket reference. It can be useful to the reasonably sophisticated business reader as well.

West's Law Finder: A Research Manual for Lawyers (1980). A booklet distributed by the West Publishing Company detailing how to use its various legal-research sources.

Special Legal Problems

Robert B. Chickering and Susan Hartman. *How to Register a Copyright and Protect Your Creative Work* (1980). A basic work detailing how to proceed under the new copyright act.

Howard L. Oleck. *Non-Profit Corporations, Organizations, and Associations* (4th edition, 1980). A legally oriented guide covering the issues facing charities as well as trade associations.

Bradford Stone. *Uniform Commercial Code in a Nutshell* (1975). A short reference to the variety of transactions, including contracts, covered by the Uniform Commercial Code.

Jerrold G. Van Cise. *The Federal Antitrust Laws* (3d edition revised, 1975). An abbreviated analysis of the various antitrust laws, designed primarily for the business executive, not the lawyer.

Particular Business Situations

Joseph Auer and Charles Edison Harris. *Computer Contract Negotiations* (1981). Deals with the negotiation of a variety of computer-equipment transactions from the purchaser's and the lessor's perspective.

Mike Major. "A Simple Business Contract for Writers," *Writer's Digest,* September 1981, pp. 39 ff. Discusses how to use a standard reply form and contract in submitting manuscripts.

John J. McGonagle, Jr. *Managing the Consultant: A Corporate Guide* (1981). A basic guide to one specialized business relationship from the legal and managerial perspectives. It includes form agreements and instructions on how to use them.

Peter S. Vogel. "Computer Wars: Vendor vs. Lawyer," *The National Law Journal,* November 2, 1981, pp. 19 ff. Highlights some of the problems lawyers and businesspeople have with computer contracts.

George I. Wallich. *The Law of Sales Under the Uniform Commercial Code* (1981). A one-volume treatise written for lawyers.

Legal Form Books

The vast majority of form books are written by lawyers for lawyers. The tend either to be specialized or to take a very broad sweep in an effort to be the sole source of forms for a law office. Those issued in binders are usually updated frequently. Some bound books are also updated, but that varies from publisher to publisher.

Robert F. Cushman, Michael S. Simon, and McNeill Stokes. *Construction Industry Formbook* (1979).

Albert Dib. *Forms and Agreements for Architects, Engineers and Contractors* (2 volumes, 1976, 1977, and updates).

Bruce E. Fritch and Albert F. Reisman, ed. *Equipment Leasing— Leveraged Leasing* (1980).

Warren, Gorham and LaMont (publisher). *Legal and Tax Planning Series.*

Plain English and Readability

Edgar Dale and Jeanne S. Chall. *A Formula for Predicting Readability* (1948, 1952). Reprinted by the Bureau of Educational Research, Ohio State University. A series of articles setting forth a formula for measuring readability and defining a list of 3,000 preferred or "familiar" words.

Rudolf Flesch. *How to Write Plain English: A Book for Lawyers and Consumers* (1979). A basic readability text, focusing primarily on government regulations as examples.

Information Plus (publisher). "Better Communication." A newsletter dealing with business communication problems.

David W. Maxey. "Fundamentals of Draftsmanship: A Guide for the Apprentice in Preparing Agreements," *Pennsylvania Bar Association Quarterly* 51, no. 1, January 1980, pp. 47–62. A brief article directed at the recent law-school graduate, focusing primarily on real-estate transactions.

Disputes

The Center for Public Resources (publisher). *Dispute Management* (1982). A handbook describing in detail minitrials, arbitration, and other alternatives to litigation.

Robert Coulson. "Arbitration In The Eighties: How To Make It Work For You." *THE FORUM,* Vol. XVII, No. 3, Winter 1982, pp. 673–81. The President of the American Arbitration Association discusses the selection of an arbitrator and the preparation and presentation of an arbitration case.

Harper Hamilton. *How to Be Your Own Lawyer in Court* (1978). A how-to aimed at the person who wants to bring or defend his own case. It is also useful to anyone involved in civil litigation; it explains many of the technical stages of litigation and shows why civil litigation can take so long and cost so much.

James E. Morris. *You Can Win Big in Small Claims Court* (1981). Aimed at the consumer with a dispute, it examines sample cases. Its major benefit is that it shows the variation from state to state in the practices and powers of small claims courts.

William Steele. "Minitrials are Cheap and Quick," *Inc.,* October 1981, pp. 49 ff. Discusses the most recent experience with the relatively new concept of minitrials.

Copyrights, Patents, and Trademarks

For information on copyrights, write to:
    Information and Publications Section
    United States Copyright Office
    Library of Congress
    Washington, D.C. 20559
For free brochures on patents and trademarks, write to:
    Commissioner of Patents
    Washington, D.C. 20231

Index